Praise for

The Game Is Hard Enough

"As a career basketball coach at St. Francis Xavier University for 46 years, as well as former Head Coach of Canada's Senior Men's basketball team, I have known Steve Lloyd for over 40 years, working with him first as a student at StFX and then later as Manager of Canada's National Basketball Team at the 1998 World Championships in Greece. In addition, Steve served as our recruiting coordinator for StFX in Ontario and volunteered as a Mental Skills coach with our team in later years. Needless to say, I am very familiar with Steve's philosophies of life as well as sports. More importantly, besides being a loyal friend, he has served as a confidant and in many ways an advisor to me over many years. I will seek his advice often when faced with coaching challenges and he has taught me a lot about servant leadership. Steve's ability to see the big picture and relate life lessons to sport is exceptional. Parents, or anyone reading this book, will benefit from a professional yet compassionate approach of how to maximize, as well as put into perspective, the real-life values that participation in competitive sport can offer."

Steve Konchalski
Career Basketball Coach, Parent

"The Game Is Hard Enough is a must-read guide for parents of today's young athlete. This book is brilliantly written from truly an insider's perspective, with experience as a parent and coach.

Steve Lloyd's own son Matt played for me in his first two years of college baseball and has moved on to a career in baseball. Steve and I have grown close as friends through the years as we've continued our relationship, at times having hours of conversations about coaching, teaching, parenting, and mentoring.

Before this book ever came to fruition, Steve Lloyd has been mentoring me for years. As a parent myself, with my own two sons who have grown up playing sports, his insights have been very helpful to me and our family. It's no different than me being a college baseball coach who played before becoming a coach and has sought out the advice of veteran coaches that I respect.

Steve has written a great book like this due to the fact that he has raised his kids who played multiple youth sports at all levels, while also being a coach and teacher. And he's applied these principles to countless kids and families that he's worked with along their journeys.

I highly recommend this book for anyone. *The Game Is Hard Enough* is a great resource for today's parents who are trying to navigate the world of competitive youth sports, schools, or just life!"

Marc Rardin
Parent and Head Baseball Coach, Iowa Western Community College

"As a mom of three incredible humans and athletes, my family and I have been fortunate to have met Steve over seven years ago when he was the baseball coach of my eldest son Jonah. Over the years, Steve has been a great support to our family as well as many other families, as we learn to successfully navigate the complex dynamics and processes of the competitive sports our boys play.

Steve is a former performance athlete, parent of a professional baseball player, coach, and educator. Steve not only has a gift of identifying early talent, but he also has the ability to elevate himself above most situations to take a long-term and calm approach, creating learning environments for athletes and their parents. By blending his experiences, passion for learning, and natural empathic approach, he provides a unique perspective to parents like us who are trying to support their kids. Steve puts you in the shoes of the athlete, the parent, and the coach to understand the "often invisible" social dynamics that play out. As parents, we are not often aware of these, nor do we have the tools to navigate them. This book provides the resources and tools that have been a lifeline for us and for many other parents wanting to do and be their best for their athletes."

Tammy Arseneau
Vice President of Culture & Talent at Suncor Energy
Wife and mom of three boys

"I have known Steve for a long time and had the opportunity to coach dozens of his players, when they had advanced to the program I was with. What he talks about in *The Game Is Hard Enough* he has more than lived up to! His work with young athletes and their parents has been outstanding. He puts complex and diverse concepts into engaging stories and meaningful lessons. You will read important stuff about the things that will really matter to coaches, recruiters, and future employers. Your walk through this writer's exploration of principles and practices, all of which will help you grow up your athlete, will be something you will come to value as much as I do. If you are a parent, a coach, or a teacher, this book is for you.

I am looking forward to asking every parent I work with to read *The Game Is Hard Enough*."

Allen Cox
Parent, College & High School Coach, Academy Director, MLB Scout

"Steve is a terrific friend and resource who I often rely upon, both with operating the program at Indiana and towards being the best parent I can be to my children. He has such a wonderful perspective on raising successful children through sport, and I am fortunate to have his council. His own son, Matt, is ample evidence that the principles in this book ring true. I would gladly hire Steve in our program if ever given the opportunity and am confident he'll provide tremendously beneficial guidance for those navigating the modern sport world."

Jeff Mercer
Head Baseball Coach, Indiana University Hoosiers
Parent of young children

"I couldn't help but think of the praise that a Babe Ruth executive said to me about Steve during one of the years my boy and I were at the Ripken World Series with him. He said: 'Steve is running more than a good baseball program; he is raising young men of character'.

Steve is a friend who has talked me through much of the content of this book. I have seen him live out these concepts as a coach on the baseball field and am now blessed to have him as a mentor to my grade twelve son, who is seeking a baseball scholarship. If you've ever wondered, as I have, whether you are helping or hindering your own child in sport, I'd recommend grabbing a cup of coffee, finding a quiet place, and reading this gentle book that is full of strong principles and practical suggestions. More than a sports book, it invites you to be a better parent for the benefit of your child."

Layne Kilbreath
Coach, parent, pastor

"I had the pleasure of meeting Steve back in 2017 when my he gave my son Dane the opportunity to play for Team Canada at the Ripken World Series in Missouri. Dane had injured his arm during the leadup to that event, and being primarily a pitcher, couldn't play as important a role as he had hoped. Steve saw past the injury and provided Dane an opportunity that has changed his life in regard to baseball. Steve recognized a kid that worked hard, treated people with respect, was a good teammate—and he rewarded him for being those things, not just for being a twelve-year-old who could fling a baseball harder than most.

These exact same traits are what defines Steve Lloyd. He's a great coach, but more importantly he's a great person. He treats people the right way, and you don't see that nearly enough in the world of competitive youth sports. I put my trust in Steve that summer to take my son for six weeks away from us, and help him become a better ball player, a better student of the game, and most importantly, a better version of himself as a young man. It was one of the best decisions my wife and I have ever made. I encourage all of you to entrust Steve in the same way with this book. We still trust him today for insight and advice. He knows what he's talking about and now he's sharing his experiences and extensive knowledge base with the world. It's long overdue and I encourage you to make this book your guide to navigating your child's journey, regardless of his or her sport."

Chris Burns
Parent and former professional hockey player
Coach, McKinney North Stars – Dallas Stars Youth Travel Program

"Steve's messages and insights in his book *The Game Is Hard Enough* are exactly what parents of athletes need to hear. His stories are real and authentic because he has lived the ups and downs of life in sport. What resonated most with me was the reference to a 'sixth' tool that involves the heart, mind, and soul. In this crazy world of sport, life is not always fair and sometimes players get the short end of the stick due to circumstances out of their control. Teaching our children to play the game they love, as well as the game of life, with their heart, their mind, and their soul will help them be resilient and persevere as they navigate the journey. If our children know that we believe in them wholeheartedly they can face the joys and tribulations with confidence. What more could we hope for as parents?"

Leah Kingston
Teacher, Administrator, Coach for 33 years
Proud Mom to a son and daughter in NCAA D1 & D3 hockey

"I have always considered myself an extremely fortunate person by way of being a parent of two amazingly talented girls, but to also be called 'coach' by hundreds of young male and female athletes over the past twenty years. Getting introduced to Steve Lloyd by a mutual friend a handful of years ago has been another great fortune I uphold.

Getting to know Steve over the years has truly been a pleasure—his extreme passion for sport, learning about his experiences with athletes at all levels, and ultimately meeting his true genuine self. With all of that, I take great comfort in knowing that I can rely on Steve as a resource for my own personal growth, not only as a coach, but as a parent as well. The principles and practices that are outlined in the chapters of this book will surely help any person looking to enhance their respective role in sport—athlete, coach, parent or mentor."

Jeff Shepherd
Operations Director, Calgary Flames Sports Bank
Parent, Youth Coach, advocate for sport participation

"Steve has been a 'constant' throughout my own athletic career, and beyond. He coached me and my parents through three years of high school, and we've remained close ever since. Whether it has been as a coach, friend or mentor, Steve has given me and my family many 'gems' that I have carried with me throughout life. Often occurring in times when I most needed guidance in my life, I have always been amazed with how Steve can articulate pertinent insights and help in a way that I couldn't properly identify through my own prior perspectives. With this, I can confidently say that all of these stories and 'lessons' ring unbelievably true, and many of these principles I saw him dispense firsthand, both personally and in our shared sport-experiences. It's been cool to have seen a ton of the things I remember during high school basketball that improved that program immensely and made it such a positive, novel, and memorable experience.

If you choose to open your heart and mind and truly analyze your own behaviours in relation to these lessons, the only outcome will be a more positive and enriching sports experience for those around you: athletes, parents, coaches, and leaders alike."

Adam Pahl
Former player, Canadian Collegiate Athlete, current Youth Coach and future parent and professional

"I was lucky enough to have Steve Lloyd coach my eldest son in baseball a number of years ago now. I would describe Steve as one who personifies the concept that sport is merely the venue through which more valuable life lessons are taught, lessons like teamwork, sportsmanship, and character. In developing these skills, you also got better athletes and, frankly, it was a beautiful thing to watch.

This book offers to you what our family experienced and can be a tremendous resource to parents and coaches alike."

Duff Gibson
World and Olympic Champion, and parent of athletes
Author of *The Tao of Sport*

"Throughout my playing and coaching career, I have witnessed the evolution of coaching philosophy and strategies and in the process have gained an invaluable appreciation for the challenges faced by parents and youth level athletes in navigating the ever-evolving elite-level sporting system. While there has never been more instantaneous access to instruction and developmental philosophy, it has at the same time never been more complicated for those trying to disseminate the proper developmental path for elite-level youth sporting participants. An early focus on outcomes has resulted in an amateur sporting system predicated on premature evaluation and projection rather than a calibrated and methodical approach towards proper mental and physical growth development. The desire to rate performance and project future outcomes early in the developmental life cycle of the athlete has created pressure on our youth to live up to these assessments and/or overcome those which are prematurely negative. Neither of these approaches are athlete-centred and/or respect the best interests of our youth who would be better served by a focus on the importance of staying in the moment when it comes to competition and development. There are very few athlete outcomes that can accurately be projected when dealing with developing youth who are by definition inconsistent from both a mental and physical perspective.

I have known Steve for a decade and coached his son and others whom he has worked with at the grassroots level. My son had the opportunity to play in Steve's Ripken Program in 2015 and participate in the Cal Ripken World Series. This experience was invaluable from both an on-field and personal growth perspective. From a parental perspective, we were impressed with the overall developmental approach taken by Steve and his coaches and thankful for the wholistic growth opportunity afforded to our son. What Steve talks about in *The Game Is Hard Enough*, he has lived up to as a coach and parent, and it will be useful to anyone involved in talent development, whether it be in youth sport, business, family dynamics or any other performance-based pursuit! One only needs to get to know his son, Matt, to realize that Steve has applied these ideas and concepts effectively as a sports parent.

This book is full of engaging stories, useful insights, and strong principles to help parents and coaches better navigate the world of performance sport. I believe you will find it to be both insightful and thought provoking."

Greg Hamilton
Coach & Director National Teams, Baseball Canada
Parent of a performance-level athlete

THE GAME
IS
HARD ENOUGH

a guide for performance sports parents

STEVE LLOYD

The Game Is Hard Enough
© Copyright 2022 by Steve Lloyd

Steve Lloyd
Okotoks, Alberta

Paperback ISBN 978-1-7780596-0-5
eBook ISBN 978-1-7780596-1-2

Printed and bound in Canada.

Published by Steve Lloyd in 2022.

For all those parents and kids who are on their journeys.

For all the coaches, teachers, and leaders who are helping them on those paths.

And for Cakes, Betsa, and Patch, who are each showing me how we become the "best versions of our best selves."

Table of Contents

Preface

A Word from Matt Lloyd

Growing up, my parents always wanted what was best for me, and they always understood the bigger picture. My dad in particular did his best to make me wrestle with the concepts of working towards a goal, dedicating myself to my craft, and never settling. My parents set me up for success, creating clear guidelines and expectations to live up to and establishing high standards, especially the standards I began to set for myself. Accountability, whether that was for chores around the house, schoolwork, sports, anything really, was always a common theme. Although there were times where I lost sight of the bigger picture, I am grateful for my parents always pushing me to be my best. I learned early on about the purpose of becoming the "best version of my best self" in everything I did. And my parents' unwavering, unconditional love for my sister and me was the foundation for all the other lessons.

On the baseball side, my dad coached me from when I started in the game until I was fourteen, the age I started with the Okotoks Dawgs Academy. Those early years, preparing and playing with him, was where my foundation was built: a foundation of working for what *I* wanted in life, setting the highest possible standard for *myself* and striving for it. Many people say, "practice makes perfect," but we always said, "perfect practice makes perfect." Another saying we would always visit while I played for my dad was, "good enough is not good enough." The theme was about setting a high standard for myself, even at such a young age, and doing my absolute best to achieve it. Dad would say, "The results are irrelevant as long as you set a high enough standard and truly tried to do your best." It was always about a process. And this is where true progress lies, when a person has unbelievably high expectations for themselves, and the building blocks in their life to reach towards them. Even after they handed my sports development over to other coaches, my parents remained a guiding force in my life. They taught me the value in having a dream, and helped me turn it into a goal. They helped me build the attitudes and the internal skills to work towards making those goals into realities.

There is no magic pill. The only way to get better at something is to do it over and over and over again. This applies to anything. Painting, learning an instrument, golf, public speaking—literally anything. This is something that I subconsciously learned through playing baseball from a young age and sticking with it all this time. Through repetition comes comfortability, and that in turn breeds confidence. My parents gave me every opportunity they could. They allowed me to face challenges and to overcome adversities. They were (and still are) relentless in their commitment to me. Whether it was their unconditional love, or their lifelong lessons of responsibility and accountability, they have been essential to my journey. I have and always will believe in myself wholeheartedly, primarily due to the countless repetitions that my dad and I did together at that young age. It was sometimes hard. Because the game *is* hard.

An important thing I understood early on was that I was going to fail. A lot. In the game of baseball, as well as in life, it is inevitable that we will fail, which is why I believe it is the best sport to play, especially while growing up. In baseball, there is always a magical balance of success and failure, where the success is pure euphoria, and the failure is the worst feeling in sport. I had to learn how to fail, learn how to succeed, learn how to be resilient. And I learned these all through the sport of baseball. And any sport can offer similar opportunities for personal and professional growth. I believe that if it were not for the foundation that my mom and dad had helped me build, my career would have been cut shorter than it might have been. It certainly would not be what it is today.

Matt Lloyd plays professional baseball with the Cincinnati Reds organization, and has been working his way through their minor league system since 2019. During his three seasons at Indiana University as a two-way player, he led the team in many offensive and pitching categories, and was a leader both on and off the field.

As a Hoosier, Matt twice earned 1st Team All-BIG10 (2018, 2019) and was 2nd Team All-America in 2018. Prior to that, Matt played at NJCAA powerhouse Iowa Western Community College, where he was 1st Team All-Region in 2016, both as a position player and as a pitcher. His youth career was with the Okotoks JDawgs Academy and included playing with Alberta Provincial Teams and for Canada with the 18U Junior National Team.

Introduction

"Let parents bequeath to their children not riches, but the spirit of reverence."

—Plato

In the film version of *Moneyball*, based on Michael Lewis's book about baseball, a hard reality about the sports world is pointed out. "We're all told at some point in time that we can no longer play the children's game, we just don't know when that's going to be. Some of us are told at eighteen, some of us are told at forty, but we're all told." This inevitability is something that I have observed in sport throughout my entire career. Within our family, application of this certainty first began when my son was little, and it carried on through his later high school years. As parents, we tried to instill in our young man an awareness that balance and perspective are important, and are part of the realities that comprise life. I have taken the same approach with almost all the young people that I have coached, taught, or worked with in the other fields that I have served. With Matt, I put it this way, and despite his occasional annoyance at my insistence to revisit it with him through his developmental years, the message seems to have taken hold. "The only thing we know about your baseball career is that someday it is going to end...and unless your name is Derek Jeter or Cal Ripken Jr, someone else will likely decide when that is going to be."

My point was always this: someday, the baseball was going to be over. So, how could Matt, with our help, squeeze every bit out of his life's pursuit that he could? We were trying to help him strive towards his fullest opportunity, to reach his dreams. This was the goal we had for both him and for his sister, Rebecca, in every area of their lives. We knew we had to be intentional—my work in social services, ministry, youth justice, education, and sports had shown me lots. Those life lessons have been enlightening, encouraging, and frighteningly cautionary. Even "way back then," when he was just nine years old, Matt had a deep passion for the game, and a profound desire to reach towards his dream. Knowing that someday it (playing baseball) would end compelled us to try to help our son maximize every possibility he could, to become everything he could be in every aspect of his life, and to help him grow in his love for the game. It was always, and still is, our hope that Matt pursues the game, to follow his dream for as long and as well as he possibly could, and that baseball could be a means to a greater end for him. And it certainly has been. Even today (with Matt pursuing his career as a professional ball player), it still is. That end is for him to continue to become the best version of his best self. It has become his North Star.

This book will be full of lessons that I have learned along the way and have applied to my own perspectives and work. One was from a dear friend of mine, Gary Moro. He schooled me with a tremendous insight about my own approach to parenting a prospective athlete. It was back in 2006 and Gary's meaningful nudge was immediate and "imprintful." We were serving together as coaches of a Little League Majors team (12U, back before LL forced the dilution of those age group teams). Matt was ten, one of a small cohort of only four underage players in that five-team division in our area (there were also six additional AA, tier-two teams). He was holding his own with the older athletes and was on the cusp of beginning the work of navigating through all the things that a young player must confront. He was still fairly entrenched in some of the perfectionism which periodically blocked him at that point in his youthfulness (which he eventually, and literally, outgrew). The team was a few weeks into the season. Matt had just hit a sharp ground ball up the middle, which got scooped up by the shortstop, who threw him out at first base. Matt was visibly upset about not getting the result he wanted, and from the third base coaching box, I yelled out to him, "hey, you're alright, you're alright," as he slouched back towards our dugout. Gary was an excellent youth baseball mentor, and as a parent-coach one of the best I've coached with. In a firm voice, he said to me that day (our dugout was only about ten yards away), "Hey Steve—let it be, he'll be fine." He was encouraging me to do with my son the things that I was already doing with most of the other athletes and students I had served—to ensure that he had opportunity and obligation to face, struggle through, and overcome the challenges that he was presented with.

In the three-year period of coaching that age group in that jurisdiction, several other coaches in our league also taught me "lessons" that stuck. But many of those were not nearly as positive in their manifestation as Gary's. There was "Glen," who had his pitcher (who happened to be his kid) intentionally walk one of our guys in a meaningless, mid-season, house league game. Our player, a strong Texas boy named Mattie V, had hit five homeruns in five consecutive at bats (ridiculously epic!), and our whole team was "up-on-the-rail" in anticipation. But with two outs and no one on base in the first inning of a scoreless game, "coach" Glen took the bat out of the hands of this twelve-year-old hitter. In effect, he robbed the young boy of an opportunity to create a legendary moment with his friends. "It was just good strategy," Glen chirped from his bench, but I was left to wonder what his real motivation was.

During a different year, another parent/coach, "Trevor," was selected to be field manager of the league's summer rep team. Several players on that team did not live up to his expectations and were relegated to minimum play, and were consistently discouraged by his approach to them. But the bigger issue was that they appeared by most accounts to regularly outplay Trevor's own child, who ended up still playing most of the innings of most of the games. Three of those mishandled "All-Stars" kids didn't play the next year. Perhaps most revealing about one athlete's experience with his parent and coach is that Trevor's own son quit baseball two years later.

Then there was "Dewey", whose gruff and harsh tones were well known around the city. Of the twelve kids that were part of "his" team that final season in which I saw him coach, five children opted to not play baseball the following spring and summer. Truth be told, up to that point in my life, I had not endured the challenge of observing so closely the attitudes and behaviours of parents from those perspectives. It was the first time in my career that I was a parent AND a coach at the same time. It was a revelation!

My observations have deepened and broadened through the past forty-plus years of teaching and coaching, and I have been profoundly informed by my experience with other high-performance sports. As an intentional and informed observer of our social constructs, it is not hard for me to suggest that sport, and schools, and families, and the justice system, and our nations for that matter, are all facing remarkable challenges. Our kids appear to have been left to swim in deep and dangerous waters, and in many cases their families do not know how to help them. Shall we try to pull them out of the water? Or perhaps throw them a preserver or lifeline? Maybe try to turn back the clock and actually teach them to swim? Can we protect them from perilous predators? Mitch Albom offers a piece of hopeful wisdom for us and our children. "I also believe that parents, if they love you, will hold you up safely, above the swirling waters, and sometimes that means you'll never know what they endured."

Why THIS book?
Greg Hamilton, Baseball Canada's National Teams director and Head Coach of the Junior National Team program (18U), has a lot of insights about the state of youth baseball in his homeland. His observations are valid for all sports. "The hurriedness of the monetized system of youth sports is creating an environment where there isn't time for development. Parents are being misled. And kids are suffering." He speaks to a larger issue. As sad as it is, children who are part of performance-sports programs have to some degree become commodified; this has become an increasingly troubling facet of our entire society. By the time they are adolescents, our student-athletes have been weighed and measured as income streams and market shares, and are increasingly conditioned to believe that this is their "normal," as abhorrent as it sounds. Overall societal constructs seem to be designed to entrench patterns of entitlement and enablement amongst and within parents and children. This is leading to more and more discord in our families and in most of the elements of the world in which they are immersed.

Yet we still have aspirations and dreams for our kids. Undeniably, we should! Author Jeffrey Archer asks: "Are parents always more ambitious for their children than they are for themselves?" I believe that the answer is yes. More often than not, we want better for our offspring than we have ever attained or achieved for ourselves. And sometimes, we even want more for them than they want for themselves. Is there something we can do to help them? How do we not bring harm? How can we guide kids into better balance and more authentic opportunities? Do they know how to "swim"? How do we keep them from drowning? How do we protect them from being eaten by sharks? Will we model for them, and help them to build, a better and healthier "normal"? How can we guide them to play "their game" for as long as possible?

The question is why "this" book? **It is because I feel deep hope for our children, for their parents, and for our world of sports and beyond.** I have hope that all of our kids can have opportunity to chase their dreams. Leadership consultant Davia Temin says: "We're all looking for a trusted voice in the storm to help guide us—one that can steer us towards the truth as it unfolds, and away from lies and misstatements, be they well-meaning or malicious. This is the leader's task—to provide that "True North" to employees, citizens, customers, investors, and stakeholders." Possibly this book can help you find your voice or be a light on your path. Perhaps this book can be a compass on your journey with your student-athlete. Maybe it can help you build a map or find your True North. Carved on Henry Aaron's tombstone is this: "I am not concerned about how I am perceived as a baseball player. I am concerned about how I am thought of as a human being." What an insightful perspective, one that we should all share.

This collection of chapters can help parents, teachers, and coaches to learn to discern, to step back and breathe, and to take a good hard look at the role they play in their children's lives. When we imagine what that role **can be** and then assess and reflect upon what it really and truly **is**, we begin to see that the dissonance between these two is sometimes vast. And that the gap from one side to the other can be bridged.

There will be some insights here that will offer to parents and others opportunities and challenges that will aid in better preparing their student-athletes towards becoming "future ready." This is intended to offer fueling for feed-forward—that is, guidance for training the generation and their parents to acknowledge, accept, and value critique. We are looking at real outcomes that reach well beyond the sport—and understand sports as preparation for life. The book can offer a chance to wrestle with concepts, principles, and practices that are worth embracing.

Dr. Bhrett McCabe specializes in sports psychology and has written a lot about what it takes for athletes to be successful in their journeys. "Parents—your kids will struggle in the sport. This does not mean that they suck, can't make it, or you need to intervene immediately. There may not be a fix, but encourage them to work through things. Don't panic! Do not panic!" This book is designed to help you to not panic. It is, I hope, a guide that can assist you in encouraging, equipping, and empowering your child "to work through things" in a purposeful, proactive, and authentic manner.

Will this book get your child drafted, or gain them a college scholarship? I wish! But I can't guarantee that. However, I truly believe that the principles and precepts here can help them to grow and to mature into better people and better players. I have faith that these stories, and what they teach, can be helpful to you as you endeavor to equip and empower your children.

We have an enormous responsibility. But as Anne Frank says: "Parents can only give good advice or put them on the right paths, but the final forming of a person's character lies in their own hands." It is our duty as parents, and teachers, and coaches, and role models to challenge kids to deepen in character and develop as well-rounded human beings. It's up to us to provide them with the "materials" that their hands need to shape and form. The insights and experiences shared here can help you to clarify and assess your own beliefs, habits, and practices. Seek to model for them and to teach your children well as you walk alongside their passions and pursuits.

And, together, we can hope.

1. The Game Is Hard Enough

"It's supposed to be hard. If it wasn't hard, everyone would do it. The hard...is what makes it great."

—Jimmy Duggan
Manager, Rockford Peaches

I was watching a cooking show on one of those dedicated specialty channels the other day. It was one of those competition-based episodes. You know the type—the ones that pit cooks against one another, with a designated set of ingredients and a time limit. For some reason, it made me think about what we can learn from (and for) parents and athletes in youth sports.

Imagine you are on that cooking show.

You have been given the task of preparing a dish, using all the required elements and any other pantry items. Time is counting down. Do you have all the materials you need? Are the right ingredients and instruments in place? Are you comfortable in the workspace? Are you permitted to go beyond the required list, and take from the pantry shelves? Will you get everything on the plates within the allotted time, and will it be "good enough" to advance?

Sounds difficult to me (and I am really quite good in my own kitchen), especially as the challenge intensifies with added obstacles or unfamiliar ingredients.

Imagine now that, added to this already daunting task, there is now an overseeing task master: a guest chef who is hovering over your every choice, every move. Will this addition to the kitchen be a help or a hindrance? You hope for an occasional affirmation, an encouragement or a suggestion along the way. Mostly though, you hear from him loud words and witness over abundant gesturing and gesticulation. Criticism and hard tones abound. I imagine it would be like this performing under the yoke of someone like "that" famous chef from England.

I am pretty sure it could turn (fairly quickly in some cases) into an overwhelmingly disappointing experience and could potentially be damaging to some people. I expect it would take a tremendous depth of maturity (and maybe even some therapy) to survive something like this. And keeping in mind, by the time most people get to these shows, they are already quite accomplished and confident as cooks.

Now, imagine that this one-time encounter was, in fact, your every-time culinary experience. Almost every time you were in your kitchen, trying your very best to prepare and execute a meal, there is that "other someone loitering," sometimes in person, but always present in your consciousness. Perhaps not constant, but this person is consistent with commentary, suggestions, corrections. I don't know about you, but I am pretty sure that it would not take me very long to begin to dislike the experience. I doubt that I could ever do my best cooking. And if I was also compelled to get back in that kitchen day after day, with this environment, well, I'm fairly certain that it wouldn't take that long for me to begin to resent it, and to maybe want to give up cooking altogether. I think it would bleed away whatever joy there was from creating food. Because it is already hard to cook.

While some folks seem quite naturally gifted in creating wonderful culinary treats, building great meals takes imagination, talent, ingredients, tools, confidence, and a desire to work at it. COOKING IS HARD ENOUGH. And none of us really wants someone barking at us when we do it!

I am sure that some of you have already begun to extrapolate the connection to youth sport. Imagine that instead of the cooking show it's a sport, and maybe you aren't that confident stepping onto that field, or court, or into that arena.

Most sports are fun; they should bring enjoyment. The reason that most of us began to play games is because we like them. The pure joy of playing and competing are wonderful experiences on sandlots and playgrounds all around the world. Without question, executing specific skills, in any of the multitude of sporting endeavors, is "hard." Don't get confused with how "easy" some people make it look, or how naturally it appears that certain children take to some given athletic ventures.

Playing sports well is hard. Perhaps that is part of the joy of playing. There are those moments of achieving that are just sweet to savour. Do you remember the catchphrase from that old TV sports digest? "The thrill of victory, and the agony of defeat." While not every baseball game is a championship type event, each outing has within it an opportunity to grow, and to learn, while we play. In each exposure, we are given moments that are mini-victories and micro-defeats. This is a huge part of why it's so fun!

In one of my favorite baseball movies, a coach points out that, of course, the game is hard. "If it was easy, everyone would do it." Perhaps it is because the game is hard that most players work so much at getting better at it. Just like cooking (or music or inventing or writing, or, well, almost anything), sport takes imagination, talent, tools, faith towards the desire to develop and grow—all integrated together, to get better at the games we strive to play. It takes a growing confidence to confront uncertainties and to overcome them. These components are building blocks of the joy of play.

I don't think I will be alone in the observation that one of the consistently burdensome variables in youth sport is the manner in which some adults conduct themselves. We don't need to chronicle what these things look like. Suffice it to say, whether it is badgering a coach, or complaining about an umpire's call, these moments add to children's levels of tension. Having dad hang around dugouts, and gibber at the athletes about "whatever," more often than not adds to the players' anxiety. Whether during games and practices, or at home, when parents criticize coaches' decisions, or "correct" their instructions, children can often get conflicted and confused by mixed messaging. And too often, athletes can end up internalizing these tensions, building layers of uncertainty within themselves, and it can begin to rob them of joy. Pitching guru Tom House has an insight for coaches that pertains to every parent. "Our first job as coaches is to provide safety. Second is to remove judgement. It's simple, but it's not easy." Parents need to carefully weigh their role in bringing tension to their children's play-space.

At the very least, a child's internal landscape can, and often does, impinge on their ability to have fun, let alone play at their top level, of being free and clear to "just go play the game." After all, I cannot imagine anything positive that is made better by adding anxiety. If I am asked to walk between two buildings on a tightrope, I have to have a "tight rope"—the cable needs to be taut. But as I step out, it is only the rope that is governed by tension. The precariously perched walker cannot be safe if they are uptight, anxious or tense. Emotional and psychological tension rarely make executing fine motor skills easier; they steal balance and perspective. And these tensions, often based in some form of fear, drive away the love for the game, and the joy in the journey is often robbed from athletes. Ironically, these all lead to fragmenting the very focus that is necessary for a successful outing! As Trea Turner put it, "You know how hard it is to play the game from game to game, at-bat to at-bat, so many things can change." Let's not make it tougher!

I asked earlier that you use your imaginations. Let's do it again.

Imagine that you were asked to diffuse a timebomb, but you have someone, maybe several people, yakking in your ear. The voices are not always audible. Sometimes they are merely a collection of past commentaries that echo in the duress of that moment. Do you feel confident? How well prepared are you to execute your skills, to deliver in that moment?

How would you feel? How would any of us feel?

Do the "voices" in our life, at our schools, on our teams, help us or do they hinder? Often, kids don't get to choose who these voices are, or when they speak, or what or how they "contribute" their messaging...the voices that they hear are often "omni-present," whether physically and audibly at hand or just virtually "there," resonant in the echo chambers of the player's collected experiences. Can we help? Can we aid in limiting the stimuli that hinder? It is most often on us, their adult influencers. It falls on us to help our children/students/players to sort out which of the noises and voices they will pay heed to. The pundits at Next Level Baseball frame it this way. "It's basically Coaching 101!!! If you can make a player fall in love with the game and competing, or stay in love with the game and competing, you're a damn good coach." Perhaps this is even more true for parents.

So, let's remember...don't make playing any tougher than it already is. Ask regularly, do you help or do you hinder? Are you building love and joy, or helping to defeat them? Is your kid having fun? It is essential to keep these foundational elements in mind.

After all...

...THE GAME IS ALREADY HARD ENOUGH.

2. The Perils of Encouragement

"Do you really want to know? Or do you want me to lie and make you feel better?"

—Steve Lloyd

I love those advertisements from insurance providers, and for one insurance company in particular. They show something happen, typically an extreme and often obscure event, and then display some sort of iconic statue that celebrates the company's handling of the scenario. And they always end the spot with their catchphrase— "We know a thing or two, because we've seen a thing or two."

We love these ads because they are "celebratorily unusual." They interact with something atypical, and bring it to our field of vision, so that we all see. They reveal that attention can be, perhaps even should be, appropriately focussed on special events and moments. And these ads hold up to the light something that I have grown to believe deeply over the years. They applaud the extraordinary, and only the extraordinary. The flip side of that coin is that they are beacons of NOT celebrating the common and mundane, and thus are examples of challenging a dangerous precept: that every moment and each action on the field should be distinguished. Unlike our youth sports world, in real life not everyone wins a ribbon. We keep score and stats and track results. Sometimes stuff happens and things go wrong. Not everything gets made into a television ad. And everything does not deserve to be celebrated. Not everything should result in an "encouragement." In fact, the preponderance of encouragement and affirmation is contributing to a growing problem in youth sports, and, I would propose, schooling and family life too. Yet, as children's writer Roald Dahl points out, "It's a funny thing about mothers and fathers. Even when their own child is the most disgusting little blister you could ever imagine, they still think that he or she is wonderful."

Steve Lloyd

Am I saying that we need to remove encouragement from the conversations with, and commentaries from, supportive parents and other followers? Not at all. Affirmation and affection are essential elements in the growth and development of all young people, not the least of whom are those pursuing excellence in their areas of passion. Kids desire and deserve encouragement (don't we all?), and it is often most meaningful when it comes from those with whom they have real relationships. However, it is important to recognize that, in many regards, encouragement mechanisms and patterns are a lot like fire. When it is properly managed and appropriate applied, fire is lifegiving. It can bring warmth, light, and protection, and even be used to help nourish. Yet, if it goes beyond its necessary boundaries, when it becomes uncontained, and uncontrolled, then fire can bring destruction.

What I **am** suggesting, is that there are real, significant perils connected to encouragement. Thus, we need to handle it with deliberateness and discretion.

Huh??? What does that mean? Let me continue with some personal observations. When my son was still in youth baseball, especially after I had stopped coaching him, I would often get grief from other parents. It was quite curious. The comments were particularly vigorous in the years in which he was playing with a really strong club program in our hometown. But it wasn't what you might presume.

There was a fairly significant cohort of parents who thought that I didn't cheer loudly enough or often enough for my son. Truth be told, he was a really good player, and while playing shortstop as a defensive stalwart, he led his team in most offensive categories. He was also the squad's ace on the mound. Facts (stats and recordkeeping, even as unreliable as they sometimes can be) would indicate that for his high school years, the lad was a top prospect in the region in which we lived. Add to that, the kid was a terrific teammate, and was highly respected by players and coaches across the country. This carried over into provincial teams, national team, Junior College (JUCO) and later at his four-year NCAA school as well. He is a high calibre person, even more than he is a talented and accomplished athlete. Even while he was involved in collegiate baseball, many parents of Matt's teammates were often curious as to why I was so often subdued, at least by their measures.

So, what was the issue? Well, I suppose in some part, most parents in the programs (those who tended to be quite vocal in the cheerleading for their own children) expected that a player who made so many strong plays, and who consistently came through in big moments so many times, would have "over-the-top" exuberance in his corner. But for the most part, I watched and enjoyed as quietly and invisibly as I could. Many of the other families chose a different pattern though. Only a few were over the top. And even fewer got out of line. In these cases, I am not referring to jeering by others or derision pointed at opposing players and coaches (though this is unacceptable in itself). If willing to admit it, we'd likely acknowledge that we have all seen cheering-on of kids that has been... well, let's just say, it has been at times "misplaced." Not everything is a "Great Play, Johnny!"

What are some of the lessons that I learned as a parent, when my son played at an elite level? There are applications for other families.

First, with more and more personal achievement accumulating on his baseball resume, it became clear to me that *my son did not want any more attention drawn to himself than was already there.* Like many young people, he was thrilled to help his team when he played well. And he was garnering lots of attention from lots of people. He thrived in the proverbial spotlight, but never asked for any lights to be shone on him. Fortunately, he was more concerned with being a "best guy **for** his team" than with being accoladed as the "best player **on** his team." As a quiet and confident young man, he was humble and content to know that, first and foremost, he was part of a team. He cherished his relationships and roles with the guys and had learned along the way that it was rare that a team was ever successful without everyone contributing. In addition to his maturing perspectives, it was clear to me from my decades of sport that things can fall apart quickly on teams when individuals begin to put themselves ahead of the group. It sure doesn't take long for a viral element to spread, and to bring a group or team or nation to its knees. Matt had heard me talk with a lot of athletes about how dangerous it was for their teams when any of them began to seek individual attention. Accolades, regardless of how impressive they may seem to be, are seductive and dangerous if not handled maturely.

Secondly, he had grown to understand and accept a new, more meaningful sense of what was his "normal," and what he expected from himself. He gauged himself according to his own hopes and dreams, and never concerned himself with being better than someone else. He understood what he could reach towards and that was how he measured what he was doing. Significant to this time in his development, he embraced a perspective that his "process" was considerably more important than any of his "results." *He neither needed nor wanted to have someone (let alone his parents) acclaim him for doing the things that he had learned he was supposed to do*. After all, would we celebrate him using the toilet properly, or applaud him for making his own bed? He did lots of things on the field (and off it) that were noteworthy in helping all his teams to be successful. But to him, these became regular, to-be-expected results that were products of his process. Please don't mistake my commitment to supporting him, however. There were numerous times that I have acknowledged, albeit often quietly, something he has done. And there are times, that I have celebrated joyously and visibly when he has helped his teams climb to those glorious moments of competitive excellence. However, we were always intentionally cautious to neither celebrate mediocrity nor bring glorification to the mundane.

Thirdly, just as it does for everyone, the principle of authentic interaction mattered to my son, especially as an athlete. It still does. There was a nineties-era writer named Josh McDowell from whom I have adopted a relevant thought. "You can fool a fool; you can con a con; but you cannot kid a kid." You see, truth matters. *What really resonated for my son from the coaches he has most admired, and I hope from his parents, are authentic responses to what he did and/or did not do.* The connections between his actions and efforts and his accountability for them have spoken deep truth to Matt. They have shaped his career and his life. So, when he saw and heard me celebrate any number of his extra-normal moments, he knew it was special and meaningful—because authenticity really matters. Another way to put it is this: If everything is "special," then nothing really is!! Likewise, if nothing is ever ineffective or insufficient or just wrong, then an athlete will never be challenged to get better. Authentic learning, and authentic teaching or coaching, are always built on real relationships which are cornerstoned by truth. **BECAUSE TRUTH MATTERS!!**

The fourth reason is that along the journey of youth sports (my son played several, in addition to baseball) *we had both seen enough situations where an athlete had been embarrassed by his parents' behaviours and choices.* I have also witnessed numerous incidences through the years of parents doing things that alienated or dismayed coaches, scouts, and recruiters. In both baseball and basketball, I have encountered too many unfortunate circumstances in which a college or pro scout has just walked away from interest in an athlete, because of what they had seen from the prospect's family. And sometimes bad stuff just happens at or near a ball diamond or gym that causes a child to experience pain or embarrassment. So, there was an inherent awareness on my part to neither embarrass Matt nor compromise opportunities for his future. I also did not care to do or say anything that could inject any possible negativity into the team's culture.

These are some lessons I have learned and tried to apply through the years. It is essential that we encourage and affirm young athletes. But because there are perils connected to inauthentic encouragement, it becomes just as essential to lead our perspective with a few guiding question areas. This is especially true in the context of a society that refutes and diminishes responsibility and accountability and, furthermore, enables individuals to blame everyone else but ourselves for our shortfalls.

1. What happens when we celebrate everything?
2. What happens when we choose to affirm and to lift up the mundane as a pseudo-sacred achievement? In this, are we creating mediocrity as a probable by-product?
3. What happens when we protect athletes from feelings about mistakes, failings, and shortfalls? When we remove adversity from the journey of a young athlete, are we really just short-circuiting their development and growth? Can we be willing to let our kids live out the consequences of their actions?
4. How can kids learn perseverance, if they always have adversity yanked away from them? Do we comprehend the connections between adversity, perseverance, and resilience?

More often than I care to admit, I find myself cringing at the way a lot of parents and grandparents interact with what their athlete is doing (and sometimes not doing) on and around the diamond and away from the field. Too often, all the messages that athletes hear is how good they are, and that nothing is their fault. And way too often, young players have mistakes and errors and failings excused away, dismissed as if these do not matter. However, authentic affirmation and encouragement, especially via the essential tools of assessment and accountability, are key for growth and development. But these must be delivered intentionally and consistently in order for young athletes to grow.

There is tremendous promise and potential that is inherent in young athletes. Often this is developed and drawn out with appropriate and authentic encouragement coupled with guidance through obstacles and adversity. But we must also be aware of the pratfalls and perils of unbridled and inauthentic praise. Good and purposeful work brings fuel, and affirmations breathe life into the fire of an athlete's passion. But let's not encourage unwisely; we don't want to let the fire either flame out or to burn down everything around it, after all.

3. The Big Lie

"And if all others accepted the lie which the Party imposed—if all records told the same tale—then the lie passed into history and became truth."

—George Orwell

I love learning from history! If we have the courage to take a thorough look at what has happened, and make the purposeful efforts to explore why these events have occurred, then we have an opportunity to make the changes we need to, so that we can improve (or at least not repeat patterns that have been problematic). As George Santayana put it a hundred years ago, "Those who do not learn history are doomed to repeat it."

An essential part of systematic development in any pursuit is having both the orientation and the ability to examine what we have done, and then to attempt to implement thoughtful and purposeful changes. This is especially true in sports, and particularly necessary when trying to grow in the game of baseball.

Unfortunately, some baseball coaches (and too many parents) often make the grave error of using incorrect approaches in addressing player improvement or evaluation. I believe this is because our general understandings of baseball, and the ability to play the game well, is based on a misconception, and if we were to authentically examine the sport, the way many view the game is in fact built on a number of misconceptions.

We are told to believe that the game is hard. And it is...it really, really is!! A lot can happen in the course of a practice or a game that could be categorized as a misplay, an error, or a result that is not perfect or prescribed. Without doubt, there are ample opportunities to see failings in baseball activities! And in some respects, it could appear that players fail significantly more than they achieve their desired outcome (consider batting statistics).

That there are failings in baseball is not the problem.

The problematic precept that deeply governs many approaches to the game, the idea that dominates coach and player psyche is this: *baseball is a game of failure.* I can see why so many folks buy into this. Like much of what happens in our world, if we tell a lie that is big enough, for long enough, eventually most people begin to believe it. "Baseball is a game of failures."

Well...it's a lie—it's a great big lie! And it is not the only one there is...(We'll get to these, too!!).

Let me share an account from Matt's youth baseball career. It comes from his second season of what was then called Bantam AAA (players 14 & 15 years old, based on birth year, an age-grouped elite league in our province). The previous season, as a first-year bantam, Matt had hit around .450, and had a pretty strong collection of other baseball numbers to go with his batting average. (Keep in mind that any statistics in youth baseball come with distinct aspects of unreliability and do not always reveal what they appear to.) That was then, this was "now"; this was a different season, and from his point of view, Matt was struggling.

It was Mother's Day, and Matt's team had just finished a weekend series in Edmonton. The squad had swept all four games Matt had pitched another shutout in his mound start and had anchored the team defensively at shortstop in the other games. Yet his offensive production was not what he had grown accustomed to, and he was not very happy with himself. In fact, he was growing more and more dissatisfied, and was remarkably and noticeably discouraged, something I had not seen in his baseball journey before.

We were having an even-more-quiet-than-usual ride home from Edmonton. As he typically did, Matt fell asleep for the first section of the trip and awoke when we stopped in Red Deer for some food. He stayed quiet as we pulled back onto the highway, and I was practicing my policy of allowing him time and space to deal with his on-field experience in his own manner. Nonetheless, I was aware enough to know that I might still be able to engage my son in some form of conversation. My experiences as a coach/teacher/parent helped.

So, I asked about his food, and he shrugged it off. And then I asked what turned out to be a gateway question, "Are you doing okay?"

I paused and waited.

It didn't take long for Matt to blurt out, "I suck as a hitter."

Well then...how was I supposed to answer that? Fortunately, I didn't answer...quite purposefully, I left his exacerbated exclamation to hang in the air.

A few moments later after what seemed to be an excruciating length of silence, Matt spoke again, this time with a noticeable tremor in his voice... "Dad...did you hear what I said? I suck as a hitter."

And I am sure, if I had been looking into his face, I would have seen that his eyes were probably full of tears. This was a moment of personal crisis for him, and he was at a crossroads.

My response to him was quiet, quick and real. *"Matt, it would be very dangerous to talk yourself into that."*

What we talked about for the next several minutes, and what he experienced through the next few days was transformative in his baseball career and I believe had a positive contribution to how he would approach the game, and his life, as he moved forward.

George Orwell wrote, "During times of universal deceit, telling the truth becomes a revolutionary act." We live in a social construct that builds on, promotes, and endorses a myriad of lies and half-truths. Our children are growing up believing so many wrong things about themselves. And here we were, Matt and me, in a car, driving home, confronting a huge matter in his life. He was on the precipice of believing a giant lie about himself, and his deep passion for the game that he loved was hanging in the balance. His hopes and dreams were at risk, and it must have seemed to him that his whole world might crumble under his feet. He was in that very precarious place that so many young players are in today.

"It would be very dangerous to talk yourself into that."

I ought to take a moment to unpack some of the luggage and circumstances that had gotten Matt to that point. I noted earlier that Matt had produced a very statistically successful season in the previous year. He had high expectations for himself, and a few other people were commenting about his lack hitting. At the point in the season that he was at, about 8 full weeks in, Matt was batting about .225, and more significantly, he was rarely feeling that he was hitting the ball very hard. Consequently, he was very frustrated with his lack of production. He was beginning to press.

Perhaps the biggest thing that had contributed to Matt's mindset and state of play was the fall and winter training sessions that he had been worked through, most notably the hitting work he had experienced with a coach at his program. "Trevor" was convinced that Matt needed to hit for more "loft power," a term he used to describe a player's ability to get the ball in the air and drive it out of the yard. He wanted Matt to pull the ball almost all the time and had him work on aspects of hitting that were neither good for his skillset nor a natural swing-path for him. In short, it was not a great fit, and while Trevor was a solid pitching coach, he was not really very effective as a hitting instructor. But Matt committed to the work, because "that's what players are supposed to do." And he struggled with it.

Spring rolled around and his team was assigned a new head coach, Allen Cox, a former high school and collegiate coach from the US (who was very different from Trevor). He is a great coach, and an even better person. At this point, Matt was just beginning to build what would become a tremendously valued relationship that has lasted for years. But on that day in May, Allen was still fairly new to our family. And Matt was still trying to do the stuff that Trevor wanted him to do.

Back to the conversation in the car that day.

"It would be very dangerous to talk yourself into that...

I know you feel this way, and it hurts you, because you think it's true." I paused briefly to let it sink in. "Would it be okay for me to explore some truth with you about who you really are as a baseball player?"

The next little while Matt and I talked about some pretty foundational things. I asked him about times he felt most successful, about situations when he felt most comfortable at the plate. We talked about all the times he had come up with big hits, and incidents that he had just trusted and executed his plan. Most of the talk led up to the question that he most needed to ask himself, an essential question that was fundamental for him to be able to move away from the lies, and into his truth. After I asked him to look back at all the instruction, at everything that he had ever heard about playing the game and hitting a baseball, this is what I inquired of him. "If you were your coach, what would you tell yourself?"

The answer he gave was bang on. "Well, I guess I would say to get my feet closer to the plate again, to look to drive the ball to left field and use the middle of the diamond, to keep my head down on the ball, and to be shorter to the ball and compact with my swing, and quick to and through the baseball."

Gently, I pushed for a little deeper response. "Matt, what are you really saying?"

He sighed the way that only a boy can sigh when answering his dad. "I'm saying I need to go back to being who I am as a hitter."

I will unpack a few of the things that unfolded as a result of the Mother's Day conversation momentarily. But we have to consider to what outcome, in the big picture, all of this will lead us. Matt and I were in the midst of dealing with not just one big lie. In fact, we were confronting and combatting three distinct, yet interconnected, mistruths and misconceptions that drive a player's feeling about themself. What follows is a lot of what Matt and I explored that day. I think this applies to an awful lot of other kids, too.

Steve Lloyd

1. Big Lie #1—"Baseball is a game of failures"

Wrong perspectives are a paradox of our times. There are remarkable gaps between <u>what appears to be</u> and <u>what actually "is."</u> Consider the condition of "virtual friendships," or that folks so often adamantly (sometimes mindlessly) believe "news" pieces, soundbites and clips, parcels of truth as told to them in portions by often biased TV networks and internet sources. Do we see the value people place on the number of likes they get or don't get from others they don't even know?

In baseball, the numbers tell a story. But it is often not the story that most folks think. The best players in the world at the highest level of competition only get hits three times out of ten at bats. "If you do this as a professional, you will be a very rich all-star player." We are taught that the top baseball athletes fail seven out of ten times. It must be a game of failures, then. But this really is a lie.

The game, certainly as players move from basic levels upwards, is a game of progression. The numbers are symbols, clues, and signals, much more than they are fact, and as standalone figures that are absent of connected meaning they do not really tell the whole story. Maybe they don't even tell any of the real story. And the real story is more about how the numbers (the immediate results) are interpreted and interacted with. Perhaps the better way to understand it is to suggest that long-term success in the game might be better built from a platform that deals with how to interact with the perceptions linked to outcomes: in other words, it's a game of learning to deal with *perceived* failures and successes.

What actually separates the best hitters from those who are mediocre is not the final outcomes of the plate appearances. Rather, what sets them apart is a combination of **Process-Driven Approach** (*that places process well ahead of results*), and a **Purposeful Perspective** (*that embraces the whole truth, as best it can, through an objective Point of View*). An athlete who embraces this mindset creates for themselves a new world order, one in which the observer refuses to allow any mere result (whether "good' or "bad") to dictate whether the execution of a skill was successful. When these two threads are interwoven with productive and sustained physical effort to acquire appropriate skills, a baseball player has produced a three-cord strand that is not easily broken.

a. The **Process-Driven Approach** embraces the reality that the results alone are dishonest: that which they can actually inform and instruct for real and authentic feedback is tainted and often inauthentic. Attending to process first, and setting aside the relative unimportance of results, is a path to freedom for the athlete. While a big-league hitter may result only getting three hits every ten at bats, a closer examination shows that to be able to generate those outcomes (hitting .300), a player must execute at least eight or nine quality plate appearances out of ten to have a chance to create desirable results. It becomes more and more imperative that a baseball player has to focus intentionally on what it is that they are doing to try to do at the plate, rather than it is to put numbers they like in a boxscore. So, they work at developing benchmarks and manageable goals to improve execution of their kinetic chain, efficient and purposeful progressive movements, and sequence of events so that they can be on-line and on-time (process). This tends to lead to more success than limiting evaluating their efforts only by determining a "positive or negative result." Focussing on the process, and refining each of the elements therein, is the only effective pathway to generating success. The destination/by-product may well still be to have good numbers, and it is fine if it is. But it is only a clearly defined and properly executed process (skills, technique, athleticism, mindset, and approach) that will make the journey possible and productive. Keep in mind that professional scouts and college recruiters are much more engaged in evaluating how a prospect approaches the game and how they execute skills. And they try to project those observations about the player's process into what they might eventually be able to do. And they almost never pay any attention to the numbers the kid has put up!

b. Perspective really matters. Rather than succumbing to the idea that it's a game of failure, let's adjust to a more fully authentic, and more articulate, understanding. Certainly, there will be lots of failings while playing the game. Baseball is a game of interacting with and processing our perceptions about the results we see. As Winston Churchill pointed out, "Success is not final, failure is not fatal: it is the courage to continue that counts."

A result is really only a failure if we stay stuck in it. **Purposeful Perspective** means that we see the truth of what has actually happened, that we honestly assess why that outcome occurred, and that we move on to the next thing, making any adjustments that may be helpful. The player does something amazing... learn from it and move on to the next task. Something goes dreadfully wrong... learn from it and move on to the next task. It also allows us to be free from the rollercoaster ride of result-dictated emotional responses that so terribly dominate youth life and youth sport. It means that we, on purpose, choose how we will see the world and the elements within it. What would the world look like if we couldn't see it in all dimensions? I have coached tons of kids who would get upset every time they made an out, and their parents were often just as misplaced in their reactions. Some players would rather have a terrible hack at the ball and reach base than to execute a nearly perfect swing and hit a ball hard right at someone to make an out. Sometimes, baseball parents and coaches put the wrong value on wrong outcomes—and this is a time when two wrongs do not make a right!

A Purposeful Perspective is when we affirm and embrace that doing a right thing right is significantly more satisfying than any mere result. It encourages players to learn that both in baseball and in life what is about to happen is significantly more important that what just occurred. And it gives the athlete a much more solid foundation to stand as they move forward in the game. After all, they are works in progress. Why would we ever want to judge a developing player as if they are exhibiting a final product?

2. Big Lie #2—"Be like Mike"

We remember the sales pitch. *Be Like Mike*...and to be honest, Michael Jordan has earned his place as a sports icon. He was a legend (still is) and the jingle was kinda cool. And it wasn't just about him and basketball. How many of us baseball fan parents would not have wanted our child to play the game like Ken Griffey, Jr?

However, I find it more than a bit disconcerting that so many parents have wanted their child to be something that they aren't. It happens way too often that children are told that they should throw just like this pitcher, or have a swing exactly like that hitter. I am not saying that we should exclude the use of really good exemplars from top level players. There are plenty of useful case studies and templates for how to do skills from which we can learn. We have done more than our share of video analysis of top players at our house. But in the same way that a hyperfocus on mechanics (that doesn't embrace a child's own athleticism and abilities) can create robotic players, it is unwise to the point of irresponsible to push towards only trying to replicate a legend. It is a little bit of a problem-area that some parents want their child to "be like Mike" in some way or another. It gets really troubling when we want them to actually "be Mike."

Perhaps worse, is when I have seen a child who is compared to a sibling or a teammate. Robbie was one of those kids. He loved the game and from the ages of ten through twelve, he was one of the top players in his age group in the region. He was blessed to be the younger brother of Richie, also a very talented prospect. Robbie was close enough in age to Richie to often have had the same group of coaches. Unfortunately, the majority of those coaches consistently and relentlessly expected Robbie to always be the same player that

Richie was. Truth be told, both boys were outstanding baseball prospects; however, they were very different talents and extremely different temperaments. Sadly, the more that coaches tried to get Robbie to more "suitably" resemble his brother, the more disenfranchised he became. The joy and passion for baseball slowly bled out of him, and Robbie never really progressed to where the game may have taken him. Comparisons and expectations from others, and being pressed to become someone other than himself, beat Robbie down. His coaches failed him. Being compared to his older brother was terrible for that player.

Fortunately, my son was not a victim of those sorts of misplaced expectations. Largely, the conclusion that Matt had to reach as a product of the Mother's Day exploration was that, in order to be on the path to becoming authentically successful, he had to stay within what we called his own "creation identity." He had to be true to himself, to pursue fulfilling all that he was designed to be and could become. He revisited and renewed his identity as a baseball athlete. He came back to his "why." He could not be any other player...he had to be him. And while he could be "like" a player that he admired or respected in certain aspects of their approach, style, play or even character traits, he should never try to "be" that guy! And this was a huge step towards Matt becoming a better player and teammate.

3. Big Lie #3—"There are shortcuts to success"

Too many people think they can get to where they want without doing all the things necessary to get there. Parents buy their children's way into a program or on to a team. More often, families ensure that they select teams and programs where their athlete can be the top player. Pro athletes take performance enhancing substances to increase their chances. Players cheat to gain an advantage. Sometimes, kids will work really hard only when their coaches are watching. These types of shortcuts typically harm the athlete and hurt many people around them. In effect, shortcuts offer, at best, short-term gain for long-term pain.

Even as a 15-year-old, Matt had seen enough and had heard enough to know that overcoming what he was going through could not be done with a quick fix, or an instant solution. When push came to shove, the question then became, "What am I going to do?" He knew that he had to get back to being himself by getting back to the work of being himself. He knew he had a lot of work to do. Lots of work.

He got in touch with one of his former coaches, Ramon, a great hitting instructor who worked with me. He did a few sessions, and started to find himself again, working hard and well at getting back to the foundations of hitting that had grown out of his identity. Matt also went to his new head coach and explained his situation. Allen was amazing in his response, and immediately let Matt know that this was the approach that was best for him, and that Trevor had been wrong to try to change him. Perhaps most significantly, Allen reaffirmed in Matt a growing belief that he was special and should only ever keep to who he really was.

And they got to work...hours and hours of extra and better work. And always with the perspective of working on perfecting the process and his approach. Matt recommitted to never relying on the game results as a benchmark for success or failings. It was also a really important time for him to more fully understand that, just like statistics, he had to interpret and appropriately discern the input and accolades that were being placed before him by others. This experience really imprinted in him a growing sense of humility on and off the field.

One of the things we most need to be aware of is that we do live in a time of systemic and universal deceit, and we have to be intentional to not have our players and students beaten and bruised by misconceptions and paradoxical perspectives. This is true in their realms of sport and perhaps even more apparent in the world of schools, social media, and interpersonal relationships.

What young people need is someone, i.e., us, to champion the truth for them and with them. Revolutionary? Or just plain necessary?

Back to the story I started a while ago... At this point, maybe you are asking, "So, what ended up happening that season with Matt?"

On Mother's Day, Matt was hitting about .225, more significantly he just wasn't squaring up baseballs, and was frustrated in ways he had never been.

He confronted the lies, told himself the truth, committed to being his true self and got to work.

He grappled with a purposeful perspective and put working on his process way ahead of relying on any results. And something clicked.

By the end of that summer, Matt's season batting average had climbed to .470 (though we will talk about the relative unimportance of statistics in youth baseball in the next couple of sections), had helped his team win a provincial championship, earned silver at Bantam Canadian Championships (where he was on the all-tournament team), and a key player with Team Alberta's 15U gold medal squad at Western Canada Games. He was also named Bantam Player of the Year.

Something really clicked...I am sure glad it did!!

4. Batting Average Is Satan

"Statistics are like bikinis. What they reveal is suggestive, but what they conceal is vital."

—Aaron Levenstein

In my life as a parent, coach, teacher, and consultant I am consistently confronted with scenarios in which a "leader" is determining the success or failure of someone who reports to them. Too often their approach to assessment is mired with misperceptions, lack of clarity regarding what is supposed to be measured, and misapplications of misunderstood "results." Sometimes we get stuck in patterns and perceptions that inhibit our full capacity to see what is really going on. Too often, especially in sports, we get trapped by the lies of statistics, the illusions of success, and the misplaced belief that results have more meaning than they actually carry. Sports in general, and baseball in particular, are fraught with these potential landmines. Sigmund Freud, in his discourse *Civilization and Its Discontents*, made some interesting observations. "It is impossible to escape the impression that people commonly use false standards of measurement—that they seek power, success and wealth for themselves and admire them in others, and that they underestimate what is of true value in life."

Results in the game are very often quite misleading, and it becomes more and more essential (especially with younger athletes and underinformed parents) to discern and decipher what these results are actually revealing. Statistics are only reliable for incomplete measures, and too often (especially with younger athletes and underinformed parents) these numbers are the by-product of "very limited" ability and execution, and underdeveloped competencies by the athletes, and incomplete or incorrect recordkeeping by parents. And consider how convoluted and confusing some of these numbers-based judgements might actually be: get three "hits" every ten times you are at the plate, and you're a star; make one error out of ten chances, you're a lousy fielder; throw four or five times off-line to a teammate, no big deal; "pitch" fewer than four strikes for every ten attempts, and you are struggling on the mound. It's no wonder that kids get locked up by the numbers. The numbers represent "results" that are not only unreliable—they are invalid.

Nonetheless, way too often, the driving force of too many parent dialogues is some form of, "My kid is so good, they're leading their team in so many stats." These folks really don't get that, at almost every level before college or professional baseball, stats and numbers rarely indicate anything valuable or authentic and are more often than not quite misleading. Putting a high level of priority on these stat packages is at the very least problematic and, in its most dangerous incarnations, it can be revolting.

To put it succinctly, BATTING AVERAGE IS SATAN!!

Please let me pause for a moment to reset.

Lynda Mullaly Hunt has a wonderful story that might lend some clarity here. In *Fish in a Tree* the author tells the tale of a child called Ally who is artistically and mathematically gifted but struggles immensely at school because she cannot read. Ally is dyslexic and, until she is diagnosed with that condition, she is inappropriately measured by an inauthentic standard, and is deemed a failure by that standard. The climax of the story unfolds when it is declared that, "Everybody is smart in different ways. But if you judge a fish by its ability to climb a tree, it will live its life believing it is stupid."

Years ago, while coaching youth baseball, I had an opportunity to organize and implement a few development camps during the regular season with the league in which I was a volunteer. At one particular camp, we had a wonderful ten-year-old boy named "Alexi." He played for a team I had not yet seen in league play, but I had heard a lot about him from other coaches in our jurisdiction. He was fairly big and quite strong relative to his cohort and was every bit as athletic as I had heard. And, my goodness, could Alexi hit!!! His hand-eye coordination was excellent, and he could flat-out crush baseballs with his powerful righthanded swing. However, his coaches were beside themselves, because despite all their attempts and efforts and rigorous instruction and drill-work, Alexi just was not figuring out throwing. And the thought of this beast of an athlete actually ever pitching from the mound in a game seemed like a pipe dream (certainly for his coach, who seemed to value winning over development).

Well, a curious thing happened…and out of all the times, it was during a lunch break—we were just hitting outfield fly balls and challenging the kids to "make a play" or to "get a highlight on SportsCenter." Part of the fun was that if a ball got over their head, the player was to make their very best attempt to throw out the imaginary runner at second base. When it was Alexi's turn, I miss-hit my fungo (a coach's practice bat) a little bit, and the baseball went a little farther and to his left than I had intended. No matter to Alexi, who was as competitive as he was athletic. He raced into the right field corner, where the ball was heading, nearly catching it. He then, without thought or hesitation, chucked the ballglove off his left hand, picked up the baseball with the same hand, and threw a laser beam to second base, which, needless to say, caught the entire coaching staff by surprise. *As it turns out, Alexi was in fact a southpaw.* He had been playing all spring righthanded. The family had immigrated with him the previous winter from Eastern Europe, and he wanted to try baseball. His mother was a high-level field-hockey athlete and had never seen a baseball game (neither had his dad, who was also a top athlete), and when she saw everyone else at practice with a glove on their left hand and throwing with the right arm, she presumed that this was a rule of the game. So, fortunately for Alexi, we figured out who he actually was, got him a lefty glove, and his enjoyment for the game almost immediately sky-rocketed. (And you should see what he did as a hitter when he began to hit from the left side…but that's for another time!)

Now, here's where the rubber hits the road. If I were to assess Alexi as a baseball player prior to him knowing it was okay to be lefthanded, he would have shown less of his full potential in the game. Or perhaps it would be fairer for me to suggest that I would have fallen short in understanding who he really was, and what he really could have been. Had we tried to evaluate him based on his numerical ERA, or defensive metrics that scored his righthanded throwing ability, Alexi would not have showed particularly well. His "stats" would have done him wrong!

Of course, it is imperative to assess. Please do not mistake what I will be trying to get to in this section. What we will be considering here is that we need to measure what should be measured. And we need to not determine how good a fish is by its ability to climb a tree. Too often with younger groups, we tend to think that accumulating statistics (whether reliable or not) is the same thing as assessment. It is not.

As parents, how often do we hear from other moms and dads? More often than not, their reports lead in the general direction of the level of skill and accomplishment that their child is achieving on the diamond. Sometimes the parent will pull a scorebook or some stat sheet out to validate with numbers what it is that they believe about their child's performance. Somehow, they never seem to understand that their subjective impression is not necessarily an accurate representation of the child's actual abilities.

Sometimes it happens between parents and coaches too. I was sitting in the baseball office of one of my dear friends, a coach I will admire till I go to my grave. As we were chatting, one of the parents from one of his program's teams arrived, stats sheet in hand. The conversation shifted and this parent—let's call him Gord—wanted to talk to the coach about how fortunate the team was to have two equal-level, top-calibre "number one" pitchers at the top of their rotation. With a bit of a startled look, the coach took the bait and replied, "I don't think I get what you mean. Mike (I have adopted pseudonyms for this) is clearly our best guy. While we have some other pretty good arms, no one else is really that close."

Not to be deterred, Gord decided to explain. "I have done all the numbers—Mike and Junior are both 7-1, both have ERA about 1.60, both have WHIP around 1.00, they have similar strikeout and walk numbers. So, as I see it the two boys are at the same level of performance." And he went on to further explain that the two pitchers were equally valuable to the rotation.

The coach shifted in his seat, in what might have appeared like he was uncomfortable, while I was quite willing to just sit back and listen. I also knew that coach well enough to know that he was about to unveil a depth of knowledge and insight to this parental statistician.

The coach started to uncoil his thoughts—it went like this... "Do you know who Mike has pitched against for us? Do you have any idea who Junior has thrown against? We run Mike out against every top team we play. He always pitches to the best programs we face and is always matched up with every team's top lineup and best arm. These are not just the better teams around here, I am talking about some of the top programs in North America!! No disrespect to Junior but he has pitched against most of the lesser talented teams we played. Mike goes against A teams, Junior faces B and C squads."

The coach went on, "So, to say that these two are even close is a huge stretch. The numbers may look the same, but they are built on two entirely different standards of measure. It is like looking at Michael Jordan's numbers in the NBA and comparing them to some kid's stats in a high school league." What the coach was pointing out in that circumstance was adeptly said in another context by Scottish poet Andrew Lang. "He uses statistics as a drunken man uses lampposts—for support rather than for illumination."

If baseball has shown itself to be consistent in any aspect through the years, it's that it does place a pretty high value on the numbers. Justifiably so, I believe, at the highest levels. A huge problem, though, with the assigning numbers and categories to young players is that we often think that they mean the same thing as they do at the highest levels. What most folks don't get is that there are a lot of things that contribute to the numbers that are not nearly that quantifiable. One of the most challenging parts of baseball-related assessment is that there are myriad variables and constructs that contribute to the outcomes of a player's statistics. These get more convoluted the younger the players are.

Consider this.

Have you ever seen a player have a day full of mediocre at bats, where not once did they hit a ball hard, and still go 4-4 on the scoresheet? How about that kid who ropes three line-drives, but each one right at someone and goes 0-3 in the scorebook? Sometimes, a player makes a great defensive play and "robs" a hit. Once in a while overall defensive play for a team is not as strong and "hits" are a lot easier to come by. We have all seen an umpire "squeeze" a strike zone, and other times the umpire have a very generous plate. Can I say a pitcher is "really good" just based on the number of outs he made, or the strikeouts he notched? We have all seen great outings result in a loss, and other times that a hurler struggles mightily and escapes situation after situation. Lots of variables and tons of variety make it hard to be entirely empirical with statistical measures. Players can have a nearly perfect swing and crush a baseball for an "oh-fer," or execute an almost perfect pitch and still have it knocked somewhere on the field where it is not an out. The result that is generated, a result that is influenced by a lot of factors entirely beyond the control of that individual, gets credited to that player, often despite (not because of) their efforts. So how can the body of those numbers ever be entirely reliable? And even if the stat was reliable mathematically, we still need to discern what it might mean wholistically. Consider the case of a young man that I had known as a youth player, who had moved on to a strong academy and had a successful collegiate baseball career. He was playing in a high-level league after he was done with varsity baseball with other former collegians and some ex-pros, and had several terrific seasons. One year in particular, he led his league in OPS (a metric in baseball that combines on-base percentage and slugging percentage—the higher the number, the better), at 1.3 or so. Outstanding!!! Think in terms that a good batting average hovers just around .300. A quick look would suggest that the athlete must have had ridiculous power numbers. Yet, the player here was able to do this without hitting a single homerun and had only one triple. How did he manage to achieve this "total"? The data requires some examination for us to truly evaluate the type of player he was and the type of season that he had. We can do this, mostly because the data that would drive our analysis was accurate and authentic and accumulated over a full season in a league of highly skilled, accomplished players. This would rarely, if ever, be the case when it comes to youth baseball.

Whenever our quantitative measurements have to be qualified, then authentic qualitative assessment is compromised. As the noted scientist Ernest Rutherford has suggested, "If your experiment needs statistics, you ought to have done a better experiment."

With baseball (think about all the statistics in MLB), and in anything that would be measured for some form of monetary import, the numbers tend to average out over time. A longer season would produce presumably more authentic statistical measurements. Situations tend to even themselves out over a season, and even more so through a full career. At the professional level, these numbers play a significant role in the contract situations of the players to whom they are assigned. But just because these hold valid status at the highest level, we must not presume that the same premise holds true for youth programs, teams and individuals. Inconsistency of play, combined with relatively meagre sample size, would suggest that numbers (were we to try to apply them to youth baseball) are actually fairly unreliable. Assessments and measurements are essential to player development—however, we must be careful about **why we measure**, **what we measure** and **how we measure** these. Perhaps we need to be even more intentional though, about what we do not measure!!

How then DO we successfully measure effectiveness and growth at executing required tasks? There are going to be various mechanisms that people will use. However, it is important that the appraisal procedures be based in principles that lead to some sense of authentic assessment.

With this in mind, there are two threads that we need to weave together. The first is balancing and intersecting our **QUALITATIVE** and **QUANTITATIVE** benchmarks. The second is engaging and embracing the interaction between **PROCESS** and **PRODUCTION**, placing higher value on the former than the latter. These are woven together and are best viewed as part of the whole-player development tapestry. We will look at this more closely in the next chapter.

We cannot get away from the reality that numbers in baseball will always matter. After all, baseball has provided the most comprehensive packages of statistics, data and analytics in mankind's history, it seems (at least in relation to sports). Some numbers are real and are virtually absolute in their measuring—things like velocity, spin rate, bat speed, how fast a player can sprint are all able to be scientifically recorded. Yet, even though mathematically calculated, the vast majority of baseball statistics are based in some way on factors beyond the execution of the player doing the task. Things like ERA and batting average are calculations derived from formulas. While based on accumulated numbers, these stats (and those like them) are influenced heavily by factors, conditions and variables outside the player to whom those numbers are assigned. So, even though they give the appearance of being empirical, especially when they concern baseball levels below collegiate and professional ranks, statistical analysis of an athlete cannot truly be relied upon. You see too often, especially as it is in youth baseball, that the numbers attached to a player's name are often a collection of images and impressions, and are too often assembled by folks who don't really know how to properly categorize them, let alone understand what they mean. It is like trying to take a photograph in a house of mirrors that is filled with smoke—attempting to focus on the real item is very difficult. At best, these can be perceptions and illusions.

Perhaps we might start with this premise—that we need to recognize that the younger the player, the less important or meaningful the "results" are. The only things that really matters are whether the children are getting more accomplished with their game play, and that they are developing their skills and execution of the game while having fun doing it. If we were creating a t-shirt, it might read "Process over Production."

Nonetheless, numbers can be quite merciless, and some folks try to apply them as sterile factors on a spreadsheet. We mistakenly give in to the perspective that statistics are objective or neutral, and could/should be seen without prejudice or agenda. This could be true at the highest levels of the game. But at every level, particularly with youth baseball, the numbers need to be interpreted and qualified. Too many people rely on these numbers to determine relative value, rank, and status of young players. Too many folks manipulate the stats to create argument and manufacture some form of consent. Too many parents place an unhealthy level of a worth on the results their children generate in games. "Batting average" **IS** Satan.

Presumably, most folks who place high importance on statistics in youth baseball may well have good intentions. But the road to hell is paved with good intentions. Maybe that's a highway we don't need to take our players down.

5. But...Assessment Is Essential

"Every line is the perfect length if you don't measure it."
—Marty Rubin

It really is imperative to assess. Please do not mistake what I was trying to get to in the previous chapter. What we will be considering here is that we need to measure what <u>should</u> be measured. As noted in the preceding chapter, too often statistical analysis is in fact measuring the wrong things, especially when it pertains to the formative ventures and development processes that are, by default, youth-aged sports. In the same manner that **you cannot fatten a pig by weighing it**, you cannot evaluate a youth player by only looking at their "numbers." This is especially true when those numbers are based on results (derived from an inconsistent collection of inconstant variables) rather than analysis of process and progress.

As fellow parents, I am sure we all hear from other dads and moms, often relentlessly. Reports about the level of skill and accomplishment that their child is achieving on the diamond, often with scorebooks or stat sheets out to validate with numbers pointing to what it is they believe about their child's performance. I can admit that I have done some stat gazing about my own son's performances at different plateaus of his career, from youth teams all the way to his professional seasons. I also realize that the numbers are more and more tempered by the need for "interpretation," especially the farther back in his journey that we might look.

Unfortunately, these numbers are often less than valid, particularly for the reasons that I have previously noted. When our quantitative measurements have to be explained, elaborated or otherwise qualified, then authentic qualitative assessment is compromised.

Of course, with baseball (particularly when we look at the higher levels of the game), the numbers tend to average out over time. The longer the season, the more authentic the statistical measure might be. Situations tend to even themselves out over 600+ plate appearances. However, when we are talking about youth level baseball, it seems apparent that the inconsistency of play, and subjective, underinformed record keeping, combined with relative meagre sample size, we could suggest that "numbers" are fairly unreliable. That being noted, I do want to affirm that assessments and measurements are essential to player development—however, we must be careful about *why we measure*, *what we measure* and *how we measure* these. Sigmund Freud framed it this way, "It is impossible to escape the impression that people commonly use false standards of measurement—that they seek power, success and wealth for themselves and admire them in others, and that they underestimate what is of true value in life." In other words, our measurement practices reveal to the player what is truly valued.

How then DO we successfully measure effectiveness and growth at executing required tasks? There are going to be various mechanisms that people will use. However, it is important that the appraisal procedures be based in principles that lead to some sense of authentic assessment.

With this in mind, there are two threads that we need to weave together. The first is balancing and intersecting our **QUALITATIVE** and **QUANTITATIVE** benchmarks. The second is engaging and embracing the interaction between **PROCESS** and **PRODUCTION**, placing higher value on the former than the latter (in both pairs). It is also important to recognize that these are woven together and are best utilized when done so with some fluidity and flexibility, with a sliding scale as it were. In other words, the relative importance of one area should be modified from player to player, and from situation to situation. And at almost all times, Qualitative benchmarks and Process development outweigh Quantitative statistics and Production numbers, even at the highest levels of professional baseball.

There is still the certain reality that the numbers do matter. Afterall, we do keep score, and sometimes players reach base and sometimes they don't. Sometimes we strike a batter out, sometimes we walk a kid. The premise of playing the game is that everything is based on some form of counting towards a rules-prescribed outcome.

Numbers can still be somewhat informative and instructive at every level. What needs to exist for statistical analysis to be a valuable tool in youth baseball is that the numbers be viewed through the more authentic lens of *qualitative assessment*. The goal becomes to examine and measure the quality of the effort and the execution being made, and learn from that examination with the intention to make adjustments and possible improvements. In order to do this, we need to develop and embrace a different system of seeing the player both practice and perform. Just as important, our system needs to promote the same value (or perhaps place greater value) on practice as it does games. A core impetus that I believe is essential is that we focus significantly more on *"ongoing" Formative assessments* (development, process, progress) than we pay homage to *"final" Summative measures* (results & scores).

One such Formative tool is Quality-at-Bats Percentage, which is a measure of how process-centred a hitter is at the plate, regardless of result. QABs include any one of the following: seeing 3 or more pitches after 2 strikes are against you, 6+ pitch at bats, extra base hits, hard hit balls regardless of outcome, walks, sacrifice bunts, or sacrifice flies. A big metric used by programs today is exit velocity. I have used a recordkeeping tool that works with players to attend to their "early pitch recognition," determining pitch type and quality early in the delivery.

On the pitching side, much of organized baseball has been using a measure call Quality Start, determined if the starting pitcher goes for at least six innings, and surrenders three or less earned runs.

One of the most basic things we try to have pitchers understand (especially when they are young) is that the best pitch in baseball is a strike!! We could spend hours designing metrics that could be used to see stepping stones of quality-based assessment and process-oriented feedback for instruction.

And perhaps that is the challenge! Can we create a mechanism that observes and measures the effectiveness of actions, and separates these from the result?

One of the things I have done consistently with the teams I have coached (that has been helpful in the players shifting their eyes away from traditional statistics and goals, and onto forward-thinking quality measurements) is the Three-Pitch Guideline. Especially with young pitchers, I have presented them with this as a challenge. For each batter, try to use a three-pitch maximum. "Out or on in three pitches or less." This is all we will quantify in this standard that we implement. The goal is to throw quality pitches, which at the lower levels are simply strikes thrown with athletic intent. It has been remarkable to see the general effectiveness of young pitchers grow as they get comfortable with this approach. And as this translates into older divisions, I have seen kids throw more quality innings later into games and generate better ERA and win/loss records. Attending to the quality and process bears good fruit over time.

Let me use another example, this from teaching. It was a grade nine Language Arts class. After some preparation work about how to take a balanced approach to research about a topic, methods to focus and develop supported arguments, and a bit of overview into technical frameworks and formats, it was time to assign a full essay. Our class was about eight weeks into the school year, and this was our first major writing work, though the class had spent some time with debates. What I wanted to challenge the class with was the process they needed to undertake; the premise was that "process" was significantly more important than the product they were attempting to present. And I asked them to think about whether they would want to drive a car that had been haphazardly thrown together without proper and necessary parts, or without an intelligent design for how it should be constructed.

How was I going to really get them to buy in and to focus on the elements of process? Though they may not use the lingo, kids understand the concept of economy of scale. It was essential that the quantitative measures we were going to use (their marks, which were very important to them and maybe even more so to their parents) matched up to the pursuit of qualitative, process-oriented work I was asking them to do. With this mind, here's how the numerical grades were distributed (there were detailed rubrics for each section). The total assignment package was worth 100 marks. Of those 100 marks, 10 marks were assigned to the final draft. A total of 50 marks was placed on the quality and organization of the research and preparation files, brainstorming and initial outline. Students earned another assigned grade out of 20 marks for their first draft, and the other 20 marks was determined by the students' engagement and interaction with peer editing, revisions and adjustments to the drafts. All of this was done with mentor level (teacher-coach) interaction, observation and feedback. Every student that actively participated improved as a writer, especially as we revisited this format several times throughout the school year.

There are also ways to incorporate this same orientation to quality-centred, process-driven work in our practices and games. One elite program for high-school-aged players has a mantra that says, "Get Better Every Day." Matt's JUCO coach challenged him to improve in at least one area one percent every day. These are incredibly good goals, but need to be defined and applied. How does a player know that they are actually getting better?

It is up to coaches and parents to develop some better feedback loops. Essential for authentic assessment is understanding the relationship between the athlete and their outcomes (and certainly their perceptions of those outcomes). Many players get handcuffed because they are focussed on results, which are inherently unreliable. As we have seen, "results" are too often illusions; in the hands of some, they become inventions that serve to indoctrinate players and parents towards wrong thinking (or sell lessons!!). Over time, what might have seemed like a harmless infection can turn into a full-blown illness. How many kids have we seen who are tremendous in practice? They make every play, crush the ball in BP, and carve up the zone in their bullpen sessions. Yet they have extreme difficulty transferring these performances into game situations. Most of us can think of one of these "five-o'clock" players!! Why this dissonance?

Perspective and perception are driving forces in how players interact with the world. Whether by design or by default, the underpinnings of our practice plans, conversations, and body language intersect with how our athletes see themselves and see their experience. They are constantly juggling thoughts and emotions that grow out of both intrinsic and extrinsic factors affecting them. Even more so is the imprint on their internal mechanisms from what they perceive that their parents and coaches value, and what we appear to make important. In a later chapter we will delve more deeply into how foundational this is for player development and how important it is for parents and coaches to be tuned in to these concepts.

What we measure, and how we communicate about it, plays a big role in how players see themselves and interact with what they believe is important. Several collegiate coaches I know routinely hold high intensity practices that are, in effect, more challenging that the games their teams play. This aids in adjusting an athlete's impression of what "pressure" is. These programs are consistent in posting practice results, celebrating and challenging progress in the team's process, but rarely put a boxscore or any season statistics up in the clubhouse. One coach labels it, "Getting comfortable with being uncomfortable."

Especially with younger teams, it can be very helpful to put extremely high and visible value on attitude, effort and focus during practice sessions, and "insisting" that the games are only to have fun showing what they are learning. This is why our programs always tried to have fast-paced and competitive practices, and why we took teams from where we are to play tougher teams in the US (and eventually some of the best teams in the world). As Mike, one of our program's coaches pointed out, "The more difficult, 'pressure-packed' situations down south that our kids participated in, the better prepared they were to play in games that 'mattered' back home...and they were better prepared for their own possible baseball future(s)."

Exposure to challenge, and authentically assessing the experiences, helps to build a new (and arguably more productive) norm.

Process should almost always take precedence over production, especially as we consider overall development in youth sports. To this end, it is essential to understand a few key concepts.

1. **Know why you are measuring:**

    A cornerstone of assessment is purpose. When done effectively and purposefully, our measures should inform and instruct our practices as coaches, and our perceptions as parents. Assessment for the sake of assessment tends to be counterproductive, especially if all we are doing is creating numbers. After all, a watched pot never boils! And measuring a stick does not make it longer.

    We also need to remember that the most important benchmarks are more towards the depth of experience. So perhaps the key aspect to regularly measure is about player joy and engagement. Imagine if a league championship was determined by who had the most fun, and which team learned the most!! Maybe we should develop a statistic for this.

2. **Know what you are measuring:**

    Have a plan, and stick with it. Be intentional. And make sure that the players know what is important. Parents and coaches reveal what they believe is important by paying attention to it. Players will benefit from prioritizing quality work and process. Also, be obvious with feedback regarding effort, attitude and focus. Intangible aspects are just as important as athleticism and skills, and this area needs to be addressed and developed.

3. **Know how you are measuring:**
   Use a range of tools, rubrics, charts, reports to authenticate the values placed on the work being attempted and accomplished. When possible, have players build a video library of their skill executions, with the intent of monitoring progress. It is important as well that we have some baseline or common standards. But it is just as important to measure a player relative to their own growth, and not only comparatively to teammates and others. It can also be a big help to have the athletes journal their development process.

4. **Know when you should measure:**
   A wise teacher once told me, "You can't teach during an exam." We already know the impediments created by primarily using game results as the standard. Ensure athletes are comfortable committing to the developing process by placing more value on progress than production. This has to be modelled explicitly in practices. And as I noted before, as the athlete is acclimatized to measurement practices, anxiety levels tend to decrease.

5. **Know what the measurements mean and how they inform:**
   Imagine a team is on the wrong side of a no-hitter. A quick, and incomplete evaluation could be that the team is not very good at hitting. It is one thing to go hitless as a team in a game, and respond by scheduling extra batting practice. However, when things are not going well, it seldom helps to 'more of the same thing'. It is entirely different when we see the causes of a problem area and make adjustments. Sometimes a team is not very good and needs to really improve, but sometimes, a pitcher is really, really good and

has a great performance. Knowing which should inform how a coach or parent will respond!

Most of the information we gather, whether stats or narratives are merely data—these are not answers, understandings or strategies. Feedback must be clear, concise and timely to be meaningful. And it must be consistent and honest, designed to draw attention to what is effective and what could use adjustment. Be intentional in unpacking any data or narratives so that it means something, and so that the athlete can adapt. The vast majority of assessment in sport ought to be formative and intentionally designed to promote ongoing development. Perhaps we should leave any summative assessments (assigning a final grade) to only the highest level.

6. **Know how the measurements apply and what they inform and instruct:**
   Players don't get better without making changes. Be in the position to lead towards those changes and adjustment. Whether as the coach or a parent, it is imperative to see what is going on and work with it. It means that we ought to know what's right and what's wrong before we barge ahead to try to fix it. This might mean a coach changing a practice plan, or the parent adjusting what they talk about with the player. Most often it is a little adjustment or a small change in perspective that can open up a world of opportunity to the athlete. Above all, the feedback needs to be simple and timely, so that it has meaning.

Measurements can be quite merciless and can be applied as sterile factors on a report card or scoresheet. The emotional and spiritual landscape of athletes (especially young ones) is not an unencumbered place. Unfortunately, stats often carry too much weight on the perceptions of young athletes, and those statistics are neither objective nor neutral. At every level, particularly with youth baseball, the numbers need to be interpreted and qualified, if identified or addressed at all. When we look at the whole package, it becomes more and more vital that parents and coaches help the player get better. Making "quality" and "process" the priority is a huge step towards that end. Adjustments and changes that come from authentic assessment are essential to the development of any athlete. And in the end, we really do need to keep the final message to young players about all of this clear and simple.

If you really want to fatten that pig, maybe it is best to figure out when to feed it, what to put in the trough, and then just step back and let it eat!

6. Make-Up Matters

"We cannot choose our external circumstances, but we can always choose how we respond to them."

—Epictetus

In sport, coaches and scouts talk all the time about an athlete's set of "tools"—their collection of skills and abilities that combine to help the higher-ups and decision-makers determine the relative value of the player, within the scope and sequence of the level at which that individual is being evaluated. In the baseball world, we hear often about the "five tools" that scouts, cross-checkers and other assessors place scores and values upon, as they grade a player's performances and potentials. Typically, these five tools include the following: Speed; Arm Strength; Fielding Ability; Hitting for Average; Hitting for Power. These are more or less statistically measurable, and in most cases as players move forward in age divisions and ability plateaus beyond high school, are fairly reliable. Nevertheless, despite some empirical devices (like radar guns and a growing arsenal of tech), there is still a significant aspect of subjectivity, and sometimes guesswork, involved as coaches, scouts and recruiters attempt to translate their current data (the player as they see them in that moment) into projectability predictions (the player they perceive that the athlete could become in the future).

Through the years, many athletes who have consistently outstanding performances in the five-tool arena have had success in moving through the ranks of amateur sport and into the realm of professional baseball. Look at Ken Griffey Jr, who coming out of high school was considered to be a "can't miss" prospect, and was. Every talent evaluator in America predicted that Bryce Harper would be a Big-League star, even as far back as when he was in junior high. But not every—in fact not many—athletes are Griffeys or Harpers. A lot of prospects turn into suspects!!

It is fair to say that almost every player that progresses beyond high school competition has had to possess to some degree all (or most) of these tools. Not all of them make it to pro baseball, and even fewer earn spots on an MLB roster. Those that do get recruited to collegiate baseball or are drafted, possess talent and athletic ability, at least to the extent that they are deemed ready to keep moving forward with their baseball hopes and dreams. Some wear the label of "top-prospect."

But...there is a huge "however."

However, we regularly bear witness to physically talented athletes (some of whom are labelled "can't miss" because of their talents) who simply stall, or wash out. This sort of outcome for a young first round pick is noted in *Moneyball*, as it pertained to the baseball playing career of Billy Beane. Intriguingly, it appears significantly more probable that "top-rated talent" ends up stalling, rather than living up to their grand projections. It seems clear, then, that there must be something else involved, an aspect of athlete development that goes beyond (or perhaps before and beneath) physical and technical proficiencies.

In respect to fully developing *projectability*, as much importance (or perhaps even more) has to be put on **the sixth tool**—the mind, heart and soul of the athlete. Is the combination of talent, ability, skill mastery, and athleticism the primary determinant for success? I think that the answer to this question is concurrently both a resounding YES and an absolute NO. "Yes," in that the five tools establish a "baseline" or foundation of observations, data and narratives that set the table for whether or not that athlete will be considered as a prospect. And "no" because something else, the sixth tool, is what separates talent from other talent, and determines how productively and purposefully a player is able to engage the process of moving forward along their path. A term that is loosely bandied about in the realm of sport, and particularly in baseball, is *"make-up."* It is not easily defined and in most regards is tough to quantify. But it is increasingly important to understand it, and grapple with it, as young athletes face continually growing challenges to their journey. In fact, internal composition is often an essential aspect of making or breaking an athlete's career. Because...

MAKE-UP MATTERS!!

How many of us know a very talented kid who may not have ever fully reached what we thought they might become? I am sure that most of us do. In Chapter 3, I mentioned a player named Robbie—a kid that sadly did not grow into many of his possibilities as a ball player, as he suffocated under the expectations of those around him.

More on point to this particular conversation is another athlete, named "Gary," who as a Junior National Team player was touted for years as a probable first-round MLB pick. Watching him in BP was astounding: the young man would absolutely crush baseballs, and regularly put on showcase displays of raw power that was off the charts. Scouts would hover around the hitting cage and batting tunnels, practically salivating over this specimen of a prospect. Occasionally, if a pitcher threw the ball where he was swinging, he would launch it, often well beyond the confines of the ballpark. When he was drafted late in the first round, he signed and then spent more than four years in Rookie ball before finally being set loose by the organization. Despite all the accolades and anticipations of many scouts (but not all, mind you), this young man could not manage to "put it together." Though electric in the pre-game cages, especially as he moved into pro ball, he was not able to translate into his game time batter's box. Somewhere in the repertoire of this "5-tool" athlete, there was a something that was missing.

And there are so many more kids all over the continent who at one time or another were the most physically dominant player in their program and garnered much of the attention in their regions; but many never got over the hump of their own potential. Too often, talented and highly regarded players begin to wither and fragment under the "pressures" of living up to everyone else's predictions.

Perhaps even more often, it isn't external pressure that buckles a prospect as much as it is that many physically dominant athletes lack elements from mental, emotional and spiritual toolboxes that could afford them the opportunity to compete competently when facing other players and teams who are at the same or better talent and execution levels.

And then there's the other side of that coin: those other players who were not as highly regarded along the way, and yet seem to squeeze every ounce out of the opportunities they earn. Consider Steve Nash in the world of basketball. Only recruited by one NCAA program out of high school, yet he somehow developed to the point of becoming a collegiate star at Santa Clara University, NBA draft pick, Olympian, two-time MVP in the League, and member of a number of Basketball Halls of Fame (both for FIBA and in Springfield). Not many would have predicted that story arc when Nash was playing high school hoops in Victoria, BC.

I mention him because I have been blessed to witness Stevie up close: we shared a number of National Team seasons when he was a young player, and when I served the program in a support staff role. While it was remarkable to watch him in practices and games, it was even more captivating to share conversations and observations with him, a collection of moments that revealed something exceptionally different about him. Something about his character and his temperament separates Steve Nash from most athletes and even most people. These intangible qualities (his make up) amplified every ability, skill, and capacity to execute and were compelling variables in his journey of raising himself up to fully realize his full capacity as a player (and as a person, I would suggest). He was consistently engaged in the process of becoming the best version of his best self!

When we think of athletes that we would say have "good make up," what is it that we think we are seeing? Sometimes, maybe it looks like they are aggressive in certain aspects of the game at certain times; they seem to have a consistently displayed work ethic; maybe they seem confident in the face of trying circumstances. There are certainly a lot of hints or signals that might suggest someone may possess some level of good make-up or bad make-up. Interestingly, it seems much easier to identify those athletes of whom we would say have fragile practices or underdeveloped skills in this area. Most of us have witnessed a young player melting down in some way on the field or at the rink. We've seen temper tantrums and/or crying over what would appear to be otherwise harmless outcomes in games or practices that probably don't mean much. Sometimes we see parents who are extreme examples of poor make-up, to their own kids and anyone else who observes them. And, sadly, too many of us have seen children walk away from their sports for reasons we would rather not have had "chase" them away. Sometimes those reasons are connected to their make-up at that point in their life.

As we hope to aid our young student-athletes to be able to actualize their own opportunities, it is imperative that we explore the Mental Game. There are lots of books and websites that promote varieties of techniques and habits to overcome discomforting scenarios or perceptions, or to perhaps have checkpoints in overcoming nervousness. Lots of these habits are useful, and truth be told, I have used lots of sport psychology methods and techniques throughout my decades of serving athletes, and even at home with my own son (and a myriad of other prospects who have lived with us through the years). Consider, though, that this is more than just Sports Psychology—it's more than just mental disciplines, more than training towards conditioned positive responses to stimuli (the concept I call pre-sponding to events and situations). Knowledge of the game, experience in rehearsing what COULD happen to be prepared for when it DOES happen, and mental toughness are all very important. Practicing these are necessary, and doing so can enhance overall growth in a young player's make-up.

Baseball writer Brian Grosnick suggested about this concept on one of his platforms that make-up is, in fact, more than just one thing, and that it needs to be evaluated as seriously and particularly as any of the other tools. He said:

"But perhaps one score for make-up isn't appropriate. Perhaps there are five mental tools as well as five physical tools: learning ability, commitment, positivity, focus, and 'maturity' (I can't think of a better term than this to describe the ability to stay out of trouble). Maybe there's even room for 'mental scouting'—a specific branch of scouting dedicated to the evaluation of a player's mental toolbox. Mental scouts could be industry folks, people who'd had experience working with players -- but maybe it'd be more appropriate for these people to be a combination of adult-learning specialist and sports psychologist. Heck, maybe these people already exist." (*Beyond the Score*)

The five tools will never not be important. They are like the walls and roof of a house. But for them to stand and be strong, they have to be built upon something even more solid. **The foundation upon which the five-tools must be built, is the sixth tool—"make-up."** And the cornerstone of that foundation is chiselled out of the core belief that an athlete holds about themself. In essence, make-up is a matter of a player's internal and intrinsic "spiritual" wellness. This is not meant in a religious connotation. It's not some new-age mysticism thing that I am talking about. What I am suggesting is that an athlete (or anyone) can only fully realize what they can do from a point of view of knowing who they really are. And it begins with their inner being. They need to ask themselves some very foundational and formative questions, and as their parents and coaches we need to ask the questions alongside them.

What is the athlete's belief about himself or herself? What is their "identity"? What is their essential core value in the understanding of "self"? Why do they possess these perspectives and are they "true" and healthy? In Chapter 3, I told a story about Matt's deeply personal struggle with hitting production one season—he was able to resolve that by asking himself these types of questions and returning to what we called his identity as a baseball player.

What are pillars of good make-up? What does it look like? What are the characteristics, qualities, and attributes? I would suggest that there are several aspects that we can identify, even if they are not empirically measurable. These are more aptly considered more qualitative elements, as it can be hard to quantify intangibles!! I would suggest that in players with good make-up we see a lot of these things: playing with joy; calmness; assurance; perspective; perseverance; resilience; life balance; courage. These athletes also tend to grasp the recognition that PROCESS is the only thing worth measuring, and are rarely bound to their results (whether positive or negative).

To help to understand some of what make-up entails, I like to categorize these qualities into general areas. Players who have good make-up tend to:

➢ Have a deep-seated drive to succeed, with an awareness of what "success" really means, and a work ethic that commits to focussed effort despite how the athlete "feels" in that moment.

➢ Consistently assert their Process Orientation into whatever situation they are encountering, and commit to the values of that process regardless of the short-term results.

➢ Possess growing technical knowledge and athletic skillsets (Baseball IQ) but are developing highly attuned mindfulness of their own emotional & spiritual well-being (Life EQ).

➢ Have a progressive commitment to put all matters into a balanced, authentic, and truth-based perspective. They possess a well-accessed toolbox of habits and techniques and are assured of their own identity.

➢ Are growing in trustworthy humility as a good teammate, understanding that everyone has the same value in the program, and with the team. Does not seek to place themselves as higher than anyone else.

> ➤ Are intensely, intentionally, and intrinsically competitive—they seek to be the best that they can be, not merely to win games or be better than another player.
> ➤ Seek to consistently be the best version of their best self.

How can parents and coaches help to challenge for growth in these areas? Coach Marc Rardin, from perennial JUCO powerhouse Iowa Western Community College, teaches his teams the essential nature of "learning to embrace challenge...to get comfortable with being uncomfortable." The success of his teams and the progression of his players to good four-year programs and into professional baseball is remarkable, and for the most part it is the character and mental/spiritual toughness of his players (as much as their talents and abilities) that make them so highly sought by four-year schools. He recruits good character and works deliberately to define and refine make-up amongst his student-athletes.

Getting comfortable with being uncomfortable means that we have to encourage, perhaps oblige, our young athletes to face adversity, to grapple with difficult circumstances and feelings, to work through failings, and to face the actual consequences of their actions and choices. "Persistence can change failure into extraordinary achievement," says Olympic swimming champion Matt Biondi. I encourage you to become familiar with his legacy. It is only through challenging situations that children can grow and get stronger. It's something that we need to talk about with them, to encourage them to develop and, perhaps most importantly, to model for them.

There's a cool Bible verse that points out that suffering (and as applied to this discussion, we can classify this as meaning adversity or trials) produces perseverance, and perseverance grows character, and it is only character that brings hope. In effect, this progression is what leads to a life (and a sports career) that is resoundingly resilient. I think this is quite apropos, especially in this day and age. And it is certainly something towards which we as parents and coaches should strive for, and with, our children.

The legendary Canadian hoops coach, Jack Donohue, had an interesting point of view when it came to these sorts of things. I was blessed to get to know Coach D in my younger days, and he was often around our National Team camps and practices well after he had retired. After breakfast one morning, as we were walking together to our practice facility, I asked him, "Coach D, what's the most important element in selecting players for a good team?"

His answer came without hesitation and has clearly stayed with me for the decades since he uttered those word.

"Don't be in love with talent." He went on. "Too many people only see the outside, the obvious talent. If you want good teams, great teams, you need to know a player's grit and character, and whether he can overcome a situation that's tough, and play for the name on the front of the jersey rather than the number on the back of it. Talent will let you down, character never will. Don't fall in love with talent."

Coach D was talking about teams, but what he said rings just as true decades later about each and every player we know. Often the first thing people will notice is the young athlete's talent, skills and ability. But these are always going to be subject to, built upon, and at the mercy of, the foundational matters of their make-up. If you really want your kid to have their best opportunity to fully realize their potential, then we have to take seriously these matters of character and maturity and struggle and perseverance and resilience—because make-up matters.

It matters a lot. And as a difference maker, it might mean everything!!!

7. The Looking Glass

"It's not what you look at that matters, it's what you see."
—Henry David Thoreau

In their worlds of schools and sports and social media constructs, our children are trying to find their way through rapidly and constantly changing landscapes that are fraught with traps, obstacles and landmines. Parents, teachers and coaches have a responsibility to help inform and instruct young people, to help them see their world through eyes that are clear and focussed.

Robertson Davies wrote that, "The eyes see only what the mind is prepared to comprehend." For decades, it's been clear to me that there are basically two kinds of people in the world. When we think about the manner in which folks see the world and decide how they will interpret those circumstances, scenarios and experiences, these polarities seem apparent. Whether we are dealing with coaches, or teachers, or "specialized experts," or parents, these two modes are set apart from one another. This seems to hold true in every sector that I have observed. There are the majority of folks, those that **only see what they already know**. And then there is the smaller of the two cohorts, the people who seem to have broader viewpoints and deeper insights about what or who they encounter. These people actually **know what they see**. We are going to look at this dialectic again later in our journey as it pertains to the coaches for whom our kids will play. In this section, we will mostly look at how the way that we as parents see our children's outcomes and abilities imprints and/or impacts upon their overall experiences in the game.

It is imperative to pause here for a moment to clarify that I differentiate these two terms. In my language choices with players and families, I define "impact" as something that is an act of force, typically one thing hitting another, often leaving a mark or some form of bruising. When I use the term "imprint," I generally mean that this is something that imparts a strong or vivid impression. "Impact" tends to lead to negative lasting consequence, while being "imprintful" is intended to develop distinguishing influence or effect for and with the intended recipient. (I acknowledge that there are limits to consolidating these terms to only these meanings, but I find the duality here to be helpful for most families.)

Perception and perspective are very important and can either open doors to freedom or be the barred windows of our own prisons. Perception is the way we recognize and interpret our experiences. Your thoughts, beliefs and awareness all help to colour your perspective. The result is an experience of viewing the world that is unique to you and only you. Lives and worldviews are influenced by the way we perceive our experiences, and the way we perceive our experiences is shaped by how we see ourselves.

While I am not a Pittsburgh Steelers fan, I do appreciate a lot of what I have heard and read about their former coach, Bill Cowher. He said, "Perception is 'reality' but may not be *actuality*, and you've got to be able to keep the difference between that." We convince ourselves that our perceptions are realities. But sometimes these are not even *actually* what happened. Sometimes we have to step back from the close-up details and immediate moments, and survey the big picture—this practice allows for a fuller and perhaps more complete and authentic understanding of the meaning of the "thing." Too often, the reactions to what happens (driven by the sometimes-conflicted overlapping belief systems—those within the parents, those internal to the player, and those that are interacting between them both) are emotionally pushed misplacements and misjudgements. In other words, something occurs, and whether discerned negatively or positively, the feelings generated by that incident propels the situation, dictating the momentum of that person's experiences. It's like that old baseball saying that if we don't play the ball, the ball will play us. Or as Immanuel Kant put it, "All perception is coloured by emotion." And whether feeling blue, or seeing red, or if there's a green light or a flashing cautionary amber, what the athlete is experiencing is governed the glass that they are seeing with or through in those viewing moments.

To illustrate, let me share a few stories from our times at the CRWS. At every one of the 12U Majors Cal Ripken World Series at which our program has had earned the opportunity to participate as Team Canada, there would be examples of situations that would happen on the field that would significantly challenge participants and parents. Especially in the area of trying to understand something that was outside their level of experience, it has been revelatory regarding the fitting together of viewpoint and interpretations of those events.

Now and again, we had a "what just happened there?" moment. Sometimes it was a reaction to something that our group had never seen in a youth baseball context. Other times, it was merely trying to overcome the dissonance that confronted us. Over time I became acclimatized to it. But our families were almost always there for the first time. We were a good team (and at home, we really were top notch for the region) but matching our program comparatively with some of the best 12U teams in the world was a deep challenge to how we actually measured up. Here we were, as part of the International Division that was made up of an assortment of National Select teams, **and us (!!!)**, playing in arguably the top 12U annual baseball championship in the world. The World Series was a growth opportunity that was tough on the kids, and sometimes even more challenging for their families.

One year, we had this really awesome kid named Dryden, one of our core guys, who was a hitting machine for us. We were playing Japan in the round robin, and Dryden got a pitch in his wheelhouse, put a great swing on it, and roped a head-high line drive into the left-centerfield gap. He sprinted out of the box, thinking double, rounded first base in full stride and executed a perfect pop-up slide at second base, standing up on the bag with his typically humble "celebration" directed towards his teammates. Imagine his puzzlement as I signalled to him from the first base coach's box to go back to the very dugout to which he was gesturing. Years later, around the same time he'd signed his letter of intent to play at a US school, while we were chuckling about this memory we shared, he confessed that, at first, he was confused, and thought I was waving him to circle the bases for a homerun, but couldn't figure out why the Japanese second baseman had the baseball. But in that moment when he was twelve, what he didn't know, because he hadn't seen it, was that the Japanese centrefielder had on contact broken to where the ball was heading and made a ridiculously remarkable catch at the wall on the full run. Nothing up to that point in Dryden's baseball life had happened like that. And quite honestly, not many twelve-year-old players have seen an outfielder make that kind of play. It was neat to hear one of the boys in the dugout say to Dryden, "You'd better get your wallet back from that kid...he just robbed you." And it was even more rewarding to hear him talk with his parents after the game, and witness them affirm that things happen on the field that we can't control, and that how we respond to them makes the difference. His mom and dad had a very healthy and balanced perspective and were helping their son grow in his. Imagine the positive imprint on this young player to have this kind of moment actually understood for what it really was.

At another CRWS, a kid on our team was a terrific outfielder, and a pretty solid leadoff man for us. But at this World Championship, Ryan's dad, Dave, thought that Ryan was struggling at the plate (another example of someone who was paying attention to the published results of a collection of plate appearances, rather than actually seeing the success in the process). Ryan had worked a couple of walks to that point of the tourney, and had had a number of Quality-at-Bats that had not led to reaching base. So, by the time we got to that fourth inning of our third game, Ryan was sitting on an oh-fer—he was zero for his total at bats for the event. Dave was growing increasingly frustrated with his son's "production" and was not very good at masking it, especially when he'd had a few "pops" (which he was apt to serve himself regardless of the time of day).

In this particular moment, we were in the midst of a tough game with Puerto Rico, trailing by a run in the fourth inning. With two outs, we had runners at second and third, and Ryan was up. Even though his dad had been "reminding" him earlier in the day that he was still hitless in this "very expensive event that we hauled our whole family to in order to watch you play," (I had heard that conversation on the concourse in the hours before the game, I am sad to say), Ryan was working hard at staying upbeat, and was still putting up good plate appearances, and playing well in the outfield. Ryan was due up, and early in the count got a pitch he knew he could handle and hit a hard two hopper into the hole between third and short. Unfortunately for our side of the scoreboard, the PR team had an outstanding shortstop, and this six-foot tall, muscular, and athletic twelve-year-old ranged to his backhand over into the hole, snagged the baseball, made a quick adjustment with his body and threw an absolute bullet to first base with Ryan still a half step short of the bag. Inning over.

"Oh-my-gawd Ryan, you gotta f***ing beat that out!!!" This was the first and loudest response that we had heard at Cal Sr yard and it happened to come from a slightly over-lubricated Dave. It didn't take a very astute observation to see the impact that this had on his perception of that plate appearance. And I can tell you that it, unfortunately, reinforced an already challenged level of self-worth in that young man, something that our coaching core had worked hard at re-shaping with Ryan.

There have been other times in which the imprint/impact scenarios have been played out more subtly. Often there are instances of kids who talk themselves into what they think of themselves. It's been intriguing throughout the decades of coaching to have seen the powerful influence of self-fulfilling prophecies and how these can abound. At one of our world championships, we had two boys have experiences with their self-prophecies, both in the same game. One lad, our starting pitching that day against the Mexican National team, very casually said as he was warming up, "It's gonna be a really good day today." And he went out and absolutely "shoved"—baseball vernacular for pitching really well—and kept us in the lead till he, unfortunately, had to leave the game with a little discomfort. The second player, as we watched the Mexican pitcher warmup, turned to one of his pals and actually said, "That kid is too good...I can't hit him." I am not about to suggest that he could have squared up that hurler (he was really good!), but my guy had already talked himself into probable situational failure. As it turned out, he struck out in each of his two uncompetitive plate appearances that day, on a total of seven pitches that included only one swing, and a weak one at that, on an out-of-the-zone breaking ball. He also made a late-inning error that led to a couple of runs before his body language "asked" the coaches to take him out of the game.

The last story is something from 2008, the first World Series we attended. Matt was pitching versus South Korea, in a game we thought we had a chance to win. The game did not go as well as we had hoped. After two & 1/3 innings, our coaches made a pitching change. Being the competitor he was, Matt was understandably disappointed (very disappointed!!) His body was slouched, he was fighting to hold back a wave of emotion, and it was apparent that he was facing some internal conflict. Even back then, I was becoming smart enough to know that Matt would need some help to navigate through the complex collection of thoughts and feelings, and to deal with the landmines of what had happened and, more pointedly, how he perceived what had happened. And just as importantly, I was becoming smart enough to know that it would be better for someone else to check in with him. Dan, one of the coaches, asked me if I thought he should talk with Matt, and I said yes, but maybe wait until practice tomorrow.

The next morning, Dan and Matt sat together for a few minutes prior to BP. Dan asked Matt what he felt about the South Korea game. The player's response was something to the tune of "It was a disaster."

What Dan was able to do in the next few moments was excellent. He pointed out that Matt had actually executed most of his pitches. Without shifting responsibility, Dan noted that our third-baseman had made two errors which had led to unearned runs, and he acknowledged that two of the three hits that Matt gave up were "dying quails" over the drawn in infield, weak contact that in most other situations would have been outs. In essence, Dan opened Matt's eyes to seeing more than he had looked at by himself, and helped to broaden his perspective, to include the reality that a lot of things were beyond his control. "So," Dan asked, "was it a really a disaster? Or was it just something you are not used to, and didn't like?"

A few days later, Matt was our starting pitcher matched up against another world class team, this time the squad from the Dominican Republic. With what I'll describe as a fairly poised approach, Matt went about his business, tossed five pretty solid innings surrendering only three earned runs. More importantly, he was able to more effectively work his way through a few errors committed by his teammates behind him, and kept everything in a much better perspective. The reframing that occurred through the conversation with Dan had informed his understanding, and imprinted positively on his approach, certainly in the short-term, and especially as he has moved forward in his baseball and life growth. A lesson from this is that while it was essential that he had to "believe in himself" in order to effectively move on to the next game, it was even more essential that he received some guidance to be able to do so purposefully and productively.

It's always been a core element of my work with young people to try to help them to know themselves, to believe in themselves, and to trust themselves in uncomfortable circumstances. The power of belief is an essential part of developing good "make-up." Sometimes, coaches tell a kid that they need to practice a concept like "fake it till you make." Truth be told, sometimes this can work, but overall, I believe it is most useful to help children see what they really are, and to empower them to learn to embrace and to own a fuller, better sense of how they interpret the situations that they have been through and be better prepared for the challenges that they are about to face. At times their confidence in this developing aspect of the process is uncertain or fragile. To this end, one of the things I have consistently reminded my students and athletes to do is this. I say, "I know this looks difficult, but trust your preparation, trust yourself. And remember that I am way smarter than you (*which I typically deliver with good eye contact and a huge grin*), so when it starts to get hard to believe in yourself, **believe in my belief in you.**"

The way that we see the world plays a huge role in how confidently we engage and interact with new circumstances and unfamiliar stimuli. Working at finding different vantage points, and truer core beliefs about ourselves, will change what we see, and how we see it. What we are looking at is still the same thing, but how we see it and how we perceive it is enhanced and deepened. It's to this end that we need to help kids embrace and self manage.

What do I mean, that we need to engage with idea of "the looking glass"—that with which the world is seen, perceived, interpreted and applied? There are three basic types of "glass" that we encounter. There are windows, there are mirrors, and there are lenses.

Mostly, we see through windows. Windows can be frosted or clear, translucent or transparent, tinted or not, dirty or clean, intact or cracked. There are a lot of possible variables when it comes to the window. Every window has its own qualities and conditions, but all of them have a designed purpose. They allow those who try to see through them to "experience" something on the other side. But even a window can be at the mercy of conditions that affect it, as the viewer attempts to perceive the world of the other side. Consider attempting to see a highway through a windshield that is covered with road guck or heavy rain, or trying to survey your backyard when the window is heavily frosted by extreme cold.

Mirrors reflect but only ever show at best a reversed image of who stands before it. And if the mirror is curved or warped in certain ways, the reflected image is often distorted. The more warped or damaged the mirror, the more grossly distorted or fractured the image that we think we see.

Lenses can alternately focus, distort, filter, or magnify what we think we are seeing, depending on how we choose to use them. They sometimes clarify, occasionally change, and often amplify. We can utilize lens settings to zoom in on an object or experience, or make it widen out to gain a greater sense of what is surrounding the focal point. What's really helpful about lenses, whether we are talking about cameras or the perspectives through which we see the world, is that we can have the power to select which lens and what filters we will use.

How do we help?
1. Know which of the looking glasses is in play. And help our kids know what each type of looking glass can do to what we are trying to see.
2. Redirect them to ask if what they think they are seeing is actually what is there.
3. Find ways to move from subjective impressions to objective observations, free from the emotional weight of other people's expectations.
4. Detach the reaction from the event (clear of the result or outcome) to move towards a better intellectual response (proactive commitment to intentional process).
5. We need to grapple with whether our efforts and exchanges are imprints or impacts.
6. We need to ask ourselves whether our interactions with our kids and their experiences is empowering for them to learn and grow, or enabling them to whither and stall.

There is a neat lesson from *The Sandlot*, and this one involves the Beast!! After Benny, during the epic final chase scene, has "pickled the Beast" (more on this in an upcoming chapter), he and Smalls have a new type of encounter with the now trapped and possibly injured animal. And in the moments that follow, their eyes are opened to the reality of what this dog (actually named Hercules) really is. The dog and the junkyard have not changed...but their perception of it has!

When speaking on the intersectional concepts of senses, appearance, essence and existence, the noted leadership guru Petek Kabakci puts it this way, "The world we see with our senses is very different than the world we see through our essence. Our senses perceive the world of appearance. Our essence perceives the deeper layers of existence. The first step of perceiving the world of essence is to have no goal other than to understand. 'Understanding' has to be the ultimate goal. Only then, can we solve the problems." *Understanding.* She's on to something here, something so foundationally and inductively pure, so simple, that it could be in the realm of profound. Inductive learning says, "Here are some objects, some data, some artifacts, some experiences…what knowledge can we gain from them?" Taking the further step of applying that knowledge to new circumstances leads to mastery and wisdom.

Engaging in the intensely fluid dynamics of what is being experienced, and how it is being seen, interpreted and internalized, is foundational to the development of our athletes and students.

We need to know what we see, in order to discern what these messages mean, and then it is imperative to apply what it means to us.

In doing so, more of us will be able to do more than just see what we already know…

…And then, we can learn to know what it is that we see.

8. How to Cost Your Kid a Scholarship

"Kids are now auditioning and not competing."

—Tim Corbin

It's tough enough for kids anywhere to get opportunities to play at the next level—it takes a lot. Any prospect in every sport needs to be talented and athletic to begin with, and in order for schools to be interested beyond a first look, the kid has to be a good student (or at least "good enough" to both gain admission and stay eligible). The student-athlete will also be assessed for matters of personality and temperament, to see that the quality of character matches up to the expectations and culture of the team that may recruit them. All of these are within the domain and self-regulation of the player themself. In other words, the candidate has control over what the recruiter will see in these matters. However, there's a huge factor that does only a little bit to enhance a prospect's chances to earn it, but if managed poorly can completely cost a kid a scholarship opportunity. A gigantic determining variable in every aspect of student-athlete development is the role of the parent. It is just as much a factor in determining the opportunities that could be either offered or withheld by coaches "at the next level."

Legendary football coach and broadcasting analyst Lou Holtz was asked a little while ago about the difference between football players of today from those he knew fifty years ago. His answer was both astounding and illuminating in its simplicity. He said, "Simple. Today's athletes talk about rights and privileges and the players fifty years ago talked about obligations and responsibilities." When we mull this over, it seems reasonable to conclude that the dynamic that parents play has been substantial in this shift. Entitlement and enablement in our society are becoming increasingly challenging to deal with, and are pillars of the problem facing many collegiate sport prospects. As we have noted, the game is hard enough, getting better is tough, and moving to the next level is extremely difficult. Parents often ask me, "Can you tell me one thing I can do to help my child get a college scholarship?"

Almost every time I tell them two things: "Number one, get your child a library card and have them read a lot more than they play games. And number two, stop doing things that can cost your kid an opportunity to earn that athletic scholarship."

Hmmm...mostly they laugh at the first suggestion—and then I explain that there is a lot more academic money at most schools especially in most sports that are not football or basketball. But the second one often confounds them. What do I mean that we can cost our kids a college scholarship? What do parents have to do with it at all?

Let's unpack this. I have always found it distasteful when parents and other supporters have "acted up" at games and practices. I hated it when I was a player, I dislike it when I coach, it's hard to stomach as a fan, and I especially found it unpalatable as a fellow parent when my children were playing on teams and I had to share bleachers with other families. There are way too many stories about parents in the stands, or on the sidelines who are "just a bit off" or perhaps even worse—we see them barking at officials, griping about coaches and playing time, questioning the system the team has, or constantly pointing out either how great their kid is or how terrible another player performs. In Canada it seems to be at its worst at hockey rinks, but it's also bad in other sports. In the US, it seems to be most prevalent in the negative sense at ballfields and basketball courts, but perhaps just as much at other sports venues. I suppose anywhere that a mom or a dad has high expectations for their progeny and aspirations for their collegiate scholarship chances, then there are also those parents who don't see that sometimes how they do what they do is actually costing their child a shot at a scholarship.

I can tell you about a number of times I have seen basketball coaches just walk away from their early interest in a player for reasons other than ability or grades. Sometimes it is about the student's character. And sometimes it's about the company they keep—there was a terrific talent I saw play lots in Toronto in the early 90's who got little interest from NCAA coaches after they found out that many of this young man's closest friends were part of a particular neighborhood "gang." There was another player whose "Dad just wore me out" (said to me by a very well known Division1 coach), "so, I told him we don't have that scholarship any more." A little later in Chapter 14, I will share the story of Tanner and what his dad did that cost him multiple opportunities that good basketball schools, programs in which he would have wanted to play.

The patterns of parental choices putting the athlete's opportunities at risk can happen earlier than one might initially think. About a decade ago, our 12Uteam was playing the Canadian championship semi-final, hosting a couple of very good teams from BC. We put together a very good squad, and were in pretty good shape to win the semi-final and play for the Canadian title, an accomplishment that would have propelled us to the world championships at the Cal Ripken World Series. Shortly after completion of the game, which we had won, I was approached by a dad who by any reasonable standards, other than his own in that moment, should have been quite pleased with the outcome of that game. His son, who we will call "Rusty," had started for us in the outfield, and through the course of the game had put together some good at-bats and ended up getting three hits on the day.

The dad, "Roger", was pacing around restlessly while waiting for me to finish up some conversations with the kids, and setting the agenda for the group for that evening and the next day. It did not take a savant to see that there was a bug up this guy's butt, and it was clear that he was about to approach me, to try to engage in a conversation that was clearly in our "not-okay zone." "Coach," he said sternly, "we have to talk." Even back then I'd been around sport long enough to know that this probably wasn't going to go very well. It's rarely a good idea, for either parent or coach, to have conversations when at least one of the parties involved is angry or frustrated. And it was obvious that Roger was upset about some thing.

My response was guarded, as I was trying to pre-empt what I hoped would not become a negative moment for our team. "It would probably be better if we waited till Monday to have this conversation."

But Roger felt a burning desire to press on.

The rest of the tête-à-tête went something like this:

"No, Coach, I need to have this talk."
"I'm telling you, Roger, it would be better to wait."
"Coach, I need to talk with you about Rusty's playing time."
"Roger, let's remember our guidelines. We'll talk about this after the championship game."

I tried to walk away and put the gear in the back my CRV. Roger decided to follow me to the vehicle. Truth be told, by then I was beginning to feel frustration myself.

"Coach, I don't know why you don't like my kid, clearly you have no respect for him as a player."

I looked at our team's lead assistant coach, who was standing by the car with me at this point, speaking with my eyes and facial expression only, indicating to him to not say anything. I took a deep breath to clear my spirit and to give myself the opportunity to choose very carefully what I would say next. Roger was about to say something else, and, honestly, I neither knew nor cared what it was going to be. I put my hand up in front of me with an open palm extended, gesturing for him to please remain silent for a moment.

"Roger, we actually think that Rusty is a pretty great kid, and that he's a good player. I know you think he's an amazing shortstop, but we have other people to play that spot for us. If this is about me taking him in the sixth inning of that semi-final, to improve our defence, you need to know that that was a good baseball decision. Sure, he had three hits, but we were dealing with a slim lead, and the teeth of their order was coming up. So, we felt we wanted to strengthen our outfield for the last inning. And it appeared that Rusty didn't object. He was fine on the bench, and seems pretty happy we won."

Rather than listen, Roger decided to try to dispute. And by this time, I had run out of patience.

"Look, Roger, we just won our semi-final game against one of the top teams here. And we are playing for the Canadian championship tomorrow afternoon, with the opportunity to earn our spot in the best youth baseball championship in the world. Right now, your son is a member of this team. But if you don't shut up, he might **not** be any more.

So let me ask you this, Roger. We are one game away from going to the World Series. We want your kid to be part of it. Ask yourself this question: **Do you want to f**k this up for him?**"

Wow...typically I make a point to not swear very often but sometimes profanity is helpful in making a strong point, especially with some people. And I really felt I needed to drive home this point. Roger walked away, and to his credit didn't bring this up again. The next day, we played and won the Canadian championship. In my younger days, I would've been tempted to bench Rusty because of his father's inappropriateness. I had matured by then, and Rusty had earned a spot in our line-up on the merits of his play. There was no need to punish the child for the indiscretion of his father.

Ironically, one of the people who overheard Roger's interaction with me that Saturday evening was a coach and recruiter with one of our area's top college prep programs. He was there to assess potential players for their teams. Later that fall, when Rusty and Roger were seeking a spot at that academy, the coach called me for a reference, as he almost always did when my guys were trying out for their teams. He had significant concerns that the dad would be a problem. Fortunately, the kid was offered a spot when I explained that what the coach had seen was an event, and not a pattern with us. Rusty went on to a solid youth career and ended up playing at college (though never again as a shortstop), without the dad ever really knowing that he had almost roadblocked his son's opportunity.

Allow me to share another story, though this one, sadly, without the redemptive outcome we would have liked to have seen. We'll call them "Jimmy" and "James." Jimmy was a really good outfielder, and when not too self-conscious or pressing too hard, could be a pretty good offensive player as well. Despite how well he could play centre field—and he was a very good package out there: terrific reads; great jumps; long, smooth strides to the ball; and an excellent centre field arm; lots of upside as a potential hitter—he had not seen much recruiting interest to this point. By this time, it was about halfway through the spring and summer schedule in his final year of high school. His dad, James, was both a little bit high strung and just as much unrealistic about the level of post-secondary baseball that was within his son's reach. This became apparent in what developed between the dad and one of the few college programs that was recruiting the son.

There had been a number of collegiate coaches who'd seen Jimmy play in the previous fall, and had liked him enough as a prospect to keep in touch with his team's coaches, but they were keeping him on the back burner, so to speak, waiting to see how other recruiting and anticipated player movement from their teams would play out. (After all, there are limits to the number of scholarships that a D1 program is permitted.) It was the early part of May, and Jimmy hadn't received a single Division1 offer to that point. But just prior to this particular weekend, Jimmy had received a call from a college baseball coach (as usual, it was the recruiting coordinator for the team), and was told that that mid-major program had interest in him as a student-athlete. They were inquiring to see whether he would want to come to their school for an official visit— clearly that school's intent was to offer the young man a spot as a freshman in their baseball program for the upcoming school year as long as things "checked out" on the visit. Obviously, Jimmy was quite pleased and hopeful that this situation could develop. Sadly, it did not. His dad, James, was a friend of mine at the time, and let me know right away. But as eager as James was for his kid's success, he was occasionally unwise about some of these things, and even more often indiscrete about what, and with whom, he talked about around baseball fields. I happened to be sitting a couple of seats away from him that Saturday afternoon when he had the last conversation on his cell phone with the recruiting coordinator from that school, the only school that had made his son a solid offer to that point. There were three things that stood out most that he said (I didn't have to be eavesdropping to hear James's bold voice). "Well, I looked at pictures of your facility and your field and they don't look as good as what we have here." "Yeah, I saw your schedule and your record; doesn't look like you guys were very good last year. And I haven't heard of some of the schools in your conference. I was thinking Jimmy would go to a better team." "Frankly, if you guys are really serious you would be offering Jimmy 100%, and I wouldn't be talking with you, I'd be speaking with the head coach."

Let me pause to be clear here—the school that was calling was a mid-major baseball program, albeit coming off a tough season, that had lots of opportunity for young guys to play in the next couple of years, in a solid Midwestern NCAA Division1 conference, and was a terrific school both athletically and academically. And this was the kid's only offer! Needless to say, the conversation was wrapped up pretty quickly by the coach. Presuming that this particular recruiting coordinator was the same gentleman that I had encountered the previous fall, it would have been done politely, but it seems enough red flags had been waved for him. Unfortunately, the school never called back or reached out to that athlete again. Perhaps most sadly, I found out after the fact that a couple of other schools (one Division1, two D2 schools) had had scholarship spots open, and had inquired about Jimmy as well with the academy staff. And while those coaches were eager to pitch his skills to these other programs, the world of college baseball is made up of men who are good friends and great colleagues, guys that talk to one another and exchange notes, especially about recruiting. When these other schools heard from their friend about this Canadian dad, they turned their interest towards other players. Even though his club team coaches were able to find a few JUCO programs that wanted Jimmy to play for them, James was stubborn—they weren't good enough for his kid. So, Jimmy ended up, despite his ability, despite his potential, with nowhere in the US to play after high school.

What's my point? I have taken the opportunity to talk with hundreds of coaches in multiple sports all over North America throughout the last twenty-five-plus years. These discussions have often been about the relationship between "player character" and the "culture/climate" of a team. Coaches, especially at the collegiate level, care about these things. One of the most significant imprints I have ascertained from these conversations is how importantly most coaches look at *the patterns of the parents* as they sort out *the projectability of the prospect.*

Apples don't fall far from their trees. People are a product of the environment in which they were raised. Good fruit comes from good trees. Examining the orchard will tell me a lot about whether a tree can produce anything at all, let alone tasty and healthy fruit. Let's also keep in mind that apple trees don't grow peaches or pears: they only and always grow some version of an apple.

In addition to lots of general comments and observations I have collected through the years, I also made a point to ask over three dozen coaches in the last year about what they watch for when recruiting, particularly when it comes to the family aspect.

What are some "red flags" with parents and families? Below is a summary version of what coaches told me.

- ➢ How the parent conducts themselves, especially in public, at games:
  - ○ Profanity
  - ○ Messaging with apparel and ancillaries, and what's in the "cooler bag."
  - ○ Is the parent always hovering around the player bench?
  - ○ What is consumed at events that might amplify or alter behaviours.

- Yelling; interaction with/about opponents & officials; how they cheer/ what they cheer about; are they relaxed or tense (especially in mundane moments); response to outcomes; level of emotional control & stability
- As a bunch of coaches pointed out—"If the parents are turds, then the kid will probably be a turd as well" (although, most of them used other words than "turd").

➢ Parents do all or most of the talking during the recruitment conversations and the visits.

➢ Misrepresent what is happening in the overall recruitment of their child. Coaches know when a player is being talked with by other schools, and most often when offers have actually been made. And coaches know when parents are overstating their child's ability.

➢ The money or scholarship is all that seems to matter & how they handle the tough conversations about financial matters.

➢ Blame game—"It's someone else's fault for my kid's shortcomings."

➢ "What can you do for my kid?"

➢ "Do you really think your program is good enough for my son/daughter?"

➢ "Let me explain/elaborate what you are not really seeing in my kid."

➢ Are they applying pressure to their child?
- Do they enable or equip the kid?
- Have they engineered outcomes, or empowered the child to compete?
- Does the kid want to be near his/her parents after the game?

➢ One coach sent me this quote as advice to parents—"Open your mouth only if what you are going to say is more beautiful than silence."

Conversely, what are some things coaches/recruiters have told me that they want to see. These are aspects that many have deemed to be seen in **Plus Side Parents**:

- ✓ Solution oriented.
- ✓ Takes responsibility and expects their kid to be responsible and take responsibility.
- ✓ They model accountability for their kid.
- ✓ Honest and open communication about their hopes for the kid.
- ✓ Reasonable understanding of their child's ability.
- ✓ Asks legitimate and insightful questions:
  - Shows commitment to aiding the child and the program to find the best opportunity for "fit."
- ✓ They want what is best for their child and are honest in seeing what that really is.
- ✓ Makes it a habit to have the child lead the conversation about the recruiting process.

Parents need to model the kind of appropriateness we've already discussed, and also have the responsibility to help their child to deal with their own hiccups. Let's take a few moments to also review a few ways that the student-athlete can short-circuit their own opportunities as well. Perhaps we can help our children grow in awareness and accountability in these areas.

There is a bouquet of indicators that coaches see in players that can cause them to have second thoughts or back away. Let's presume that we all understand that talent and athletic ability (relative to the level they are recruiting towards) will always be an initializing variable and will drive the recruitment early on. And that the matters of academics will "never not matter" to college programs (and that it's even important as a bell-weather for pro scouts).

What are some things that can put on the brakes, or cause the vehicle to careen off the road?

> ➢ Body language.
> ➢ Body type and composition—and evidence of their commitment to health choices.
> ➢ Attentiveness (to coaches, tasks, teammates, etc.).
> ➢ Eye contact and communication patterns/habits.
> ➢ Behaviour off the field and around the field/community.
> ➢ Making excuses/complaining.
> ➢ Getting stuck in "a moment."
> ➢ Are they tough? Resilient? How do they respond to adversity, challenges, setbacks?
> ➢ Social media presence.

Part of the reality of the present-day recruitment landscape is the aspect of professional services. Even though we need to put some of what these agencies do into better perspectives, we can learn a lot from some of the fulltime recruitment consultants. Pro Baseball Reports (PBR), for example, is a large scouting service that evaluates and promotes youth baseball players around North America. Families pay for their camps and other showcase events and get in return data -driven scouting evaluations on the PBR websites, which are regionally sorted but internationally displayed. They (like many of the others) have also become a resource for college coaches at all division levels, who subscribe to their service for presumed-to-be-reliable information and data about prospective student-athletes. This type of service provider, that delivers evaluations, scores, reports and rankings for players, is common among most sports, and are used fairly broadly.

Dan Cevette is President of PBR New York and has over 35K followers on Twitter and even more subscribers to their recruitment service. And that is just one segment of that organization. He pointed out on a podcast that, "Poor body language on the field is a billboard screaming at everyone with eyes 'I can't handle this'; 'I'm giving up'; 'I'm a shitty teammate'; 'I don't respect authority.' It's bad, and your performance will suffer. Understand this. In baseball you're going to fail, a lot." And body language (for both player and parent) is only one of many observable traits that coaches and scouts are assessing!

On another one of his other platforms, Cevette notes for prospective college athletes and their families the following "warning":

Ways to Not Get Recruited
> Poor attitude
> Poor body language
> Not running everything out
> Arguing with umpires
> Disrespecting your coaches/teammates/parents
> Not practising
> Showing NO growth
> Ignoring college emails
> Poor grades

PBR is just one among several baseball-scouting groups (such as Perfect Game) and shares a similar role in the same "marketplaces" that we see in other sports—football, basketball, and hockey all have them—and it would take up pages to list them, and then there are those services connected to other sports. Most of them would offer to their clients very similar precautionary thoughts. Please understand that in telling you of these realities I am neither endorsing them nor discouraging you from paying for them. But be aware that they do exist, that they play a significant role in the sports recruiting marketplace, and that when they offer insights such as those note above, we can learn valuable lessons!

A final story for this chapter. It was the summer of 2013 and it was Matt's first opportunity to travel and compete with the Junior National Team. As a matter of fact, it was the final opportunity that summer for a cohort of players (Matt and a number of others) to earn a spot on the final roster that was going to the 18U World

Championships. Most of the core group was set, but Coach Hamilton was still in search of filling the few last spots. The team had assembled in New England and were training and playing competitive match-ups with several summer collegiate teams. As parents, Matt's mom and I regarded this opportunity as a huge privilege for him; we thought he had a shot but knew that as a seventeen-year-old it would be tough to crack that roster, let alone get inserted into the lineup. We took the opportunity to travel to the Northeast US and were able to watch a large portion of the practices and games.

Because of its proximity to central Canada, this particular training experience for JNT offered access to a large number of families to be able to attend. Perhaps naïvely, I expected every other parent to hold the same perspective, that even being invited to this was a privilege for the athletes involved. For the most part it was quite enjoyable, meeting so many baseball parents in this context. This was, after all, the core group of most of the best talent in the age group from across the country, and I presumed that everyone would be a top-notch parent. But not everything was sweet and lovely! There was one parent in particular who stood out for me and really forced me to catch my breath about the potentially dangerous outcomes for student-athletes that can be spurred on by the choices of their family.

I can't remember the name of the mom or the athlete; even if I could I probably shouldn't write them down anyway. I do recall, though, that this young man was also seventeen and was in the same academic class year as my boy. Mrs. "My Son" was harping constantly. "My Son would've made that play," whenever there was an error or a non-play in the field. "My Son can hit that pitcher; I don't know why he's not playing." "My Son is one of the best players at home, in the best program in the country. Maybe these coaches will figure out that he should be playing." Honestly, it was exhausting. (By the way, it's not just that I don't remember the player's name—the mom actually referred to him almost exclusively through the entire time we were there as "My Son"!!) Making matters worse for the kid, Mrs. My Son spoke loudly and often enough that several members of the coaching staff were able to hear her relentless commentary. I am not about to say that this boy would have made the final roster anyway. Regardless of what his mom thought, at that level he was at best a bubble player. And he did not make the final squad. Neither did our Matthew, because he hadn't earned it, yet. However, the two things that were most breathtaking from that ongoing encounter with Mrs. My Son are these. First, that player was never invited back to a national team development camp, while the other five of the six seventeen-year-olds were all invited back. And secondly, and I only knew this after the fact, that a collection of the college programs that were following that JNT tour all crossed that player off their list of kids they were going to recruit.

All of this to say, it's already a tough, tough thing to accomplish—to get considered, let alone be offered, a college sports scholarship is really, really hard. As parents, we want what's best for our kids. We want them to reach for and to attain their dreams, and their goals. But sometimes, and probably more often than we are aware, parents need to back off. They need to seriously consider what those decision-makers are really seeing when they look at the parental behaviour and choices. Our conduct has significantly more influence than we may know. So let me encourage you to begin with the end in mind, to carefully weigh what you do, and do not do, on the scales of the whole parcel.

Because someone else is deciding whether or not your kid is going to be offered a scholarship, or even a spot on a team.

So, ask yourself, "Do I really want to mess this up for my child?"

9. Find Your Yoda

"Great leaders put people before the number."

—Steve Jobs

Once in a while, a piece of wisdom gets "stuck" in my consciousness. The proverb about iron sharpening iron is one of those. Early on in Matt's baseball journey, years before any semblance of organized participation with a league, it was becoming clear that, not only did he truly love to play, not only did really love the game of baseball, he was showing signs of being good at it. He was strong and athletic, could hit and throw with what seemed to be a natural ease. And he loved to try to do newer and harder things. He thrived with challenges and opportunities to try to do tough things.

Without really doing it on purpose, something of a "system" began to develop at home and carried on even after he started to play on teams. Matt and I worked on skills, and while both of us really enjoyed it (for the most part), the general orientation was something like, "This is how you do it, this is how you do it correctly, this is how you will need to do it when you are big, and this is why we try hard to do it right." His appetite for play and practice was voracious. So, we went to the backyard and <u>did</u> it; we went to the school gym and did stuff; we went to ballfields and practiced; and we went to cages and hit. And bit by bit, piece by piece, Matt learned sound mechanics, proper techniques and efficient physical pathways and mental practices. It rarely seemed like work, but there were some expectations, disciplines and structures that were in place, even though we almost never talked about them, and they were rarely onerous. Meanwhile, just as often Matt would just explore and push his athletic limits and capacities for exuberant play with his mom. "Mom, throw me some divers!!" "Wanna play whiffle-ball?" "Can we go to the park for some catch?" Let's do homerun derby." These times were free and fun and fabulous. Their shared joyfulness was absolute and apparent, often included his sister, sometimes me, neighbourhood kids, and later on any teammates who wanted to be around.

Interestingly, as I gaze back at those earlier times, I recognize that both of these themes are essential to the player that Matt has become. And as I reminisce, I picture the "two Matts," and see how the boy would wear his hat in those early years. There was the focussed and purposeful kid with the bill of his cap straight over his eyes, locked intently on doing everything cleanly and purely and well. And then there was the Matt who was our pseudo-version of "The Kid," hat backwards, exuding joyful passion while at play. His mom played with him "where he was." Alongside his dreams, I imagined with him "where he wanted to go," and we practiced towards those "future-ready" aspirations.

When we were finally able to join an organized youth league, and as Matt began to play, he was displaying more aptitude, and was having even more fun. We started looking for more opportunities for him to immerse himself. One of the earliest and most important things we did was to respond to his hunger for the game, and to find places for him to be challenged to grow, to support him in his budding passion. It was about the time he was nine or ten years old that Matt first told me he wanted to play in the Big Leagues.

And I believed him, and believed **in** him—that he could do that one day. Or at least back then, I believed that he had the desire to do what he needed to do in order to reached towards his dream. He wanted to build something, and we needed to figure out what it was going to be, and where we could build it. We needed a plan. He was ten years old when we made our first trip to Phoenix to take part in a Christmas development program (with Ben Boulware of America's Baseball Camps), and it was remarkable. Matt was put into the midst of a tremendous group of young players and worked with a collection of expert level coaches, all of whom were former pro players, and minor league or college coaches. The most illuminating observation, and to some degree most invigorating for both me and Matt, was that he fit right in with this top-level talent and athleticism from around America.

It was around this time that the old proverb began to take on deeper significance. But what was the best way to get "iron to sharpen iron"? This theme would be a foundational question and guiding principle throughout his baseball journey. It should compel and direct all parents and coaches.

What seemed clear then, and has become even clearer now, was that if Matt was going to have a chance to turn his dream into a goal, and his goal into an opportunity, then those opportunities into realities, we were going to need help. And we knew that for him to reach his fullest potential, he had to be surrounded by like minded kids and guided by gifted mentors. And we knew early on that he needed to be on teams and in programs that were populated with players who were bigger and stronger and better than him. It was also clear that we needed to find more than just technical expertise and skills-teaching ability.

Since learning is vital...And finding the best teaching and mentorship fit is absolutely essential...

We had to find somewhere and someone that would help him get the most out of himself.

Like a young future Jedi, Matt was the Padawan in search of a master.

So, we needed to help him find his Yoda.

Every player, every young and developing Jedi, needs to find someone to help them see all that they can be. Let me share a story about a kid that had the opportunity to develop under the tutelage of an exceptional coach who knows what he sees, and sees what could be. Alejo Lopez is a young man who came from Mexico City to where we live in Alberta when he was in ninth grade. At the time he arrived, he was an athletic, average-sized, fifteen-year-old, a decent right-handed hitter, and had good hands and even better feet. He came here specifically for the Dawgs Academy baseball program, and to attend school to learn better command of the English language. And he had a dream to play professional baseball.

Alejo was not at the Academy very long before the primary hitting coach, Allen Cox, connected with him, and suggested that Alejo consider something that would more effectively prepare him for his possible future. Allen asked Alejo to learn to hit lefthanded. So, Alejo committed to this process and worked and worked and worked, all the while not reducing his efforts to get better from the right side and to hone his defensive skills. Conversations between the eager player and the Yoda-type coach were steeped in considerations of "what could be" down the road, and what it would actually take in order to get there. In other words, they imagined Alejo's possible future, and worked at his future by becoming "future-ready."

Alejo moved from Okotoks to complete high school in Phoenix after tenth grade (and reclassified to enrol in sophomore year in America), and in 2015 he was drafted by the Cincinnati Reds. And I can tell you that this young man (who had never taken a lefthanded swing in a game prior to being fifteen) was named the 2021 Red Minor League Hitter of the Year and also experienced his first call-ups to the big leagues that same season. While I couldn't say for sure, I wonder if this would have been even remotely possible were it not for the foresight of a coach who knew what he saw and believed in a young player. What a blessing that he and his Yoda found each other when he most needed it!

***

An awful lot of my passion for encouraging players and parents has to do with a deep belief that we must work at seeing what others can become, rather than just settling for what they currently are. I have tried to apply this through the coaching I have done, and the program leadership and support staff roles that I have been blessed to undertake throughout involvement in both of my primary sports. And I endeavor to take this same orientation into whatever I have done with teaching and the community service agencies I have served.

But what does this actually look like? What are we looking for so we can find "it" in the coaches we might select to train our kids? Perhaps I can unpack this by relating a few more lessons I have observed in being part of my boy's journey. I believe we will see a pattern develop as we encounter some of his best coaches.

Matt has been blessed to have had a lot of tremendous coaches in his life's pursuit of baseball. He had first been equipped by me and his mom, and then through a number of pretty solid community league Dad-Coaches (like Ramon and Gary) as a young player. Dawgs Academy was steeped in great baseball, and with coaches who placed high values on character and school, especially in the years he was there. And he's been wonderfully guided by a handful of provincial team coaches with those select teams, from each of whom he has learned something that he's applied to his development. His exposure to exceptional coaching through the Baseball Canada Junior National Team (18U) has been an incredible growth experience and Greg Hamilton, Chris Reitsma, Corey Eckstein, and the other staff have left indelible, positive imprints on Matt's game and on his character. Almost to a man, the entire coaching staffs at Matt's JUCO and, following that, the four-year school he attended have been very good for him. To a large degree, our son and our family have been "spoiled" by consistently having had coaches who are not only high-calibre baseball technicians, but are even better people. More than just that, they have been an amazing assortment of coaches who both "know what they see" (more on this idea to come) and have invested richly in Matt's process.

Of all these coaches, three in particular have stood out (at least to me): Allen Cox, who was Matt's primary coach from eighth grade till high school graduation with the Dawgs Academy in our hometown; Marc Rardin at Iowa Western Community College from 2014-15; and Jeff Mercer at Indiana University for Matt's final collegiate season, his senior year. What separates Allen, Marc, and "Merse" from the rest? What has made them Jedi Masters in the life of our young Padawan?

Allow me to share three narratives, one respectively involving each of them. All of these accounts are about a coach who knows what he sees.

I have already told you about the coach who had tried to change Matt's swing and approach to hitting back when he was 14-15 years old. That guy only saw what he already knew, and wanted our young prospect to set up according to his mold. Though still a quality coach, Trevor was not the right match at that point in the fledgling Jedi's life. Fortunately, Coach Allen Cox was instrumental in helping Matt move out of, and away from, the quagmire in which he'd gotten "stuck." More than that, Coach Cox began to build something very special with this athlete. He helped to build a sense of virtual "invincibility" that was based in trusting the process, and putting any results in their proper perspective. *I should point out that Allen has done this for countless players across North America, and this is not a story in isolation.* He did it with Matt, in this instance, by doing things like telling him that he would be the shortstop everyday, even if he made an error, and in fact that he needed to work hard enough that he put himself into situations that he would make errors. He told him that he'd be hitting in the two or three slot every day, and it didn't matter whether he got hits or RBI, as long as he was working at generating quality at-bats and getting better. In this commitment from Allen, it was helpful that the athlete played better and better as the season progressed. Notably, it wasn't just words and philosophy. It was also sweat equity! Allen also worked his butt off, together with Matt, who was working his own butt off. It never mattered how much extra work Matt wanted to do, Allen made himself available and rarely let Matt limit himself to only doing "extra work." Allen has a knack for redirecting and refocussing athletes to pursue "better" work. Matt and Allen even had a long-time "tradition" of hitting together on Christmas Day, something they did almost every Christmas from the time Matt was fourteen, till Allen moved back to the US in 2019—seven Christmases. The only time they missed an actual December 25 was the year that our family did Christmas in Ontario with Matt's grandparents, and even that year Matt and Allen hit together in Owensboro, Kentucky (after Allen had set up an unofficial recruit visit to Louisville a few days before) on December 22 that year!! All of these moments point out something that is a separator—Allen saw something that Matt could become, helped

Matt to believe in it, and facilitated a growth track that would see Matt become more and more self-directed and self-determined as a potential elite athlete. Their shared commitment grew into a share conviction. It's clear that this rooted a very deep bond between them. And Coach Allen continues to play a vital role in Matt's life and career today.

***

Marc Rardin was Matt's JUCO coach at Iowa Western. Lots took place at that school in his two years there that helped Matt become a much better player, and even more that helped refine him as a person and grow into the man that he has become. Nothing from that experience has been more substantial than the character of his head coach. Perhaps the most telling account that reveals the kind of person that Coach Rardin is can be seen in how he handled my son's freshman season. You see, Matt had spent most of that summer prior to enrolling at IWCC with the Junior National team, representing Canada in several events leading up to the Pan-American 18U "Tournament of the Americas," the world championship qualifying event. In fact, even after he arrived on campus in the middle of August 2014, Matt had to leave the school for a short while to join Team Canada, to prepare and play in that final event in La Paz. While playing for his country he developed an elbow issue, something that he tried to rehab back to health but never really got better.

Let's put this into some perspective. When they recruited him, IWCC's expectation in offering Matt a pretty significant scholarship package (they only have ten to offer) was that he would play a central role in their drive towards another national championship, as a two-way player. Their plan was to have Matt both play in the infield and hit in the teeth of the order, and for him to hold down a weekend starting pitcher spot. I have seen lots of other college coaches whose first priority would have been to protect their program and keep one of their valued scholarship athletes on campus. I've seen situations in several sports in which collegiate staff would not permit their student athletes to participate outside of their own controls, even with national teams. So, in many regards, it's remarkable that Coach Rardin blessed Matt in allowing him to play for his country in that event, and permitting him to miss three-plus weeks of school and fall practice, particularly as an incoming freshman.

But that's not even the most noteworthy aspect of what this story reveals.

When the bronze-medal-winning team was finally able to leave Mexico (and that in itself was quite a post-hurricane adventure!) and Matt returned to Council Bluffs, his elbow had not gotten better. In fact, it was becoming increasingly clear that what initially appeared to be something that he could rehab from was most likely a fairly significant issue with his UCL. He could still hit (and to that end, the swing was still pretty good!) and could do some light tossing so he could still have played first base, or been in a lineup as a DH. Playing any other defensive position was unthinkable, though, and there's no way he could have pitched. Coach Rardin had Matt see one of the top orthopedists in that area, they did the MRI and other diagnostic things and confirmed that Matt would need Tommy John surgery. It was at this point, despite the fact that he was giving up a key cog in their hopes to win another championship in the following season, Rardin pulled Matt into his office and told him he had to get the surgery now, or at least as soon as possible. He told Matt that as a future pro prospect (which he believed Matt was) he would be unwise to hold off on this career-impacting surgery. And there was no way that he would be comfortable holding Matt's career goals hostage to his own win-loss record. Matt's job as a Reiver, then, would be to do well in school, get healthy, get strong, be at every practice and event, and be a good teammate. And to get ready for the following fall season and to prepare himself to compete with and lead his team as a sophomore. And he told Matt in late September of his freshman year that his scholarship would be honoured for that year and renewed for the next.

This coach put that player's best interest ahead of the short-term goals of that team. In a world that dictates job security for a coach by wins and championships, this is not as common as one would hope. And he continued to invest deeply in Matt's life, his growth, and his character. Coach turned an adversity into a time of incredible enrichment. So, it should come as no surprise that Matt continues to be in close contact with Coach Rardin even today.

***

Matt first met Jeff Mercer on the phone in the summer of 2018. It was the first encounter in what would become a deeply meaningful relationship. But the year that they worked together at Indiana University almost never happened.

The end of his junior year as a Hoosier, 2018, developed into a convergence of circumstances our family did not anticipate. Hoping to be selected by a major-league organization in the first-year player draft that spring, Matt had done careful academic planning and had managed to put together all the credit requirements for his degree track and had qualified to graduate that year. After another successful collegiate season, most of the folks in our baseball world thought Matt would be drafted, and that he would begin his professional career. All that came to a screeching halt when the draft passed and Matt was not selected. Just after all of this had transpired, the then IU boss, Coach Lemonis, was offered and had accepted the head coaching position at baseball powerhouse Mississippi State University. Indiana Baseball was in limbo.

Matt was in a uniquely challenging and unanticipated position. Should he seek a spot with pro ball as an undrafted free agent? Or should he go back to school and play his senior year? Who would be the new head coach if Matt went back? What none of us at home realized at first was that this would turn into a tremendous self-directing moment. As a player with a final year of NCAA eligibility remaining, and having already earned graduation status at his four-year school, Matt was able to transfer to any school in the country that was interested in him, free and clear of any redshirt requirements (and thus wouldn't have to sit out a year if he moved schools). With the now uncertainty of the Hoosier coaching staff on the table, Matt decided it would be wise to consider what his options could be for the next calendar year, and his mom and I both agreed this would be prudent. Around the same time that he put himself into the NCAA transfer portal, Indiana Athletics announced that the new head coach of Hoosier baseball would be up-and-coming coach Jeff Mercer. And as soon as Matt was in the transfer portal, recruitment calls started coming in, all from some significant top-ten baseball schools.

Shortly after he was hired, Coach Mercer called Matt. They had what appeared to be a very good conversation and agreed that if Matt was to go back to Bloomington for his final campaign as a college baseball player, he would visit and get to know Coach Mercer face-to-face.

The summer of 2018 had changed substantially. What was supposed to a be a few weeks at home to regenerate after a gruelling Big Ten season, and to get his feet under him after the way the draft had played out, Matt was now immersed in an unexpected recruiting journey and was considering multiple other schools. Coach Mercer planted seeds and had shown enough of his principles and character in that call that Matt knew that he needed to make his decision about going back to Indiana, based on confirming his first impressions of the new head coach. So, the arrangements were made, and he boarded an airplane and flew to Bloomington. What did he and coach Mercer talk about together while he was there? The truth is that I will never really know, but this is what I have discerned from both Matt and Merse. It went something like this:

*"I know you are disappointed with the draft, and we are just as surprised as anyone that your name wasn't called. But I want you to know **you will** play pro ball.*

We would like to help and be part of you reaching your goal. Everyone knows you're already really good and we have a plan to help you get even better.

We are working to put in new styles and systems in place here, we're going to build you up and we're going to build your senior year around you.

We are going to do a better job for you. Everywhere you've been you have put the needs of the team before your own. We are going to focus on you.

We know what kind of leader you are, and we are going to embrace it, honor it, and watch it grow even more than it has."

Perhaps what most resonated with Matt was Coach Mercer's authenticity. He was anchored to who he really was, with a deep passion for a clear and simple vision. And Matt figured out in short order that this new head coach was the real deal—the real deal in teaching the game, the real deal in being in relationship with players, and the real deal in leading his guys into better ways to self-determine their own outcomes. It was apparent early on that Mercer was steeped in authentic character and would endeavor to deliver on everything that he was purporting to offer. As a person who is innately gifted in figuring out people quickly, Matt still took a couple of days to sort out all the data about all the opportunities He decided to follow both his head and his heart, and took them, along with his hands, back to Indiana Hoosier Baseball.

A rigorous fall program that was specifically and individually crafted for him, and new relationships with a fresh and dynamic coaching staff, appeared to have re-invigorated Matt. When the season came around in February of 2019, Matt had another great year in his two-way role, helped the squad to a Big Ten championship, played again in the NCAA tourney, and then got drafted. Most important, Coach Mercer not only delivered, he worked with Matt, and he worked *for* Matt. And he and Matt developed a tremendous relationship that is both immensely professional and deeply personal. Their bond is so strongly entrenched that Matt still goes to visit Coach Mercer every off-season, and, in fact, insisted that he and I go to Bloomington on the long drive from Chattanooga back to Alberta at the end of the 2021 season, despite the reality that it was not really on the route!

***

Not everyone will have an opportunity to, let alone "can," play for these particular men.

But it is possible to seek out coaches that exemplify similar traits, patterns, and character that they exude. Allow me to summarize and suggest the key aspects of what has made these exceptional men the exemplars that they are—coaches "who know what they see." Noted leadership consultant Simon Sinek asks, "How do great leaders inspire action?" I will paraphrase his answer. When you talk about what you believe passionately, authentically, others may begin to believe you. But when you model and live out those beliefs, you will attract those who also want to believe what you believe. Because what you do is the only true evidence of what you believe.

"People don't buy what you do; they buy why you do it," Sinek says.

What a succinct manner in which to begin to understand these three incredible influencers! To further unpack this, I suggest that the following items are each worth including on the lists we might have for coaches who "know what they see." We can name these as character traits, best-practices, habits, principles, or perspectives. Regardless of how they are labelled, any player and their family would be blessed to have coaches who are practicing and producing a range of these aspects.

HABITS OF COACHES WHO KNOW WHAT THEY SEE
(or "How to recognize a Yoda!!")

- ✓ Each is purposed by "the Why" in their life and work—How and What are centred in Why.
- ✓ Their players' long-term success is in the centrepiece of their Why.
- ✓ They are driven by passion, beliefs, and values.
- ✓ Culture matters to them (good culture is paramount, and nurtured).
- ✓ They engage and coach the whole person—parts of life outside the sport are equally important.
- ✓ They work to define and refine athletes to become "the best versions of their best self."
- ✓ They value process over production.
- ✓ They strive for progress not perfection (but don't shy away from attempting to perfect techniques and approaches).

✓ They offer frameworks of authentic loyalty, and defeat enablement and entitlement.

✓ They possess a remarkable blending of technical expertise, ability to teach to the student, and empowerment of the learner to own their career—and they help players to become more self-determining.

✓ They are good role models for children away from the game.

✓ They are relentless in seeking out each person's greatness.

The educational theorist, Thomas Carruthers, surmised, "A teacher is one who makes himself progressively unnecessary." This idea is certainly true when it comes to coaching. As our student-athletes grow into autonomy, as they become self-directing, they are able to self-assess and self-correct. Therefore, being tutored by mastery-level coaches becomes more and more essential. Recognize, as well, that long-term sport development, regardless of the particulars of the discipline, involves four wholly integrated aspects (Quadrants) that need to be developed in order for the individual to have the opportunity to become the best version of their best self. We will look at these interlocking and overlapping aspects in the next chapter. It is important that we unpack what the scope and sequences that this kind of coach (one who knows what they see) takes on. Then the threads that these coaches weave together offer an opportunity to achieve the best possible outcomes for their players. The athlete has opportunity to actually become "the best version of their best self."

There may be bumps and barriers along the journey, even when future-mastery students are taught by mastery-level guides. No doubt, there will be. The *Star Wars* anthology paints this picture for us. There is help available; we just need to figure out where it is.

I encourage you to read through the list of Habits I have noted about.

And use these benchmarks as you help your athlete to find their Yoda!!

10. Because...Coaching Is Huge

"A good coach can change a game. A great coach can change a life."
—John Wooden

Coaching is huge, and finding the best teaching and mentorship fit is absolutely essential. A little while ago, I suggested that when (figuratively) we boil all teachers and coaches down, we can categorize them into two distinct groupings that are on separate sides of the coaching spectrum.

Prior to getting into the two distinctions, it is important to remind ourselves of something that is basic, but can too often be overlooked. Whichever category of coach that your player has with their team, it is very important that the coach is committed to treating everyone with core dignity. David Klein from @MenloParkLegends writes, "The best youth coaches of today's kids motivate with encouragement and positive reinforcement, instead of punishment. There is rarely a need to yell or punish when you learn to inspire kids with positivity and a connected learning environment." In other words, it doesn't matter what gifts, skills, or rings or resume that a coach has, if they don't have a positive connection to the learner.

Let's revisit what the two types of coaches are.

THERE ARE THOSE WHO (ONLY) SEE WHAT THEY KNOW.
Psychologist Alexander Maslow is noted for his Hierarchy of Needs work. He wrote, "I suppose it is tempting, if the only tool you have is a hammer, to treat everything as if it were a nail." Too many of us have seen too much of this kind of "leadership," whether it is in schooling, sports, business, or government. How does his treatise apply to our discussion? Imagine that you want to build a custom home. Who would you want to have design and build it? Curtis Fentress pointed out that, "Some architects have a **preconceived notion** of what a building should be." Would you be satisfied with a

cookie-cutter version of your desired-to-be-custom building? Or would you prefer something planned for your specific hopes and dreams, created with your present and future needs in mind? (See Chapter 11 for more or this concept.)

A lot of coaches and teachers lack creativity and imagination. They limit what they can ask players to be or to work towards, based on their own lack of vision and foresight, unable to see the possibility of a future that is outside the boundaries set by their own parameters. As metaphorical "cooks," they may be able to look at a recipe, find the right ingredients as per the prescribed list, and follow the instructions to make a fairly good meal. But it won't go further than that. And every plate is the same.

While these coaches are quite often very adept with skills training or athletic development, it is typically only manifested within their own teaching style. And they mostly are not particularly comfortable with instructing children or methodologies that are "outside their own box" or beyond their comfort zone. They only *know* what they already "know," and tend to *do* what they always "do." Players, then, are typically expected to form-fit within these prescribed patterns and predetermined systems. Where is the room for the creativity and entrepreneurial drive of a self-motivated and self-determining young athlete in this?

It seems that the majority of coaches in most sports fall under this domain. Do we truly want our kids to train only with and play only for coaches who don't really imagine or explore what individuals and teams "might be" if they work towards skills and abilities that they don't yet have within their reach? Along the journey, I have had the opportunity to see lots of coaches who have great credentials, but who cannot help kids get better at their sport. We have seen folks with MLB pedigree, some with World Series rings who are a nice draw at a camp, but are pretty mediocre instructors. It's important to really think through whether someone can actually connect with your athlete and has both the toolbox and the mastery to teach. And then to ask, can that person help my kid get the most out of themselves?

AND THERE ARE THOSE WHO ACTUALLY KNOW WHAT THEY SEE.

These folks work deliberately at not lumping certain types of players into predetermined notions or expectations. The coaching type that I am talking about here are those who have an orientation to gaze into a student-athlete's possible future and work with the partnership group (player/parent/program) to provide that child with every opportunity to become everything that they could possibly become. This coach-type, in basketball for example, sees the players he can assemble and builds his systems for defense and offense according to their talents and athleticism, rather than pre-setting a system and selecting players that fit into roles in that structure. These "Yoda types" see beyond what the player already is, and try their best to encourage and empower the athlete to not settle for just being "good enough." If you have not yet seen the film, it is worth the investment to watch *King Richard*, the story of Richard Williams' at-the-time-deemed unorthodox approach to the tennis development process for his daughters, Venus and Serena. He and his wife both knew what they were seeing and refused to subject their daughters only to coaching and programs that were driven by rote, longstanding habits, standard forms of practice, and "doing what we have always done." He had a "plan" (the film is clear on this) and had the conviction that the girls could rise to levels of greatness through that plan and because of their passion for the game. Williams searched for and eventually found a coaching program that would support the conviction of that design and would personalize the program so Venus and Serena could be future-ready for their own possibilities.

This premise has cross disciplinary applications. While he was speaking about his artistry as a thespian, Ryan Reynolds' comment has just as much to do with growing athletically. "I don't think you can help but personalize a role. You almost play to none of the preconceived notions of it. It's more or less a personal experience and journey." The best players who have had in their lives the best coaches, those athletes that came closest to fully maximizing their potential, have at least this one thing in common. Along the way, they have been mentored by someone who has personalized the experience and journey for them and with them. These mentors are like great chefs. These chefs are masters of the kitchen—they survey tables and pantries full of ingredients and imagine and execute a fantastic meal that most other cooks could not conceive.

Both types of coaches can bring some good stuff to players and teams and can offer at least some value. Both types are able to develop varying levels of deep and meaningful connection to their teams. But whenever it is possible, I would encourage all of us to seek out those mentors who will look at the ingredients and know what it is that they could become!

In the preceding section we looked at a checklist of qualities, characteristics and skillsets that I have deemed as "Yoda-like." Complementary to these features are a number of elements that would be looked-for in a coach or coaching staff. Let's unpack what some of the aspects that every coach, especially those who "know what they see," is called upon to address. Here are a few significant checkpoints that we want to see in our coaching staffs.

- ✓ They put First Things First—because things which matter most must never be at the mercy of things which matter least.
- ✓ They possess technical expertise that they can teach and possess a proficiency in the game-management facets of the game. HOWEVER, they understand that relationships and communication are essential. Because young players want to know how much their coach cares, more than they care how much their coach knows!
- ✓ They prioritize Process ahead of Production.
- ✓ They exhibit Character more that just Charisma.
- ✓ They value Principles over Prestige.
- ✓ They have a track record of growing better people, concurrent with building better players.
- ✓ They embrace and nurture the partnership relationship triad—Player-Parents-Program.

Additionally, it is important to recognize that long-term sport development, regardless of what we are working towards, involves four linked-together aspects (Quadrants) that need to be designed, developed and implemented with an integrated plan. This affords that the individual may have opportunity to become the best version of their best self.

THE FOUR QUADRANTS

Every athlete has four distinct interlocking aspects of their whole being. These four aspects intersect and overlap, like multiple plot lines in a great novel. They operate concurrently and each affect and are affected by the others; each imprint upon and/or impact on the other three in everything the athlete experiences. This interlock may be viewed by some as puzzlelike pieces, that link together to form a whole picture. While this is an apt enough representation, I think that there is more to the interconnections of these four aspects.

They work together more like a **tapestry**: a heavy handwoven reversible textile used for hangings, curtains, and upholstery and characterized by complicated pictorial designs. A tapestry is an interlocking, intersecting, interconnected assemblage of threads, cords and cables. When intentionally designed and proactively fashioned, it creates a pattern that reveals a story. All the elements work together structurally and artistically. No thread of colour, texture, or experience is wasted. Everything connects and contributes to its meaning. A tapestry is crafted to tell a story, and made to endure.

The plans for our children are tapestries. Each part is an essential aspect of the whole athlete. Investing in, building upon, and drawing from the distinct yet connected materials (as if they were all coloured and textured threads) in each and all of the FOUR QUADRANTS is key to having the tapestry woven and completed. Seldom would any two individuals have the same need to draw from the same baskets in the same way at the same time. "No two persons can learn something and experience it in the same way," suggests therapist and life coach Shannon L. Alder. Thus, the time and space dedicated to everyone's individual tapestry is unique. It is part of our jobs to help our child's tapestry, their journey, become completely and totally their own.

The coach, therefore, needs to be purposefully immersed in nurturing, developing, and accessing all four quadrants, with wholistic and integrated principles, plans, practices, and programs. They must be observers and assessors and have insight into the athlete's process, so as to regularly inform and adjust their instruction. And coaches, parents and players work must work together to use elements from all the areas to weave the tapestry most effectively. Weaving these stories is both art and science. As Sheldon Glasnow puts it, "Tapestries are made by many artisans working together. The contributions of separate workers cannot be discerned in the completed work, and the loose and false threads have been covered over. So it is in our picture of particle physics."

Below are the four quadrant "baskets" pertaining to baseball (easily adapted to other activities):

ATHLETIC CAPACITY	BASEBALL IQ (Intelligence Quotient)
❖ Size ❖ Speed ❖ Quickness ❖ Balance ❖ Agility ❖ Strength ❖ Eye-Hand Coordination ❖ Reaction times ❖ Visual acuity	❖ Implementing the WHAT and HOW ❖ Brain power - the game ❖ Cross-transferring skills and abilities ❖ Develop an approach to particular circumstances ❖ Understanding and executing plays ❖ Applying prior learning to new situations ❖ Discerning strategies and scenarios
These can be trained.	*These can be learned.*

SKILLS AND SPORT SPECIFIC ABILITY	SPORTS EQ (Emotional Quotient)
❖ Footwork patterns ❖ Throwing mechanics ❖ Pitching progressions ❖ Catching and fielding ❖ Hitting techniques ❖ Applying athletic action to situations ❖ Running and running the bases ❖ Game play ❖ Practice habits ❖ Rules of the game	❖ Embracing the WHY ❖ The spiritual and social aspect of sport ❖ Both introspective and interactive ❖ Awareness and actions ❖ Personal well-being ❖ Responding to personal emotions ❖ Interacting with others' emotions ❖ Probing for other perspectives ❖ A habit of "deep listening"
These can be practiced.	*These can be nurtured.*

It has been perhaps unusual to have had all of these quadrants addressed so well and so purposefully delivered by those three coaches that have served as illustrations in the previous section. Our family's experience has included even more coaches and teachers along the journey who have also been tremendous, as I have noted earlier. Truth be told, this was often the by-product of some very deliberate choices by our family. But sometimes we were just very blessed, because you can't always know what it is that you are getting into until you're in it! However, it is not unreasonable to seek out as many coaches who fit this "job description," whether the decision-making that your family is undertaking is at youth or school tiers of sport, high performance academies, or post-secondary levels. So, allow me to encourage you to undertake your due diligence.

Sometimes it's very difficult to find one coach who can reach into all four baskets and grow a player equally well in every aspect. This is why it's so important to be part of a team or program that has a variety of coaches as part of its staff, and that those individuals bring different talents and abilities and that they practice differentiated teaching styles.

It is also important to note that "the great coaches" will never let the athlete settle for being good enough. And in this regard, they offer consistent challenge for the player to proactivity integrate the exponential nature of their Head, their Heart, and their Hands. We will unpack both "H³ integration" and not "settling," in Chapter 12.

So, what **are** we looking for?

Our kids need coaches who know what they are doing in terms of teaching the sport; players will learn best when the coach is able to "connect"; athletes are best served when they are mentored by coaches who "know what they see"; and their "tapestry" will unfold most purposefully and completely when all four quadrant-baskets are attended to by the triad of player-parents-program.

Steven Spielberg sums it up wonderfully. "The delicate balance of mentoring someone is not creating them in your own image, but giving them the opportunity to create themselves."

Since learning and growing ARE so vital, and finding the best teaching and mentorship fit IS absolutely essential, coaching really is **HUGE!!**

11. Zoning Makes a Difference

"Wherever you are, be there totally."

—Eckhart Tolle

How a neighbourhood is zoned determines the kind of properties that will be developed in it. Municipal zoning guidelines and by-laws decree whether a neighbourhood is commercial, residential or industrial. The guidelines connected to each type of property are usually clearly documented, so people know what to expect for permitted construction in any of these designated areas. An individual can choose a neighbourhood based on what it is that they want to develop, whether it be a home, a store, or a factory. However, those choices are still under the domain of municipal rules, environmental restrictions and geographic realities. We all have some capacity to select where we want to work, live and play. Naturally, activities and structures are dictated by where you are.

Wherever you are, then, is where you need to be!

Consider your child's sports world. Is it a playground, or is it a workplace? How would your child label where he goes to play and practice? Would she say it's like "home," or perhaps that it is more like "school"? Is it a place to go to be "immersed in joy" or to show up to endure the "daily grind"? Is it a place to "belong" and thrive? Is it a minefield, or perhaps a circus? It is essential that we pause periodically and look over our child's zone and to honestly assess whether they are in the best situation for them, to perhaps consider if we need to do some landscaping for change, or to just move to another spot. In *Wherever You Go There You Are*, Jon Kabat-Zinn says, "To allow ourselves to be truly in touch with where we already are, no matter where that is, we have got to pause in our experience long enough to let the present moment sink in; long enough to actually feel the present moment, to see it in its fullness, to hold it in awareness and thereby come to know and understand it better."

We all want the best places for the best experiences for our offspring, in whatever endeavors they are undertaking, especially when it is something for which they are passionate. It is up to you and your athlete to figure out what type of zone you want to go to in order to "build". Whatever activities they want to commit themselves to, it is imperative that the situation "work." But before a parent goes out to find the "ideal program" for their student-athlete, or select the best coach for their kid, they should assess and address some matters related to "being where your feet are." And to do this, we first acknowledge that our "feet" are the means through which our whole self connects to the ground and circumstances around us. This is both literal and metaphorical. Our feet are carrying us through the journey, and move us towards, into, and around the zone in which we are building.

How do we get our feet on the road, or into the best zone, and get them moving in the right direction or set firmly at their most productive positioning? Pursuing excellence in any venture involves outlays, and this entails more than just money. When it comes to our construction project, we devote time, focus, energy, hopes, feelings, and lots of other additional resources, both tangible and intangible. For this journey, perhaps an appropriate starting point is to ask about how we view the matter of costs. Thoreau shared an interesting perspective, penning that, "The cost of a thing is the amount of what I will call 'life' which is required to be exchanged for it, immediately or in the long run."

Do you consider the costs, incurred both by you and your child, to be *expenditures or investments*? Do you understand the difference? Does what you "spend" result in only short-term gratification and perhaps merely fill a schedule? Or is a purposeful use of resources to generate long-term benefit? What returns do you hope for, or expect? Is your perspective based in immediate results or do you exercise patience to wait for the interest to accrue?

In order to witness a player's voyage from the starting point of their hopes and dreams and follow their work towards (and possibly reach) their goals, we, as parents and coaches, have to commit to the long game. It is necessary, then, to invest wisely and commit ourselves to being patient and purposeful in why and how those goals are pursued. There are three key interconnected areas that have to be addressed to assist in proper design planning and construction in the applicable zone, as we examine the building project intended for a student-athlete. Just as any structure has a foundation, so too must this process be built on solid ground. This base, these roots, this heartbeat must lead the planning for and implementation of the project. Please consider these guiding questions.

1. What are the athlete's responsibilities? What do **they** want to build? **Why do they want this**?
2. What parent/guardian **responsibilities are connected to contributing to this**? How do families and supporters actually help?
3. Where do we build, and **with whom do we partner** to help build it?

THE PLAYER

In terms of understanding the intrinsic nature of expertise development with young athletes, I have learned a lot through observing and reflecting on my son's journey. Recently, I began to articulate a more particular understanding of what Matt's path can teach me, this time via watching a TED Talk featuring Dan Pink. The presentation had to do with his (Pink's) progressive way of thinking about professional development tracking and talent optimization in corporate structures. It was fascinating and has much to say about athlete development. In a nutshell, Pink suggests that organizations are better suited for success when they adopt a new self-determination approach to motivation. Transferring this concept to sport is a natural fit.

To maximize their potential and create opportunities to become the "best version of their best self," student-athletes are most optimally served if they work at becoming self-determinant. Part of this includes the individual being driven by *intrinsic motivation* (an "internal longing" leading to personal satisfaction), rather than compelled by *extrinsic incentivization* (external factors that point to the hope of receiving a reward or, conversely, avoiding a less positive outcome).

If it were displayed linearly and as a stage-to-stage lay-out, this progression would look like this:

ENGAGEMENT → AUTONOMY → MASTERY → PURPOSE

This model suggests that the individual begins the "process of progress" at the point of **engagement**, and is initiated by the *desire* to be involved with something (an activity or project), with the dream/hope/plan to develop in that area, and partnered with the intention to do better and better as time and effort are invested. Typically, the initiating desire plants the seed for possible/probable future and ongoing passion.

Autonomy refers to the human *longing* to lead a life of their own, of moving beyond merely doing what they are asked or required to do. The autonomous athlete, then, while still working within the structures of their program, their teams, and their coaches' instruction, works above and beyond those expectations to strive towards becoming the best that they can be.

Mastery is the *commitment* to improve something that matters to you. These athletes continue to work at the tasks that they already do well, but also identify areas that need development and work intentionally to grow in those areas as well. These individuals grapple with and take ownership of their own journey, and in essence are self-initiating and entrepreneurial. Players at this level typically only feel that they are doing worthwhile work if they are moving forward or improving. Pink suggests that mastery level athletes require tasks that suit their current capacity, but also that they need the space and support to promote improvement and growth, and that they ought to be encouraged to take the initiative to do so.

Purpose is about the *conviction* to believe towards, and achieve, something greater than just yourself, to be better tomorrow than you are today. The athlete at this plateau is unlocking their highest level of motivational potential. Purpose includes putting your nose to the grindstone every day, showing up to do the work every day, grasping opportunities to tackle more and better challenges and complex problems, regardless of how you feel that moment, what has transpired the day before, or what other people may think or say. It means striving, as one of Matt's coaches put it, to "be one percent better at something every day." Purpose makes a habit out of the idea that what happens next is significantly more important than what just happened. Elizabeth Kanter, from Harvard Business School (agreeing with Daniel Pink), writes that purpose-centred people are more apt to take on strict goals and "impossible challenges," especially if they are successful in making progress in them along the way.

What, then, would a "checklist" for a player's responsibilities in their development include, as they move through the process of becoming self-determining? Let me suggest the following items.

The player will:
- ✓ Design, determine and deliver on goals.
- ✓ Assess capacity and commitment to reach towards them.
- ✓ Identify and embrace the "cost"—time, money, sacrifice—and invest rather than merely expend.
- ✓ Develop all aspects of their life—be a good person/citizen, good student, good athlete, good player, good teammate. Grow in the awareness that everything matters, and all things are interconnected.
- ✓ Do the work, even when it gets hard or boring.
- ✓ Trust the process over the production.
- ✓ OWN IT!!!

THE PARENTS

What are your responsibilities? How do you contribute a positive outlook on and input to his/her baseball world? How can you really help them deliver, through the sport, on the best possible outcomes that imprint productively in every aspect of life? As the part of the athlete's world that is typically most present, most involved, most influential (directly and indirectly), families have profound imprint/impact potentiality. It becomes imperative to work at nurturing an environment that supports the growth to self determination. And it really helps to focus on patterns of interaction that point to intrinsic motivation, and puts extrinsic matters in their appropriate places.

What might that checklist look like?

✓ Be encouraging but not excusing.
✓ Be empowering and not enabling.
✓ Teach them to "earn it," and that they are not entitled.
✓ Insist upon and model a balanced life. Other aspects matter as much as the sport.
✓ Offer authentic, meaningful unspoken challenges—get them in programs where they're not the best player right away, and have the chance/expectation to improve.
✓ See the big picture, and keep all the elements in sight. Recognize the distinction between opportunity and experiences.
✓ Identify and embrace the "cost"—time, money, sacrifice—and understand it is an investment!!
✓ Be honest about your athlete's ability and their realistic placement in the game, especially beyond your immediate geography.
✓ Help them to love the game by loving all the aspects of the journey.
✓ Practice some of what we have already talked about, and will continue to address.

THE PROGRAM

What sort of "place" should you and your athlete invest in?

First and foremost, it needs to be **"the right fit."** At every stop along the journey, the zone needs to be the right place at the right time for the particular individual involved.

In the context of building in the zone that is best for each athlete, we begin with a few foundational queries. How does this place/person at this time help your child reach their goals and dreams? Does it challenge the player in every aspect that demands growth? Does this zone direct towards self-determination?

What are some of the pillars of the program that will help the athlete grasp the best experience from the opportunities provided? What actually constitutes a "good fit"? And, as it is very important to begin with the end in mind, do the goals of the organization match up with the goals of the individual, and do they align with the values of player and their family?

Here are a few guiding ideas to consider as you assess a program:

a. ***Seek to understand the foundations and frameworks of that program.***
   - ➢ Is it "development-based that performs" or "performance-focused that also tries to develop"? Where is the "cart" in relation to the "horse"?
   - ➢ How do they define and refine competition? Is it extrinsic or intrinsic?
   - ➢ To what extent are these people and this program "purpose maximizers"?

b. ***Seek proficient, intentional, differentiated, high calibre instruction.***
   These coaches:
   - ➢ Are not just coaching the sport, they are coaching young people.
   - ➢ Embrace the "future-ready mind set."
   - ➢ Have a purposeful plan and offer authentic feedback.
   - ➢ Take a differentiated approach, recognizing diverse coaching and distinct learning styles.
   - ➢ Of the two types of coaches, are led organizationally, philosophically and in their principles & practice by those who "know what they are seeing."

> ➢ Address and develop all four quadrants of whole player growth. (See Chapter 9.)

c. Seek good culture.

People and principles that are steeped in good character and positive values make a huge difference in sport, in society, and in the life of your child. These are matters that are reflected in how the program is executed. This is just as important (perhaps in some regards even more vital) as the actual programming that is delivered. After all, "The things that we love, we grow to resemble." And we want our kids to resemble things that are worth loving.

What are some of the characteristics worth looking for, that any of us would want to have in a culture-strong program?

A robust and positive culture exhibits that is:

- ✓ Authentic and Reliable, and is a place that engenders conviction towards the athlete's goals.
- ✓ Grows Trust and "Trustability" as building blocks. It knows what really matters.
- ✓ Derives and delivers both meaning and connection.
- ✓ Is Purpose-driven and Process-centred.
- ✓ Is a Permission Giving Network, & Risk-Taking Environment that promotes the freedoms to fail that can lead to opportunities for long-term success.
- ✓ Where Relationships are important—all are respected, honored and protected. There's no point in developing a good player, if they are becoming an a-hole.
- ✓ RESPECT—for self, for others, for stuff and places, for opponents and officials, for everything!!

d. Seek a challenging schedule and a diverse & strong talent pool.

"Something deep in the human heart breaks at the thought of a life of mediocrity." C. S. Lewis may not have meant this to apply to youth sport, but his premise sure does seem to work here.

Mediocrity is fatal. And not many things in sport lead to mediocrity more virulently than winning a lot of games against bad teams and/or always arranging for our kids to be the "top" player on their squad. Programs that play soft schedules and easy teams may win games but rarely develop players that maximize their fullest potential. It is imperative that kids are given the opportunity to be challenged in order to become self-determinant. The unchallenged athlete or student grows complacent and is at risk of losing motivation (or interest altogether). As General George S. Patton put it, "Anyone in any walk of life who is content with mediocrity is untrue to himself."

In the same way that a weak schedule can contribute to overall under-performance, being in the midst of mediocre talent can be detrimental to personal development. How many stories can we find in which mom and dad carefully select the teams for their kids, or bounce around from program to program, just so that they can ensure more playing time in key spots for Johnny or Jenny? Some folks try to manufacturing more "happiness" for their athlete by creating situations that allow their child to seem like they are the star on that particular team. In effect, especially as it pertains to long-term athlete development, these patterns rob the player of day-to-day challenges and growth and take away the possibility of future opportunities, turning a potential prospect into a probable suspect. As I have noted throughout this book, iron sharpens iron. Good players only get better by training with and competing with others whose skills, abilities, and execution outcomes are at higher levels than their own. As Coach Rardin at Iowa Western has asserted, "You become the average of the five people with whom you spend most of your time." So, if the five teammates you child spends time with are mediocre...well, you can do the math!

In order for the student-athlete to be able to work towards becoming the best version of their best self, it is essential that they take on the responsibility of self-determination, and that they are working through engagement, autonomy, mastery and purposefulness. But they rarely can do this in isolation, or outside the partnerships we have laid out. Much like a good rope is made up of three strands, and becomes something that is not easily broken, it takes all three aspects of Player/Parents/Program working together for the prospect to become "future-ready."

Each of these should offer an opportunity for the student-athlete to be challenged and grow. And they are best managed within a partnership that is common-interest focused and collegially framed. After all, it still takes a village...

There will be challenges to those who are involved, and events and circumstances that are encountered must be navigated, worked through, and overcome. Eckhart Tolle discusses this in *The Power of Now.* He writes, "Wherever you are, be there totally. If you find your 'here and now' intolerable and it makes you unhappy, you have three options: remove yourself from the situation, change it, or accept it totally." In this he is not advocating that the individual run from adversity. Quite the contrary. Sometimes a place or situation is untenable and unhealthy—if so, it may become necessary to find a new location to build. But in those other times and places, when the challenges are valid but not unsafe, where struggling with them is going to become valuable, it is better to grow through them, and because of them.

I like many of the lessons from *Field of Dreams*. I won't go into the plot of the film, but suffice it to say that the protagonist, Ray Kinsella, undertakes an interesting and unusual journey in order to fulfill a deep passion that has swelled within him. He is compelled, in the midst of his cornfield, by an ethereal voice: "If you build it, he will come." So, he does: he builds it. He chooses to pursue this calling, this dream, fraught with obstacles and obstructions along the way. Yet, he has the courage to "stay the course." It's tough, for him and his family. Staying the course puts him at risk of losing everything—or at least "everything" in the purview of those unrelenting critiques and unbelieving critics that surround him. The payout in the film's conclusion is archetypically romantic and uplifting to all of us who dream or have dreamt. (If you don't know what this ending is, then let me encourage you to watch this movie with your children!!)

This is no different for us and our kids. We all have our own fields, fields of hope and promise in which we dream. We are all in a neighbourhood of some sort, and we can design and determine what will go there, to our heart's desire and to the limits of our imaginations. We have the power and the responsibility to choose where we build, what we build, and with whom we build it. But wherever you are, wherever you decide to build, is where you need to be! Be deliberate...

Because what's in the zone makes every bit of difference.

12. Don't Settle for Good Enough

"The enemy of what's best, is what's good."

—Goethe

I was recently listening to a coach named Evan Russell who was pointing out to young players that there are two questions that they need to ask themselves when it comes to their own development. Number one: *how bad do you want to be good?* Number two: *what are you willing to do to get to where you want to be?* These are great questions. A lot of players, when examining their careers, and the varying levels of their successes and failures, can match their answers to those two questions with how far along in their sport they have journeyed. Answering the second of the two is a lot tougher than replying to the first. And certainly, it is significantly more challenging to actually become accomplished in a pursuit of any goal than it is to merely want to be successful in it!

"The greater danger for most of us lies not in setting our aim too high and falling short; but in setting our aim too low, and achieving our mark." Michelangelo, I am sure we can all agree, knew something about the pursuit of passions and goals, and by most accounts seems to have achieved a remarkable level of success. He never seems to have settled for anything other than doing his very best work at whatever it was that he was doing, and appears to (using my lingo) have sought to consistently be the "best version of his best self."

What application might this have for us as parents of children who are playing sports, and hope to be "good at them"? There have often been times that the teams that I've coached arguably had the collection of the best age-group players in the province in which we lived. Our 10U & 12U select teams (in those olden days!!) quite literally dominated play in this region and sometimes we were able to comfortably handle some older age group teams, if they would play us. We thought we were a big fish, but, honestly, we were swimming in a fairly small pond with even smaller fish in it. We really had no idea how much better baseball was in the rest of North America, and around the world. I mean, we sort of knew that baseball is very good in a lot of places, but we actually thought we were a really good team with really good players. And to be certain we actually were…well, at least here where we lived. What I did not understand was that we were actually barely a medium-sized fish in an even smaller pond than I realized.

We did know that we wanted to get better, and that it would be hard to do that if we only stayed home. We started to play events in the US at some pretty solid youth events. When our "elite" group first went to play in Phoenix it was wonderfully eye-opening, and a little painful for some of the dads and moms. We could compete against some of our opponents for some innings at a stretch, but overall, their level of talent and experience superseded ours by a pretty strong margin. This "acquired dissonance" was even more deeply entrenched when our group arrived in Aberdeen, Maryland to compete at our first Cal Ripken World Series. Our group of players were confronted with a paradigm-shifting reality—that if we were going to play with and against top programs, and in the future compete for baseball opportunities in the greater marketplace of the game (that included a talent pool that stretched across North America and included a lot of great baseball from around the world), we really needed to see how prepared we were. And we found out that we were not!

That first epiphany occurred in 2008. In the years since then, the programs that I led took dozens of teams and hundreds of players to tournaments, games, showcases, and world championships at venues around the US and Canada. And while my eyes had been opened to the breadth and depth of talent that we would face when leaving the safe and familiar confines of local baseball, and have to measure ourselves honestly against it, it was very intriguing to see so many other families (both children and parents alike) have the scales shaken from their eyes and see their own relative position in the baseball talent hierarchy.

What's been very interesting has been coming to the realization that to a large degree many of the best players that our program had been developing locally, while head and shoulders above their age cohort here, were being outcoached by other staffs, and outworked by tons of other kids in other jurisdictions. It was also intriguing to begin to address and to confront the prevailing perspective that our parents and their players held about their talent level. To a very large degree, many on our rosters were just better athletes than most of the other kids their age here in Alberta. Most of my guys and gals were simply better skilled and better prepared to execute those skills at game speed in our local area. And perhaps without realizing it, most of these players were quite comfortable being good enough to be the top players in our local region. "Success is a lousy teacher. It seduces smart people into thinking they can't lose," said Bill Gates, and he was right. Our "successes" were not real, at least in the scope of what many of our players wanted to pursue. What they didn't know then that we learned very quickly, and we know intimately now, is that they were putting their baseball futures at risk. If they were willing to settle for being good enough here, they would never have the opportunity to completely fulfil their possible baseball futures. We needed to find ways to not just be better, but to be committed to being the best that we could be, and to not settle for being "good enough."

While I had had this perspective for a while from my years of playing, coaching, and administering teams and programs, the first time that it came into my awareness that Matt wanted to be the best that he could be at things was pretty early on. I recall a time in May of his first year of school. We were living in Nova Scotia at the time, and he had just come home from his school's annual sports field day. He brought with him several ribbons and certificates from having "won" a number of the athletic events in his grade group. At the time, he was in grade primary (the NS equivalent of kindergarten), and as the only elementary school in our town there were four or five classes at that same level. When my wife got home from work that day, and we sat down for dinner, we started to ask the kids about the different activities that they had participated in. Matt's older sister attended the same school (in second grade) and likewise came home with a handful of awards (she was also a very good youth athlete before turning her interests to music and other things). When their mom and I suggested, "you two must be very proud of what you did today," Matt's response was thought-provoking. His sister shared a similar perspective, but it was his particular phrasing that caught my attention. "Well, you know, they gave out ribbons to everybody. It's not like it's big a deal."

What's interesting about this, from my point of view is that even back then this child, like so many other children, "got it." What I mean is that kids know the relative value of what awards and affirmations mean, especially in the world of striving for accolades and affirmations. They understand that not everything should be awarded a prize. And while kids may not articulate it in the way that I just did, they really do get it. Part of it for my children may have been framed by all the meals and meetings that they had sat through at our house, or in the gyms that they had been in when I was helping out with basketball teams. Inevitably the conversations that they had heard, with "those big kids" as they referred to them, had left some sort of impression. They witnessed athletes talking to one another and with me about striving to be better teammates, discussing how to become the best that they could be, and striving to achieve the goals that they had as a team. I can only presume that as Matt paid witness to these moments and these patterns, the lessons by osmosis imprinted positively on his perspective in his pursuit of personal excellence through sports. This sort of opportunity is not isolated to our family though. It is just as possible for any of us to help our kids learn the value of excellence over the measure of "better than" someone else. It just takes some intentional choices.

Author Mark Sanborn writes that, "The greatest danger a team faces isn't that it won't become successful, but that it will, and then cease to improve." He's clearly on to something here that applies both to teams and to individuals. I have been remarkably blessed to have been around a plethora of athletes and other professionals who make it a habit to pursue their own excellence as part of team greatness. One such time took place back in 1996 during a Basketball Canada development camp that we were holding, to work with about fifteen of the "top-big-man-prospects" from around the country. During one of our staff meetings, someone inquired of one of our guest coaches, Bill Wennington, about his championship experiences with the Chicago Bulls. It was fun listening to him answer questions, and I was most interested when he was asked about what separated the Bulls from the rest of the league. The Bulls were dominant in that era and were in the midst of a string of championships that was remarkable. What pushed them beyond being merely good enough to win lots of games, and their conference, and the NBA title? While the start of Bill's response was no surprise to anybody, what he was really getting to after that was quite profound, at least from my point of view. He started with the obvious. "Well, of course it's Michael Jordan. He's the difference maker." Then Bill went deeper. "But it's not just that he's the best player in the world—it's that he won't let himself settle for being good enough, and he won't let our team be satisfied with that either." He elaborated that Jordan was unrelenting and every practice the team had to be as close to perfect as they could get so that there would no question that the Bulls would beat their opponents. "We don't leave practice till we get it right. There's no settling for anything else."

Navy SEALs are roundly acknowledged as being elite performers, albeit in a different arena than our children. Everything I see or read about these people is that they strive to be the very best that they can be, as individuals and especially as a team. Clearly their passion is driven by a deeper sense of mission. I have seen posted in various spots one of the compelling ideas that they use in their drive to excellence. "Navy SEALs say when you are under pressure you don't rise to the occasion. You sink to the level of your training. So, train well."

Marcus Luttrell, former "team guy," and noted writer of *Sole Survivor*, elaborates for us. "What the SEAL teams do, what our training does, is it chips away the outer layer and shows you what you're capable of and not capable of." Interesting. What about us as parents? Are we willing to help our kids see what they can be? If so, what are some key ways that we can help our children to not settle for being "good enough" and to reach towards being "their best version of their best self"?

1. MAKE IT ABOUT THEIR WHOLE LIFE

And not just about their sport. Not sure to whom the quote should actually be credited (I have seen a few sources) but I like the thought— "The trophy is earned in the hours that no one is watching." Let's remember that the bottom-line is that we are trying to help our kids win their life, and that the sport is only a part of it! School and relationships, and rest and nutrition, and other interests are very important. Ever try to stand on a ball? It's tough, and takes lot of balance and strength. If we really want them to "be on the ball" with their sport, we need to help them thrive within the balanced and complete life that they need to live. Being unbalanced is not typically very fun, so let's always keep in the centre of our plans the foundational value that kids want to have fun. Much of the most important aspects of a person's development happens when no one else is watching, and where we don't always realize folks will look. Encourage them in all things, because at some point, they will have to account for every part.

2. RECOGNIZE AND ADDRESS YOUR OWN PRECONCEPTIONS AND PREMISES

Every so often, take stock of your own thoughts and hopes for your child's pursuit. Step back and take a broader view of what their talent and ability really is, and how it fits into the bigger picture of the real world of that sport. Evaluate what you are modeling in terms of their pursuits. Are they seeking personal excellence, or just being better than the next kid, or being "good enough" to win here? Does what you think

The Game Is Hard Enough

about your child's talents match up to what the rest of the world sees? How do we help ourselves and aid our players to learn to see and deal with reality?

Craig Noto, head baseball coach at NCAA D1 Wagner College points out, "Building coping skills is where the foundation of growth really stems from. We have to nurture those as parents and coaches first, then growth comes." Of course, he is talking about helping student-athletes develop coping mechanisms to aid them in navigating all of life. But this has just as much import to each of us as parents. If we can learn to cope with our own preconceived notions, then we can help our kids to overcome theirs as well. After all, it really is the truth that sets us free!

3. MAKE THINGS THAT HAVE MEANING, HAVE MEANING

And everything HAS meaning! We just need to be deliberate in seeing, interpreting, and understanding what it really is. Putting things into proper perspective is essential. Place more meaning on the things that really matter. Goethe said, "Things which matter most must never be at the mercy of things which matter least." It's also good to be aware that the musician Sting was right about something—coaches and recruiters see a lot more than what we try to show them. "Every step you take...every breath you take..." Well, you can finish that thought!!

4. SET THE BAR HIGH

And make it known that you're not the least bit interested in letting your child make excuses, especially to you! Accepting excuses, coupled with low expectations, is destroying kids. Stop telling kids how good they are and help them push to be as good as they can be. Byron Pulsifer writes, "Excuses are only for those people who are unwilling to find the solution, who find greater solace in the loudness of their complaints rather than in the action they are taking to

139

implement the actions that carry them steadily forward to their achievement." (*My Excuse For My Excuses*)

An aspect that is sadly lacking for so many of our children in so many areas of their lives is that of accountability. As parents, it is extremely important to hold them accountable for their choices and to model accountability to them.

5. STEP OUT OF YOUR COMFORT ZONE

For our kids to grow, they need to learn to be comfortable with being uncomfortable, but how can they do this if they never see us do it? How often do we seek out opportunities for our kids to "be the top player" on a team, or to be part of a group that wins a lot, even if these opportunities actually lead to mediocrity or under-development? Whose ego is it really for? We need to seek change and learn to guide our kids towards change.

We usually react to change in stages:

    i.   shock/disorientation
    ii.   anger
    iii.   coming to grips with the new normal
    iv.   acceptance—moving forward

We need to get through these. We need to face the reality that for our kids to become the best version of their best self, they will need to be challenged. They will need to work through failings. They will need to struggle. And that they will be much better off when we oblige them to do so! It doesn't do them much good if we remove them from it or do the work for them.

6. TEACH AND MODEL "INTENT."

It was really a neat experience to hear David Price and his former college coach, Tim Corbin, talk together as part of a workshop in Nashville. This was several years ago, and Price was at the top of his game. He was asked how he was able to throw with velocity so consistently throughout the season, and so often deep into games. His answer? "I throw hard because I throw hard." He talked of the concept of training and playing with the basic premise of maintaining his own standards **AND** with the intent of getting better each day than he was the day before. He talked about practicing with purpose and living with intent. If you want to be competitive, you have to compete—this begins within the self—it is an intrinsically driven motivation rather than extrinsically compelled responses to what others say or do. For us as parents, it means we encourage and empower towards self-determination. It also means helping our children move away from "I didn't mean to" into a habit of "I chose to mean to and mean not to."

7. PREEMPT PATTERNS AND PREDISPOSITIONS TO PERFECTIONISM

Remember that "process" should always be more valued than "production"—there will be a whole subsequent chapter dedicated to dealing with this! Sometimes in sport we have to seek after "perfection"—but there are circumstances in which perfectionism (especially when it is centred in results-only) can be crippling. It's imperative to know the margin between those two concepts.

8. BEGIN WITH THEIR END IN MIND

But let's work hard at helping them own that it is actually "their end" that we all have in mind. Purposeful choices are important as our student-athletes reach towards their futures. Check in regularly with them to assess if the dreams and goals are actually theirs. Then their dreams can set the journey in motion and be the wind in their sails. Antoine de Saint-Exupéry puts it eloquently, "If you want to build a ship, don't drum up people together to collect wood and don't assign them tasks and work, but rather teach them to long for the endless immensity of the sea." It really is our children that need to lead the way.

Francis of Assisi pointed out that, "The labourer works with his hands, the craftsman works with his hands and his head, the artist works with his hands, his head and his heart". Pursuing excellence in anything, and certainly in sport, is as much artistry as it is science, it is as much spiritual and emotional as it is physical. The best version of our best self has to be a "whole person"—complete, integrated, and intentional. It must be passionately pursued.

There is a tremendous educator-writer named Jane Roland Martin who I particularly like when it comes to understanding the nature of whole-child development. I think she has a bearing on our conversation here. What could we say is the foundation of helping kids develop into versions of their "best self"? It is the amalgamation of Head, Heart, and Hands. These, together, are the beginning of self-transformation, and then self-determination. What we think about what we do, how we feel about ourselves as we do it, and how we put into practice doing the things we do all work together to help us move from knowing about, to really knowing, and then into actually doing. There is more on this idea in the chapter "Coaching is Huge."

I call it **H³ integration**—this means that not only are each of the aspects present, each and all are intersected and integrated together. Rather than add to one another, they exponentially increase each other (please forgive my limited math expertise). Think of deep-sea bathyspheres—how glass fibres intersect and interlock in a fine weave and get stronger when under compression as the vehicle descends into the depths. Imperfections are overcome by design of the glass because it is exposed to growing pressure. Likewise, H³ integration is an internal psycho-spiritual version of the "whole" being greater than the sum of its parts. It is that proverbial rope, the linking of three strands that is not easily broken.

Theologian A.W. Tozer suggested that we, "Refuse to be average. Let your heart soar as high as it will." Our kids—whether in sport, or the arts, or at school, or in their friendships—are predisposed, I believe, in wanting to become the best version of their best self. We see it especially when they are young, and their innocence has not been tainted by all the things in our society that crushes in on them. We see it in their passions and their pursuits. Let's help them continue to want this. Let's help them to not settle for being "good enough."

Let's help them soar!!

13. Pickle Your Beast

"We cannot choose our external circumstances, but we can always choose how we respond to them."

—Epictetus

Folks who know me, know that one of my favourite storylines is in the film *The Sandlot*. The build to its climactic scenes, and the "payout" as the film begins to reach its resolution, is a fantastic piece of storytelling. Leading up to these climactic moments, Scotty Smalls has taken a prized possession belonging to his stepfather, an autographed baseball, to use on a beautiful afternoon so the boys could continue playing their never-ending game. Because he has brought the ball, it's Scotty's turn to bat. "Your ball, your ups." On the first pitch, Scotty manages to hit the baseball better than he ever had hit one before and launches it into the adjacent junkyard that lays beyond the left-field fence. In a cool piece of cinematography, as the ball is sailing out of the sandlot, we are given an up-close image of the autograph. By this time in the story's progression, the audience is well aware of the history of the junkyard, and the legacy of every ball that has landed there; of course, the mythology of "the Beast" has been well constructed. Likewise, the audience is aware just as much about to whom the autograph belongs.

Scotty is beside himself. He knows that the ball is something that his stepdad, Bill, really values. But as a still neophyte baseball fan, he still doesn't know the actual value of the baseball. He scrambles to climb the fence and is pulled back by his friends. Desperate to recover the ball, he is asked why he is in such a panic, why the ball is so important to him. He explains to the boys that he took it from his stepdad's study and that the ball was signed by some girl named Baby Ruth. Naturally the boys join Scotty in his abject urgency to want to recover the ball. Referencing back to an earlier scene in the film, they discuss the actual autograph signer: "Smalls, you mean to tell me you went home, swiped a ball that was signed by Babe Ruth, brought it out here and actually played with it?" Timmy Timmons verbalizes the incredulity of the situation for the whole crew. They, and the audience watching, are struck with the depth of the dilemma that they face. Benny's observation cuts just a little deeper. "Smalls, Babe Ruth is the greatest baseball player that ever lived. People say he was less than a god but more than a man. You know, like Hercules or something. *That ball you just aced to the Beast is worth, well, more than your whole life.*"

The boys proceed to concoct a series of elaborate rescue and recovery attempts, relying as best they can on their own intellect and engineering. Nothing manages to work, and the majesty and menace of the mythical beast magnifies in their minds. They are running out of time. They were in a real jam, and the Beast was what stood in the way of getting out of it.

It seemed that there was no way out.

Later that night, in a dream sequence, Benny "the Jet" Rodriguez is visited by Babe Ruth himself. He is there to help. The Babe leads Benny to see what he has to do. The Babe tells him, "Remember, kid, there's heroes and there's legends. Heroes get remembered but legends never die, follow your heart kid, and you'll never go wrong." While the film doesn't use the terminology, the Jet is presented with his own version of Occam's Razor. Benny is confronted with the idea that the simplest answer is probably the truest one, regardless of how ridiculous in may appear.

So, he decides to execute the simplest solution. Benny shows up at the sandlot the next morning with a new pair of PF Flyers and explains to the others that he was just going to hop over the fence and retrieve the ball. He was going to pickle the beast. What happens next is epic.

We'll return to *The Sandlot* in a few moments.

***

A few years ago, I first worked with a student-athlete named Adam. One day, in the first season that we were together, he said to me, "I cost us that game." Allow me to be clear at the start of the episode that Adam really is absolutely one of the best people I have

145

ever coached in any sport. A good athlete with remarkably well-developed skill sets when he arrived in tenth grade and made our varsity basketball team, Adam also had a fairly mature understanding of how to play the game, and possessed an atypical level of experience for his age group (as a result of having played in the provincial team program for a couple of summers). Despite all this, and notwithstanding having earned a spot in our starting lineup early in his first year with us, there was still lots to work on if this young man was going to become "his best version of his best self."

Back to that moment with Adam...It was just after Christmas break, and our team was playing in a high-end tournament, and having won our first two games we had advanced to the semi-final. We were matched up against one of the top high school programs in the province. We knew we had to play extremely well, and that we had to compete at both ends of the floor to have a chance at victory. We did play well. And our guys competed wholeheartedly, and within the structures of our game plan. Late in the game, we were down one with only a few seconds remaining, with possession of the ball. In the proceeding time-out our head coach had designed a play, and to their credit the squad executed that play almost to perfection. We got the ball to our best player, at the spot on the floor we wanted him to have it. Adam caught the ball cleanly, lifted up an elbow jumper (a 15-foot shot from the right corner of the free-throw lane) and we watched the ball sail towards the basket as time expired and the buzzer sounded. In the movie *Hoosiers*, Jimmy makes the basket and Hickory wins the state championship. But on this night, we were not Hickory and Adam, as good as he had been that game, was not Jimmy.

Adam's shot bounced softly off the rim, and the other team won the game. But this is not what the story is really about. When we had concluded our team meeting after the game, and were all done our postgame stuff, the guys filtered out of the room to meet up with their friends and families. But Adam lingered, clearly bothered. I could see that something was on his mind, so I pretended to be doing something while the other coaches exited. "Coach, can I talk with you for a minute?" For the first time in our coaching relationship there was a hint of tremble in his voice. Whatever he needed to talk about was clearly important to him, and my guys are always important to me. So, I asked him what was going on.

"I cost us the game, Coach."

I took a few seconds before I answered, looking at him quite intently, and then in a soft and gentle voice I asked Adam what he meant. He went on to explain to me that missing that final shot at the buzzer was the difference in the game and that if he had only made it, we would've come out victorious. That he had let the team and the school down, and he felt horrible because of it. He felt even worse because everyone had trusted him in that moment, and he didn't come through. And then he lowered his teary eyes, trying to catch his breath.

I was deliberate in my pause before responding to him, and even more intentional in the words I chose. *"Adam—just how good a player do you really think you are??"* He began to answer, but I signalled for him to stop speaking. "How good a player do you really think you are? We play for 40 minutes a game with 12 players on our team. Do you really think that you are good enough player to win a game by yourself?" The terseness is in my voice was apparent, and Adam was taken aback. His response was steeped in a personal urgency that told me that he was ready to engage in this teachable moment. "Coach, I would never suggest that!" I looked at him, making strong eye contact and said, "But you do think you could lose a game all by yourself?"

The point of the story is that Adam had some barriers and obstacles that he needed to overcome. And in his case "the beast" was hyper-responsibility. We went on to unpack that moment, one that became a key learning moment in his journey towards self-determination as a tremendous high school player who earned a college scholarship two and a half years later.

***

Thomas Edison is an intriguing study in perseverance. He pointed out that, "Our greatest weakness lies in giving up. The most certain way to succeed is always to try just one more time." There are plenty of stories about Edison's "failed" experiments and efforts—most of which were not entirely failures, but rather progressions to the achievements that he was seeking to develop. I don't think it is a stretch to discern through his work that situations can be overcome when we choose to not give up.

More often than not, we need to overcome situations, circumstances, and sometimes our own perceptions and perspectives. It seems that along this path, we have to get out of the comfort zone(s) that we prop up around ourselves. Our student-athletes need this just as much or more as we do.

The power in overcoming is found in examining and reframing the perceptions that our kids have about what they think that they are seeing and experiencing. In the same way that sherpas guide and support climbers, as parents and coaches it is our responsibility to assist our wards to ascend their own versions of Mt. Everest.

Dan Coyle in *The Talent Code* talks about the fluidity and flexibility of the development process, and the necessity of moving out of and back into comfort zones. This is apropos for working with students and athletes, and especially important as we seek to aid them in their growth, and to model process progressions for them as the adults (that is, "expert learners") in their life. He suggests that we can understand that there are three "zones of practice," and that individuals could/should slide from one to another. This pertains to skills development and applies just as much to social-emotional growth.

    A. **The Comfort Zone**—This is when/where they work with ease, and things are more or less effortless. They are working but not really reaching or struggling. The percentage of success according to Coyle is at 80% and above

    B. **The Sweet Spot**—If it were represented as a Venn diagram, the sweet spot would be that crossover area that overlaps "ease" on one side and "strength" in the other circle. In this zone we will see some frustration, difficulty, and that the athlete/student is alert to mistakes. They are fully engaged in an intense struggle; like you're stretching with all you have for a nearly unreachable goal, brushing it with your fingertips, and then repeating. Percentage of success: 50 to 80%.

C. **The Survival Zone**—Confusion, struggle and sometimes desperation are present in this zone. The student-athlete is overmatched: they are scrambling, thrashing and guessing. Sometimes they guess right, but it's often luck. Percentage of success: less than 50%, and most often significantly below that.

It is key that athletes be in a position and mindset that they spend most of their time in their Sweet Spot but are given opportunity/challenge to slide on the scale from zone to zone. And it is essential to remember that if they don't sometimes have to journey into the Survival Zone, that they most likely will see limited growth and development towards actualizing "the best version of their best self." Persistent and purposeful visits to the Survival Zone (particularly when the participant achieves some success there) adjusts the geography of the scale. In fact, it redefines the boundaries of their Sweet Spot, expanding that area to include skills and attitudes that were previously beyond its limit. It moves the range of the entire scale.

***

Let's return to our film-based lesson. *The Sandlot* is more than just a fun experience. The film tells a deeper tale, with significant meaning. At the point that we left the plot, The Babe says to Benny, "Let me tell you something, kid. Everybody gets one chance to do something great. Most people never take the chance, either because they're too scared, or they don't recognize it when it spits on their shoes."

As I pointed out earlier the "payout" of the film is epic. Or at least it is for this purpose, as this sports-based children's movie can teach us an important lesson. Benny accepts the challenge. He commits to the simplest answer to their problem—but let's note that simple answers are not often easy to attain.

Benny jumps over the fence and sprints to pick up the coveted baseball. This accomplished, he races back, leaps over the fence and

149

with the treasure secured, faces the other eight. What happens next leads to a few minutes of chaos displayed on the screen. The Beast—in fact a very large dog—has followed, soaring over the fence and is chasing Benny through the neighbourhood. The hero's quest to escape the Beast eventually leads him back to the sandlot and again over the fence into the junkyard. As the dog follows over the wooden wall, it dislodges the panel which then topples and falls on him.

Scotty realizes that the Beast is pinned and possibly injured. His sense of mercy and kindness comes to the surface and he, with help from Benny, is able to lift the fence so the Beast can be freed from danger. The dog moves towards Scotty and licks his face profusely in appreciation.

As the story moves towards its resolution, the boys discover that the Beast is merely a dog named Hercules: less than a beast, more than a dog. We see that it is not the dog that has been their Beast—rather, the Beast has been an exponentially growing fear of something that they did not really know, or yet fully understand. Their Beast was an imagined illusion, and the myth had grown out of their own anxieties. And that was what they had to overcome! They befriend Hercules and his owner, Mr. Merkle, a former Negro Leagues player. Their new friend schools them in the legends of the game, enriching their lives, and also helps them out of their "pickle" by giving Scotty another collectible ball, this one signed by the entire 1927 New York Yankees. And in the end, what was once their beast had become their redemption.

It is probably pretty obvious that I love stories. They have greater value than merely being entertaining. Part of the power of story is that often there is symbolic or underlying meaning in them for humanity. This is certainly the essence of the heroic tale. Every hero story is the same—the protagonist is confronted by a situation that they must work through, in order to achieve an end. The pattern of these stories can be simplified to look like this:

Challenge → Adversity → Struggle → Perseverance → Resilience.

This can just as simply be the foundation of the journey through which we and our children are traversing.

One of the unfortunate aspects of our current societal context is that we appear to be moving away from the power of myth, and the value of the journey. It has become a significant issue in the overlapping worlds of sports, schools, and family dynamic that children are being taken out of situations in which challenges are present, let alone that they are allowed to be faced with any sort of adversity. For our kids to become the "best version of their best self," in order for them to fully embrace and execute a life pattern of self-determination, they need to learn to become resilient. The reality is that growing in resilience takes perseverance, which comes from struggling through adversity (and sometimes adversaries!!). If we remove challenges and adversities from the pathway of our children, then they will have a difficult time in ever reaching what they can actually accomplish.

Here is the question with which we must grapple. How do we guide our children towards the outcome of overcoming their obstacles? How do we teach them to "pickle their beast"? **It comes with a commitment to PERSONAL AWARENESS AND RESPONSIBILITY**. Everyone's journey is their own. Each person's beast—their obstacle, challenge, adversity—is unique to them. Yet, the principles we need in order to journey through them are the same. When I have worked with individuals, teams and groups in dealing with these types of concepts, typically we will work through a progression of questions and analysis.

1. *"If everything is as it should be, what would you be experiencing?"* It is often a great starting point to have the student-athlete explore their utopia—to describe what they would like to be as a player and a teammate. Sometimes it helps to create a perfect world that we would like to live in, if we want to plan towards building it!!

2. ***"Opportunity" and the peril of "potential."*** It has been intriguing over the years to have heard so many young people, especially those who are in pursuit of some aspect of excellence, tell me how much that they have learned to hate the word "potential." When it comes to their development, they often view the term as an indictment, rather than an encouragement. Hundreds of kids have told me that when they hear "potential," they feel like the adult saying it to them is pointing out that they have not done what they are supposed to do. The feel it is an indication of present failings. More often than not, I suggest we put aside that word, and replace it with the idea of "opportunity to reach capacity." John Quincy Adams wrote, "Courage and perseverance have a magical talisman, before which difficulties disappear and obstacles vanish into air." The questions for the prospect then become:
   a. Do you know what your capacity to achieve in this area actually is?
   b. Are you willing to attempt to reach towards those opportunities?

3. ***IDENTITY.*** The foundation to working through adversity, and growing in persistence towards resilience, is having an authentic sense of "self." With the individuals and teams with whom I have journeyed, I encourage them to regularly revisit these question areas (see below), and practice journaling to record and mark their process. We often begin this as a personal exercise, but as trust is nurtured within the team, they are encouraged to share with others. This builds the type of accountability we will talk about in Chapter 16.
   a. What do you believe about yourself?
   b. What do you want from this?

      c. What skills and abilities do you bring to the team?

      d. What qualities and character do you bring to the team?

      e. To what extent is your contribution in line with what is best for the whole?

      f. Do you believe in yourself? In your teammates? In the system? That the program wants what is best for you?

4. ***What holds you (us) back?*** What are your (our) challenges? What obstacles and/or adversity do you (we) need to address and overcome?

      Lessons from *The Sandlot*—

        1. Identify the Beast

        2. Confront the Beast

        3. Pickle (Conquer) the Beast

        4. Embrace the Beast

            i. Why is embracing necessary? Because it becomes part of your journey!!

5. ***Learn the power of "YET."*** Along the journey there will be failings and shortcomings. Your children will say these things a lot: "I don't get it" or "I can't do this" or "This doesn't work." The road to resilience is marked with obstacles to overcome. We must endure and teach our children to endure. Discouragement will be real but can be reframed.

Take a deep breath. Go for a short walk.

Then add "yet" to the end of your sentence: as in, "I don't get it...yet"; "I can't do this...yet."; "This doesn't work...yet."

And then add to those thoughts this affirmation, "And I will work to do it better."

6. Remember these **three takeaways to keep in mind** while working with young athletes (borrowing from Coach Ben Ehrlich):
   a. Normalize mistakes/failures. They're not just normal. They're necessary.
   b. Celebrate struggle. It takes courage to go for it, and going for it is the only way to get it!!
   c. There is value in comfort, too. Help them find it, but not always hide in it.

Stephen Hawking was no stranger to adversity. It is not particularly difficult to view all that which he has accomplished, and to discern that he confronted his own beast, and pickled it! For him, perseverance began with perspective. He wrote, "Remember to look up at the stars and not down at your feet. Try to make sense of what you see and wonder about what makes the universe exist. Be curious. And however difficult life may seem, there is always something you can do and succeed at. It matters that you don't just give up."

If you really hope for your kid to be resilient, to have the capacity to persevere, then you need to allow them to struggle. Help your child to embrace their whole story and learn to be their own "hero." Sometimes the story doesn't need to rewritten; rather help them to see through a better lens, perhaps a more simple and clearer perspective. Just like in *The Sandlot*, the process of overcoming our biggest obstacles takes intentional thought and choices. Often, it is a matter of relooking at what the problem really is and defeating our own perceptions.

And, while it does take some effort, let's also remember that it will take time. As the Roman poet Ovid put it, "Dripping water hollows out stone, not through force but through persistence."

14. Unfortunately, There Is an "i" in Team

"It's better to have a great team than a team of greats."
—Simon Sinek

Does anyone else remember when your favourite childhood player started **and** finished their career with the same team, your cherished team? Do you recall the era when "loyalty" and "team-first" and "sacrifice" and stuff like that mattered and were essential parts of our sports experiences? The world that I grew up in was very different than the one in which my son was a child a decade and a half ago. And the world of children today is remarkably distant from the one that he experienced. In so many ways, it is easy to see that the world is getting faster, more furious, and in some regards more overtly and obviously precarious to navigate. Or at least it seems to be much more immediate and in our faces.

Information technology is bringing the world "together," presenting data and images and ideas (whether true or not) much quicker, more prevalently, and significantly less filtered than many of us could ever have imagined when we were young. However, despite assertions that it is supposed to bring us together, it appears that mounting patterns of generally unwise and un-tempered use of these mediums is actually tearing us apart.

Social media, and all the "stuff" connected to it, is wreaking havoc on multiple facets of our humanity, and is particularly damaging to the psyches and perspectives of adolescent students and athletes, both individually and collectively. Within the world of sport, add to this already disheartening dilemma the growing problem of "performance-showcase orientation," and the "get mine" outlook. We can discuss and debate what may be the causes of this virulent phenomenon in another time and space, to perhaps explore the depths and natures of their impact on our children and on our civilization. Without needing to go into detailed dialogue, we can at least presume that the situation is real. The issues stemming from the "look at me" generation that seem to be spawned and splayed on platforms like Tik-Tok, Instagram and Twitter are self-evident. In terms of sports culture, while performance and showcase events are not in their purest and simplest forms the whole problem, it is the submission to, and perversion from, the perceived meanings that these types of events portend that have become increasingly challenging. It is just as perilous that many families are conformed to the patterns of this costly world, and have resigned themselves to believing that all of this is "just the new normal." But it does not have to be this way.

There is a consumeristic individualism in our society. We cannot deny it. This consumerism devours money almost as hungrily as it swallows souls. What are some words that I could use to best describe what this represents? Dangerous; acidic; poisonous; rugged; mercenary; malevolent; ravenous. This is a huge issue. There is too much "me focus." We have been encouraged to believe that what we want is what we need. It seems to have swallowed up coaches and parents. And it is eating our children alive.

Throughout this tome, we have been exploring ideas about why we play and why we coach. Hopefully it is for positive reasons, things like the enhanced experiences of growing up, working at getting better, being part of a team and community, facing and overcoming challenges, and learning about ourselves. Perhaps some of us are still in the purest stages of pursuing the ideal: "for love of the game." But this may not be the case for some families. And, truth be told, the sports performance marketplace is making it more and more difficult to just love the game, and to be happy to learn through it. So, there is this other big picture question that we need to ask. Not just "why do we play?"

Who **DO** we play for?

Is it the name on the front of the jersey, or the name and number on the back of it?

And here, at this crossroads-centred guiding question, is where we begin to wrestle with what could appear to be a pair of opposing viewpoints. We still need individuals and individuality, but not to the point of self-adoration and self-worship, which are core elements of individualism. What does it mean to be part of a team? To what extent are they oppositional? What **is** the relationship between "self" and "team"?

Let's begin with this. I want to share a cautionary story of the dad standing at the back of his SUV in a parking lot, who uttered the words, "Well, YOU got YOUR three hits." It was when one of our 13U teams was playing at a pretty significant event in Las Vegas one fall. Our guys were just arriving and starting to get prepared to play our contest. I had gotten there early and had watched the previous game at the diamond on which we were scheduled to be competing. That matchup had featured a squad from San Diego and a group of kids from Phoenix, purportedly both very good teams. The California team, in the end, had manhandled the group from Arizona. What was most interesting, however, was what I got to hear in the parking lot between games. One of the dads from the Phoenix program was talking to his kid. "Well, at least **you** got **your** three hits." Let me put this into context. While the boy's team had lost, and not by a small margin—and not only that, the outcome of the game was determined mostly in the third frame in which that particular lad had made a two-out error that had opened the floodgates to a big inning for the other guys—all that seemed to matter to the dad was his son's individualistic outcome in one area of that particular game. And in that one statement (along with the general tenor of the conversation), he enforced for his son the misplaced concept that his individualistic production was significantly more important than the team's overall result on that day. In fact, he was clear that it was the only thing that mattered.

There was another event, this time from while watching a high school basketball, in which I witnessed from the stands something that made my head shake and my spirit sink. This involved the dad of a fairly decent prospect, a big kid who wanted to play after high school and who had both the size and the talent to be able to consider to do so. In this particular game, "Tanner" was not putting up numbers that his dad was happy about. *Talk about bad body language from a parent in the stands!* And not only this, Tanner's father began barking out instructions during the game to players on the floor from his perch in the bleachers. Pretending that it was for the good of the team, he was yelling at a couple of the guards to do a "better job of getting Tanner the ball"; to get him more touches; to feed him the ball so he could score more easily and more often; "come on, help your team!!" What he did at halftime was even more objectionable to me: just as the half ended and the team was heading for its off-court meeting, the parent pulled his player aside and in a loudly obnoxious "whisper" said to the boy, "There are gawd-damn college scouts here to watch you play and you'd better get your head out of your ass so you don't lose those scholarship opportunities."

Clearly that parent was putting the individualistic hopes that he had for his kid ahead of the overall purposes of and general wellbeing of the team. And in this situation, he in fact was undermining the opportunities for his own son as well. Unfortunately, it was this moment (in the scope and sequence of a pattern of moments like it) that actually cost Tanner opportunities to play at several of the schools that had earlier expressed interest in him. And I can tell you this with assurance, because those college coaches were folks that I knew (through my national team years), and they told me over a beverage later that evening in no uncertain terms, that this type of player with that type of parental baggage could not be part of their university teams.

Given that individualism is problematic, how do we still affirm the individual and their individuality within the function of a team? Where **does** the individual fit as part of a team? This is an essential question, and not just for groups that are an assemblage of players that compete in team sports. Kids who participate in individual sports are also a part of a team. How each part of the collective interacts with their own role and responsibility, and concurrently intersects these within the constructs of the overall program, is instrumental for their own progress and for the success of the team. And while each individual must be affirmed and developed within their own plan, for their own good, and on their own merit, it is essential that we work at defeating aspects of individualism which can creep in to poison the culture of the team and the program.

Allow me to illustrate. With almost every group that I've ever coached, I do some version of a simple exercise with both the player pool and the parent group. Typically, on a whiteboard in large block letters, I draw out the word TEAM in block-style capitalized letters. **TEAM.**

As part of this interactive dialogue, we talk about what "team" means. The overall idea of the collective is explored, and the concept of "we" being more important than "me" is introduced and discussed, which leads to asking the question, "Is there an 'I' in that word? Is there 'I' in team?" Almost to a person, the answer is no. I asked them, "How many of you have ever seen a situation in which one person puts themselves ahead of the rest of the group? Most often, how does that turn out?" Many folks are able to come up with accounts that reveal unfortunate stories and circumstances of teams or groups that have come up short of what they were trying to do, and typically these people use the terms "selfish," "egotistical," "self-important," or "individualistic" in their storytelling. And together we reflect on the dangers of allowing those forms of self-centredness to dominate plans or subvert the team's goals. So, I ask again.

"Can there be an 'I' in team?" As the participants are formulating their responses, I will go to the whiteboard, and using a different colour marker, shade in the open sections within the capital letter A, clearly showing that it resembles a lower case 'i'.

"So, there is an "i" in TEAM and it's often hiding in the A-hole."

By the time we do this, those moms and dads and their kids have heard from me a lot of stuff about how we are going to individually design specific programs for the best interest of each player, and build this within a general context of what is best for the team and the program. Typically, we hope that what is best for the child will also be best for the team. And we begun to talk about the importance of team goals and team outcomes, and how these provide a framework for the individual aspirations of each of us and for all of us on the team.

It's within this foundational premise of the value of individuality that we talk about the danger of individualism, and how it can be poisonous, or even cancerous to the health of the team.

The purpose of this exercise is to show them that while the letter 'i' can be found in the overall construction of the word team, it is best that it only be a support to the overall substance of the word. In other words, it is hidden within team. And we never should see it ahead of or instead of TEAM. So, if there is an I in TEAM, we had better work on it not only being in that A-hole!!

It is important to differentiate between healthy and productive self-determination (we have seen lots about this in earlier chapters), and the destructive selfishness that we are talking about here. British writer Richard Whately asserts, "A man is called selfish not for pursuing his own good, but for neglecting his neighbour's." Individualism is striving for our own betterment, and only our own betterment, competing (and sometimes conflicting) against one another regardless of being a teammate or opponent, rather than for the advancement of shared values and outcomes, and is sometimes done at the expense of the group. It not only places a higher value on the individual than the group, it positions the individual as the **only** person of value in the group. We still need individuals and individuality, but not to the point of self-adoration and self-worship. Individuality affords that a player seeks to make themselves better with the constructs of the team—individualism will do this at the exclusion of and expense of anyone else. The former is part of collective community, the latter is cancerous.

How do we do this, then? How do we build individuality while defeating individualism? How do we keep the 'i" in TEAM from hurting our programs and our players?

I think the answer is simple—and note that I am saying it is simple, not that it is easy!

As I have noted in previous sections, Reiver baseball mentor Mark Rardin says that you become the average of the five people with whom you spent time. This is just as true for our coaching associations and parent groups as it is for our players and students. If you want to be a better sports parent, identify, seek out, and spend time around better parents!! **Whoever walks with the wise becomes wise.**

We need wisdom, insight, and healthy and wholistic perspectives in order to save our children from those dangerous teeth that are being flashed about in the world of performance sport. We need to make some very deliberate choices if we are to defeat the patterns of the world of youth sports, and not conform to them. We need a transformation instead of accepting conformity. Our sport worlds could really use this sort of renewal!!

Great teams are built with and by teammates who are individuals that are committed to getting and being "better." Let's look at three pillars of what this looks like.

1. **GETTING and BEING BETTER REQUIRES GOOD COMPANIONS**
   a. Together Everyone Achieves More
      i. You can't play catch alone.
      ii. "No one can whistle a symphony. It takes a whole orchestra to play it." —H. E. Luccock
      iii. "Individual commitment to a group effort—that is what makes a teamwork, a company work, a society work, a civilization work."—Vince Lombardi

b. Think about The Fellowship of the Ring
   i. There's a lesson to be learned from hobbits, humans, elves, and dwarves that collectively are willing to set aside personal feelings and individualistic aspirations for a shared vision and commitment to the greater good. In the *Lord of the Rings* universe, it meant that their world was saved. For us, it might just mean the difference in a person's life, or whether they can actually reach towards a goal or a dream. It may not be easy, and it most certainly is not free of moments of struggle, but it sure is worth it!
   ii. Connected to this idea, Jamy Bechler has a neat note for coaches and parents: "One of the best ways to get your athletes to buy into the program and have a team first attitude is by inspiring them to be part of something greater than themselves. Experiencing success together as a cohesive group when doing something is exciting for athletes."

c. The journey is Collegial and Collective in nature
   i. "When there is no enemy within, the enemies outside cannot hurt you." — Winston Churchill
   ii. We sometimes forget that we're all in this journey together. There's a young man from here in Alberta that was a good player in high school but was not getting much interest from college coaches. But when a coach from a school in upstate New York went to watch Alberta play at Canada Games, he (that coach) saw this player and began to recruit him. (He had actually gone

to watch someone else, an Alberta teammate.) The before-that-encounter-unknown-to-that-coach player accepted the scholarship offer that followed, had a good career at that school, got drafted, and is playing pro baseball.

What's my point? When teams strive together, then unpredicted and unforeseen positive outcomes often follow. And you never know whose kid is going to be that "that" kid on the day that coach shows up!

d. Compete within yourself rather than against others. This goes for both kids and parents!!

    i. Do you remember that old advertisement for the US Army? It didn't promote the idea of being better than that other guy. Rather, it pitched. "Be all that you can be!" Same idea here. One of the best sayings I heard was, "Get one percent better at something every day."

    ii. Duff Gibson in *The Tao of Sport* calls it the common exploration of elite operators as they seek "purpose, passion and growth, as it relates to achieving high performance, or as a means to an end itself."

2. GETTING and BEING BETTER REQUIRES COMMUNITY BUY-IN

a. Think about a rowing crew—everyone needs to pull together, in the same rhythm and same direction, with similar patterns of force for the boat to move at its optimum pace. No one wins the race on their own.

b. Iron sharpens iron.

      i. The actual verse from the Book of Wisdom is, "As iron sharpens iron, so one man sharpens another." We have a responsibility to ourselves and to one another to be sharp, to be sharpeners, and to be sharpened!

      ii. Another piece of insight suggests, "Though one may be overpowered, two can defend themselves. But, a cord of three strands is not easily broken." (Eccl 4:12) In other words, we are all in this together, and together is much more productive than alone.

  c. Tools are best used when we learn how to use them purposefully and properly.

      i. But let's remember how hard it is to build a good house by ourselves, or without a good foundation and strong materials.

  d. "There's nothing more dangerous than a dull knife."—Gordon Ramsay

3. **GETTING and BEING BETTER REQUIRES AUTHENTIC ACCOUNTABILITY**

  a. "Faithful are the wounds of friends."

      i. Succeeding and failing, when done in community are binding elements. A shared experience deepens relationship, and can bring much deeper learning, and much more significant growth.

      ii. A sport journey, just as is life, is more a marathon than a sprint. And over time, we need to count on others, and be counted on by others.

      iii. While we may not always be "happy," the joy of the shared journey is marvellous.

Sometimes, we can only move forward with a little help, whether it means getting fuel, a gentle push when we're stuck, or a few guiding words of direction.

b. It takes a village to raise a child.
   i. Consider that sometimes it needs to be okay to correct and affirm others.
   ii. And just as much, and perhaps just as often, we need to be admonished or affirmed.
   iii. "We are each other's harvest, we are each other's business, we are each other's magnitude and bond." —Gwendolyn Brooks

c. "We must learn to live together as brothers or perish together as fools." —Martin Luther King, Jr.
   i. Authentic accountability helps lead to genuine unity.
   ii. Very little in sport is done in isolation, and even less is without ripple effects for others.
   iii. "Alone we can do so little; together we can do so much."—Helen Keller

d. "The rule of 4 to 1."
   i. For the most part, individuals have two eyes and two ears for each mouth. This is a four to one ratio.
   ii. Great learners, and great teams and teammates tend to listen and watch significantly more than they speak.
   iii. Discipline—both internal and external—are essential components of authentic accountability. As the legendary John Wooden so eloquently framed it, "Discipline yourself so someone else doesn't have to—it's a form of accountability. The more

accountable you become, the more disciplined in life you will become. When you are tough on yourself, life becomes easier."

Here are some interconnected principles that are also helpful:
- ✓ The game (and life) is about more than what you can get; it's about what you can give.
- ✓ It's not about being better than someone else; it's about being the best you can be.
- ✓ It doesn't matter whether a player is the best talent on his squad if they are not a "best teammate" on that field, on the bench, and in the room.
- ✓ Flounder alone or flourish together—those are the only two choices!

One of the things that is most sadly and damagingly unfortunate about modern sport, is that we see an increasingly prevalent movement towards individualism and monetization within the sports. This environment all too often chews players and families up and spits them out.

This is not just about the money that we pay (and I am sure we all know all too many people who have spent all too much to chase an all too elusive windmill). Sometimes families only look at the price and don't really comprehend what the whole entity might actually cost!! It is just as sad that there are ample people out in the marketplaces of youth sport who are unabashedly promoting themselves or their programs to exploit the hopes, dreams and aspirations of children and parents. But the reality is still that we cannot buy for our children the dreams that they may have. They still need to earn them. Perhaps, as well, we need to remind ourselves that the process of getting from "here" to "there" takes time, and we can't hurry it along, even if a snake oil salesman tries to convince us otherwise. As C.S. Lewis wrote, "The future is something which everyone one reaches at the rate of sixty minutes an hour, whenever he does, whoever he is."

The monetized, consumeristic individualism's treachery is also about the false token economy that is stacked around the games our children are supposed to be playing—they are being conned into not seeing the essential differences between actually earning something or always thinking they are entitled to it. Combating it means becoming aware that numerous organizations promote rankings and ratings, as gospel truth, mercilessly creating the impression that a person's relative value on their list will make or break a child's opportunity for advancement or placement. And too often a player's self-worth is impacted by this sort of approach, and just as detrimentally, it appears that parents are falling into this very same trap—*that, if only I do this, or spend on that, then my kid will be good enough, or be seen enough, or been deemed as enough*. This conformity pattern is abundant and unrelenting, manifested in everything, from to believing they have to buy the most recent and advanced equipment and apparel, to signing up for every possible scouting service they can find, to attending every showcase and camp they can get to, to paying for more and more lessons with any coach who will just tell them how great their kid can be (if they just get a few more lessons!!).

Don't conform any longer to that dangerous, seductive and illusory pattern. Instead, seek to be transformed!!

Don't settle for consumerism—it will just consume you.
And it will devour your child.

15. Individuality...Is Not Individualism

"At the heart of excessive individualism is a broken heart."
—Robert Holden

Let's try to be clear on this: the "i" in the A-hole of team is not the *individual*, it is the ***individualist***. The margin between the two can either be razor thin, or it can be a huge separator for the player (and family to which it applies). But know this—it is 100% necessary for every athlete to be treated and trained as the individual that they are! "You cannot hope to build a better world without improving the individuals. To that end, each of us must work for his own improvement, and at the same time share a general responsibility for all humanity, our particular duty being to aid those to whom we think we can be most useful." **Marie Curie,** in *Pierre Curie,* her biographical work about her husband, was not speaking specifically about athlete development, but if she were an observer of today's sports team environments, she may well have added a few thoughts to her statement. It is imperative to improve. It has to be done as an individual. And this is best (perhaps only, really) done in the collective, collegial, and cooperative culture of effective teams. It is just as true, however, that we can't do this effectively when the individual is drowning in individualism.

So how do we help kids to grow as individuals without becoming individualistic?

We looked earlier at the idea that it takes a unified approach, a partnership between all the stakeholders for young players to fully maximize their potential. A major issue for us in adopting and adhering to a unifying approach is that individuals are being compelled by undercurrents in numerous areas of life to pursue their individualism to the point that it is building to a pseudo-religious fervour—a de facto "individual-anity" (yes, I have made up this term)—that propels youth and their parents towards the precipice of self-adoration and self-worship. Another problem we see is with some pay-for-play type programs is that they (inadvertently we hope) erode the basic concepts of team-first, program-first, development-first, process-first. Ironically, even though they most often will promote unity/build-the-complete-player mantra in their literature and advertising, they will more often be steeped in practices that muddle the differences between individuality and individualism. This is often under the surface, and seen first in what the overall priorities of the program seem, actually, to be. The telltale signs that are most easily seen are often in what items they deem to be newsworthy or promotable. Is the program about more than just wins, or player placements in brand-name schools? It can also be readily observed with programs, coaches and instructors who just keep on adding more and more fees to families, with the intent of promoting that player to "all the right places."

This is not to say that all pay-for programs lack the practices and principles of growing the whole athlete, with individualized premises that are not individualistic in nature. Many are very good, and several are excellent, at developing the individual in all the essential areas, and do so within the community context. But there is a fine line separating the orientation to be the "best you can possibly be" from "be better than the other guy." So, I want to encourage everyone to think seriously about how we can best help our children grow.

Those that teach towards healthy individuality are hard to find in the general manifestations of our society, let alone in the confines of structured programs and teams. "Nobody can be exactly like me. Sometimes even I have trouble doing it," was the way that the mid-20th century actress Tallulah Bankhead said it. We have to help our children to not conform to negative patterns, to aid them in not just being either cookie cutter replicas or self-centred individualists. This, though, is not isolated to our children only. We as parents and coaches must model what appropriate perspectives and behaviours are necessary for our young people. The manner in which we invest in the involvement of our children, how we engage with our own concept of "self" as parents and coaches, and how we engage others will make or break us personally, it will determine the outcomes of our families, and it will bless or blast our teams, both separately and organizationally.

Tom House says that any development program ought to be built on a primary premise, that "Being honest about what you're bad at is the first step to becoming your best." Being honest begins with assessing our own motives and aspirations as parents and as coaches; it includes stepping back from our own subjective beliefs about our child's abilities and opportunities; and it continues into the realm of checking our thoughts, feelings, and commentaries (both private and public) about others. We will see more on this in Chapters 16 and 17.

All of this takes us to taking view of a unified approach. To live in unity, we must grow in humility, because unity is not individualistic. Authentic humility, as defined and unpacked in the context of community, is the key not only to unity within the domain of the team/program, it is also the key to unlocking an athlete's full potential in their individual pursuit. Brené Brown is a research professor at University of Houston, specializing in behaviour and growth. She writes, "Authenticity is the daily practice of letting go of who we think we are supposed to be and embracing who we are." She addresses in this single statement the essential distinction between pursuing what we are told we ought to be, and who we are created to be.

This is the essence of humility. Humility is **the integrity and courage to be who you actually are**. Humility is a character strength, and as a strength, it is an integral aspect of character that is demonstrated in traits like modesty, empathy, and respect for others. Just as much, humility is seen in the quality of understanding our own strengths and limitations, and owning them.

In that humility is a cornerstone of positive and productive temperament (both for the individual and for the team), it can be viewed as the opposite of pride or arrogance, and it defeats that inflated sense of self-importance, individualistic talents, and personalized accomplishments that are so often seen in youth sports. It is built upon the foundational premise of caring for others, and growing in compassionate attitudes towards others, just as much as caring about or for oneself.

Humility is a specific mindset and is the fruit of some intentional choices by the athlete and their family. Described by Carol Dweck in her work as "growth mindset," humility and authenticity are building blocks of great character and real, long-term success. It does not just admit shortcomings, but actively works to overcome them. Thus, it is a commitment that becomes the conviction to acquire knowledge from the best practices of others and to learn from our own failings, and is a point of praxis (combined approach-practice) that underwrites our process. This mindset-driven-action-plan embraces constant self-correction and self-improvement. Humility is, therefore, intimately intertwined with learning and teachability, and is an inherent and essential part of self-determination. It is necessary to understand that you don't know it all. As a result, it is imperative to remain open to gaining more information about the vast world around you through other people, places, and experiences. And while this is essential for young athletes, it is even more important for their parents. We need to be, then, lifelong learners in order to be long-life learn-ed. This is foundational to humility. Or as Dr. Anna K. Schaffner, Ph.D., puts it, "A humble mindset has significant positive effects on our cognitive, interpersonal, and decision-making skills. Humility is directly related to our ability and willingness to learn. Humble people are better learners and problem solvers."

What does humility look like? Writer Rick Warren says, "True humility is not thinking less of yourself; it is thinking of yourself less." There are three inter-related threads that help us to put together what humility looks like. These are, in effect, characteristics and qualities that are identifiable and growable, especially when we become intentional about them. The contrast between "self" and "other" are important for us to grapple with as we seek to grow towards, and to model, authentic humility.

Authentic humility is:

a. "Self" forgoing, and otherly-minded

    i. "We" is greater than "me.". Can you think of any team in any sport that has achieved any thing at any time on the shoulders of just one person? While every championship run typically has an MVP, the team can only win when it has multiple and varied contributions from the whole squad. Don Larsen pitched a perfect game (27 up 27 down, with no one reaching base) in the 1956 World Series. But he would not have done so, were it not for his catcher and the other seven players on the team!

    ii. The 'me first' attitude is a succubus that crushes teams and programs. Selfishness is most often, I believe, an attempt to fill a void. And like most vacuums, once pierced they will suck in and destroy any material outside them. And perhaps even more dangerous than just being "energy vampires," individualistic aspects of a group effort can become black holes, dragging into themselves all the energy and efforts of the entire system around it. Nature abhors such vacuums, probably because they bring destruction.

    iii. Individualism erodes individuality from within, and eventually can lead to implosion. Think about a submarine: in order for it to function, in order for its crew to survive, the submarine needs to remain intact. If the hull is breached, the pressures of the ocean will crush it, and the vessel will implode, collapsing in upon itself. So, it is pretty important no one inside the sub does anything to weaken it from within. Individualism does this to teams and groups.

iv. But the work of the individual is still absolutely necessary. Michael Jordan points out that "You have to expect things of yourself, before you can do them." High expectancies within the growth plans of the individual, as applied to considering and working with others to raise their own expectancies and individual goals, makes each and all better within the team construct.

Authentic humility is:

b. **"Self" forgetting, and otherly-reverent**

i. "Humility is attentive patience." This basic principle of human interaction as noted by Simone Weil, is all too often overlooked in our modern, self-indulgent practices. She also wrote that "attention is the rarest and purest form of generosity." Attentive patience looks at and listens to the other, because they are as valued as the self. We seem to have forgotten in our society that others matter, and they matter as much as we do!

ii. Consider that the needs and goals of others are as important as your own. This is not to say that what we want for our children is any less important. But the aspirations and work of others has to fit in with that of own kids, and when these are worked towards together, it can be magnificent for all of them.

iii. We can all learn from Spock—that "the needs of the many, outweigh the needs of the few, or the one." Remember that iconic scene from *The Wrath of Khan*? Someone has to sacrifice themselves (and in the case of that story, he pays the ultimate sacrifice), in order to save the ship. In that case, Spock expects of himself to do the right thing at the right time for the right reasons...and he "saves the day." Literature, film, and theology are rife with such stories. Not just because they entertain and comfort us. But, more so, because they reveal the truth about what we are really all about.

Authentic humility is:

c. **"Self" sacrificing, and otherly-focused**

    i. Booker T. Washington, the historically noted educator and activist said, "If you want to lift yourself up, lift up someone else." This is the opposite outlook of a lot of parents and players that I am sure that we all have encountered. We have witnessed those folks who have to tear down others to feel better about their own or their child's status. If we really are "all in this together"—and we really are—then doesn't it make more sense to help each other be better? After all, the tide should and will raise all the boats in a harbour. And it will, unless we put holes in some of the other boats.

    ii. Putting self aside, and focussing on others, chooses Courage over Comfort—and it trusts that the process of growing individually, as part of the team that grows as a whole, will be seen over time. But the risk of taking the courageous steps of focussing on "others as being as important as your self" is a tremendous move in the right direction. It was really imprintful for me during one of our team meetings to listen to Bill Wennington talk about what it was like to be a member of the Chicago Bulls in their primetime championship years. Most notably, he told us that the most significant aspect of those teams was Michael Jordan's dual convictions to both be the best player that he could be, and to also do everything he could to help everyone else be the best player they could be. And that Jordan's modelling of these ensured that everyone else on that team bought into this as well.

iii. "The way a team plays as a whole determines its success. You may have the greatest bunch of individual stars in the world, but if they don't play together, the club won't be worth a dime." Babe Ruth, who said this, was a part of some of the greatest teams of all time. He's remembered for this, almost as much as he is regarded for his outstanding individual accomplishments. It's interesting to ask how many great players there have been in history who are not remembered very well or at all, because they were on bad teams, or because they were selfish.

iv. Though both are extremely detrimental over time, "selfish" and "self-important" reasons are not the same, even though they may have common roots and similar production outcomes. *Selfish* is when we are putting our own ambitions at the forefront, and pursuing these exclusively, or even primarily. This is substantially more dangerous for young athletes and their teams, as it is much more challenging to redirect. *Self-important* is a highly developed sense of hyper-responsibility; when we think that it is only me that can create the circumstances necessary for the team to achieve its goals. I remember coaching a high school basketball player, extremely talented and athletic, who consistently tried to win games on his own, believing he was helping the team. Our long-term success as a team, though, was determined by how much he learned to surrender to the plan and trust his teammates. If not for tempering this pattern of his, he would never have developed into the true leader he became in his collegiate career in football. Both aspects of self-first foci can take away from what a team is working to accomplish. Once in a while, players get a favourable result, but over all these are aspects of both individual athletes and teams that under-achieve.

Intriguingly, there are stories after stories of times when individuals have put aside "self' for the greater good, and not only has the group or team or world been better off, but the individual themself has benefitted. From this foundation of humility, of authentically knowing who they are and how their individuality fits in to the purposes of their program, these people have led with their character and conviction. "Humility is a great quality of leadership which derives respect, and not just fear or hatred."

Seeking after and teaching towards humility is a challenging and ongoing process. It takes time, effort, and sustained focus. And it, even though we may be purposeful in trying to nurture it, does not always take root right away.

Allow me to share with you a story from the summer of 1998. It was the night before our Senior Men's National Team was scheduled to leave for what would become an arduous adventure representing Canada that summer. It was our last night of training camp, and the next morning we were leaving for New Zealand and then on to Australia, on a multi-game tour of those two countries. That was to be followed by our preparatory events in Europe, and then we would arrive in Athens for the FIBA world championships. None of our players, and only two of our staff, had ever been through something quite like this. We had a long, demanding, and grueling seven weeks ahead of us.

Our final team meeting of training camp was scheduled with our sports psychologist, the notable and accomplished Cal Botterill. After he had gone through a few summative remarks, and a few other general principles and practices for all of us to be able to be fully immersed in individual and team wellness, Cal began to work the squad through a team-building exercise that I will never forget. Some of it was deeply personal to me and I'll hold off on sharing that imprint from that moment, at least at this point. Nonetheless, what he worked the team through was profoundly meaningful, and I believe pertains to what we are learning here.

As part of training camp, Dr. Botterill had observed and participated in a ton of our practices and exhibitions and had met a number of times with the players and staff, both individually and in groups. And as part of what we had already done that culminating evening, Cal had masterfully guided us through a discussion about what it is that we had hoped the team would accomplish that summer. Remember, this was prior to our current era of abundant and available NBA level players, but our guys were still a collection of Canada's best basketball talent. And even though we wouldn't be able to go to the world championships with our best player and leader Steve Nash (because of the surgery needed on his foot), we still had hopes and aspirations, as the quality squad that we were, and believed we could reach a top-eight finish. And it was interesting to note that the individual members of the team all seemed to share (or at least they said so in this meeting) the perspective that this summer, and what we were working towards overall, was all part of the greater forward-thinking "Mission 2000," our vision of qualifying for and competing at the Sydney Olympics. It seemed like we were pretty good shape to depart training camp with a unified goal, and a team-first perspective. I thought we were done for the evening, and I got up to leave so I could get back to final preparations for our departure the next morning. But Cal asked all of us to stay for just a little while longer, and to take a moment or two for some personal reflection.

I did not anticipate that Cal would ask the next question. But I'm glad he did.

"What do YOU bring to this team?"

He asked us each to think about that question, and one by one, player by player, coach by coach, he asked each individual, what do you bring to this team? It was wonderful to hear each person articulate what they thought their role with the squad was and then to listen to Cal help each of them to unpack the more significant question he was asking. He guided each person to share what they believe (really, what they hoped) that their character and commitment could bring to enhance the quality and completeness of our team. It was deeply personal. It was remarkably vulnerable and intimate. It was shared in trust and togetherness. And it was inspirational.

In fact, it was foundationally and integrally important for the success of any team or program. What Cal seemed to be trying to do was to show each of us, and all of us, that while each of us and all of us had to be individuals within the construct of our program, that this individuality needed to be woven together, much like the tapestry idea that we have talked about earlier in this book. What he was trying to show us is that while each thread needs to be in and of itself individual, it is only in the commitment to the strength and unity of the weaving that the beauty of the tapestry can be unveiled. It was a marvellous lesson for us all.

Unfortunately for us as a team, a couple of the threads unraveled at a few unfortunate times while we were competing at the world championship. While it was only in isolated instances, there were just a few times too many in which one or two of our individuals became individualistic, and whether it was for selfish reasons or for self-important reasons, those glimpses of individualism hurt opportunities for our team to overcome some tough obstacles and opponents. We ended up losing a couple of games that we may otherwise have been able to win, in no small part because of those individualistic choices. At that level, there is not a lot of forgiveness for not winning, regardless of the reason for it, or the growth the team has from it. But while the shortcomings of that season (we finished twelfth), and the fallout from it, were hard to swallow, it is very reassuring to know that the lessons of those threads and that tapestry were well learned, and that the team got better from them.

The moral of Cal's question bears meaning for us all. We all need to ask it for ourselves, and to encourage those with whom we are in the journey together to ask the question as well. "What **DO** you bring to this team?" Writer and conservationist Terry Tempest Williams may have most articulately summed up for us the importance of defeating individualistic pursuits in terms of what is best for teams and for the individuals that are part of them. "Abundance is rooted in community, not individualism. Abundance is what is before our eyes. We cannot see it when we are blinded by greed."

Despite all the messaging and conditioning in this world around us, we still desire deep down to do the right thing at the right time for the right reasons. And we can do this by no succumbing to individualism and individual-anity. And perhaps to adjust Spock's words just a little, "the needs of the many outweigh the wants of few, or of the one." This is not just logic; it is anchored deeply in emotion and spirit as well.

These really are matters of the heart, and not many of us want our kid's athletic careers to end with broken hearts.

16. Sticks and Stones

"Be mindful when it comes to your words. A string of some that don't mean much to you, may stick with someone else for a lifetime."
—Rachel Wolchin

There is an often-overlooked sequence in *The Sandlot* that occurs early in the film. This particular segment is important for us though. It establishes an initial observation regarding the importance of interpersonal relationships and communication between kids, and among athletes and within the team settings. The film's main character and narrator, Scotty Smalls, has just moved to a 1960's suburb in the Los Angeles area. The young boy is in the midst of significant life changes. A new kid in a new neighbourhood with a new stepdad, his life is fraught with uncertainty. Scotty Smalls chances upon a neighbourhood baseball "game", being played in an otherwise empty sandlot by eight local boys, and he is mesmerized. He watches for a while and, in his uncertainty about himself, decides to go home.

The scenes that immediately follow set the tone for the entire film through a pair of character choices that leads to deepening relationships between a group of boys. These two seemingly minor plot points embody tremendous lessons for all, if we are willing to embrace them. The first occurrence is when another neighbourhood boy, a kid who was part of the sandlot crew comes to the door of the Smalls' house. Benny Rodriguez invites Scotty to join them in their never-ending game, explaining to Smalls that his inexperience doesn't matter for him to be their ninth player. The second incidence transpires when they get to the makeshift field, where the new kid clearly is uncomfortable, and most of the other boys don't do very much to make him feel at home. He tries to play some outfield and is struggling with things like how to throw the ball and even where to stand. At this point in the story, we don't know yet that Benny "the

Jet" will be the hero that he is. Nonetheless he steps up to the plate (quite literally in this case) and saves the day for Scotty Smalls. He shows him where to stand, saying to the new guy, "Just stick your glove out in the air. I'll take care of the rest." He proceeds to hit a high flyball, landing it in the middle of Scotty's outstretched ball glove. At that moment the rest of the sandlot group completely and unabashedly accepts Smalls into their cohort. He is made to feel as if he belongs. And he most assuredly does.

The Sandlot is among my very favourite "coming-of-age" movies. It is chock-a-block full of life lessons and is a remarkable "text" for beginning dialogue with athletes, teams, parents, and businesses about a myriad of matters. Let's start with what it can springboard us into; it speaks in regard to how we interconnect with others. It also has a lesson about the necessary role which adults have in help shaping children's patterns of communication. What (and how) our children present as messages to others—whether it is verbal, or virtual, spoken or shown as body language—makes a world of difference. This is true for how they imprint or impact upon others. It is just as valid in the ways that others will perceive them. Others are watching and listening (for more on this, see the chapter "How to Cost Your Kid a College Scholarship"), so it becomes increasingly important to be aware of the need for intentionality with our words and deeds.

Paulo Coelho in *The Alchemist* writes, "It's not what enters men's mouths that's evil. It's what comes out of their mouths that is." Though it seems to be a small part of our physical being, it is remarkable how influential the tongue can be. Someone once said, "The tongue has no bones but is strong enough to break a heart." It is imperative that we guide our children towards being careful with their words. Because...

"Death and life are in the power of the tongue." This incredible piece of wisdom is found in the Bible (Proverbs 18:21), and it carries just as much truth today as it did when it was written. The things we "say," whether verbal, written, or visual, have remarkable rule over our lives, and upon the lives of those around us. Words and thoughts are as powerful as anything that we do; perhaps, at times, they are even more so. Too often in school, teams and even workplaces, a pattern of oppositionalism can be seen. The habit of "othering" (creating a sense of "us" versus "them") is prevalent in a range of situations. In those, we see that the sense of belonging of one person or some small cohort is attacked by another segment of the group. They do so by creating a false sense of equivalency and attempt to establish a token economy of inclusion or exclusion. With it, they hold immense power, in the same way that a virus or cancerous tumor has presence within a body.

An example of the power of words is easily seen in bullying, and the problems that it brings. Consider "Emma's" story. I first met Emma when she was in elementary school, and we were part of the same church group. She's one of those really bright athletic lively kids, with tremendous parents (her dad is a terrific youth football coach). She loved to play hoops and through her junior high basketball experiences was becoming a pretty good player. Though skilled and athletic enough to have been close to making varsity in her tenth-grade year, Emma got assigned to junior varsity, mostly because she was still a little smaller than and not quite as strong as some of the older girls at her school. She was set up for what she and her family hoped would be a terrific season. Sadly, despite her love for the game, Emma had a terrible experience in her first year of high school basketball. There were three girls on her JV team, all a year older, that began a pattern of teasing and tormenting her shortly after tryouts started and carried on through the course of the season. At first, she tried to tolerate it, and to let things slide. But these three girls carried on, their bullying began to intensify, and the impact on Emily began to deepen. Emma took her concerns to her coach who suggested to her that "these were just girls being girls," and that if she just ignored them, it would go away. It did not.

Emma's experience began to worsen, and her parents began to notice more and more anxiety developing on the part of their young daughter, especially as it pertained to going to practices and games, and even attending school. It took more than a little patient and purposeful digging on the part of mom and dad to get out of Emma what was going on. And when their efforts to intervene on behalf of their daughter with the coach bore no results, they took the matter to the school principal. That school principal, unfortunately, more or less dismissed the matter—as it turns out, one of the purported bullies happened to be his daughter. His position was that "she (his daughter) would never be a part of something like that," so if words were being exchanged between these girls it was most likely that Emma was an equal participant in it. More likely though, he thought, Emma must have been "imagining this." I do not think I am alone in thinking that this adult, in his conflicted dual role here as parent and school "leader," exhibited a response that was reprehensible in this circumstance.

Not unexpectedly the bullying intensified even more, though now it was done in more secrecy and subterfuge. The offending parties had in fact recruited other members of the team to pick on and isolate Emma even further. By the end of the season, Emma had found that being part of that team and attending that school had begun to grow unbearable for her. And she ended up transferring out of the school. She also opted to not play the following season at all, primarily due to her heightened anxiety. Her capacity to trust in players and coaches was fragmented, caused by her short, intense, and destructive experience with that one high school JV team.

Here's another story that can show the detrimental and/or damaging effect that words, attitudes, and behaviours can have on others. There was little stretch of time a few years ago in a program that I am familiar with, through which the organization endured a period of some player personnel turmoil. Almost every culture has its hiccups, so thankfully that seems to have passed for them. While this is an example that we would like to have avoided, it's important to acknowledge that bullying is not as uncommon among sports groups as many people would hope. This organization seems to have learned from it and made themselves better.

The problems that this association suffered through was centred primarily within one age group. What was happening? A small group of boys in the program (most of whom appeared to have some issues related to their own self-worth and belonging) began to "put down" other children on their teams. It was most often subtle, and rarely done around the coaches or other adults. Occasionally, though, a few of the parents seemed to endorse and/or encourage some of the attitudes, behaviours and word patterns coming from their children. Those parents held tightly onto their own habits. They were undermining some of the other kids or suggesting that one athlete really was not as good a player as another, often doing so in front of their own kid. Trees bear fruit, and parrots repeat words and sounds.

Among the athletes, there was ample teasing and tormenting, and plenty of verbal jabs and barbs were presented by this small but poisonous core group. As an outside observer, I cannot be sure if these words and gestures were intended to be harmful, only that they brought harm. Nor can I really assess whether the boys were actually conscious that their words and actions were as detrimental as they in fact were. It was obvious, however, that the perpetrators were aware that they were saying things to their teammates that those kids did not like. When asked about it, they claimed that their actions were "just attempts to be funny," or that they thought they were "meant to be something to laugh about." And a couple of the boys even said, "Well, my dad/mom thinks so too." Over time, it became increasingly clear that those recipient children (those who were feeling impacted negatively) began to feel more and more that they were being targeted. The level of discord and discomfort continued to grow.

When several of the athletes brought some of their concerns forward to the staff, it appeared the coaches were unprepared to acknowledge the depth of disrespect and discomfort that a portion of the group was feeling. Parents began to get involved. Some spoke up in regard to their dissatisfaction. Others, though, did not feel like there was any problem at all. Because the coaches, in their response, had been somewhat inert early on, and inconsequential later, the parents of those boys who were involved in the bullying denied that their children were doing anything beyond "what a typical early teen would do" as part of a team. The situation was neither authentically nor effectively resolved within the program. One of the targeted lads ended up leaving the team around the time the team began to play games and actually had to be convinced to not quit the sport altogether. At the conclusion of what they deemed as a dysfunctional season, a rather large cluster of other families migrated to other playing situations, in the hopes of finding a better experience for their children. Joining that exodus was a significant handful of very high-level players that left as well. And while not all of them said that the bullying (and the organization's "response" to it) was the reason, each of them reported that they were not entirely comfortable with the environment they had observed. Words are sometimes code for other feelings, after all, and it is not very difficult to interpret what they meant. The ripple effects of that one season managed to affect the program for a few years after, as a number of prospects opted for other organizations, at least in part due to the reports that they had heard from families connected to those who had departed.

Not everything is seen, that is true. I have worked with young people long enough in a wide enough range of circumstances to know that coaches, teachers, and parents can miss things, or misinterpret matters. Sometimes behaviours can be ignored by coaches and parents. That is like overlooking or ignoring symptoms because we don't want to believe that an illness is present. Missing things is not the same as pretending that they are not happening. If we chose to do so, I am certain we could come up with a litany of times in which a negative behaviour was overlooked. These would not only be isolated to times when it involves top prospects or is perpetrated by high-end talent. There are lots of negative behaviours are disregarded at the highest level, aren't there? It's not only a problem for an organization who seem to sweep things under a rug and are trying to keep fees coming into their accounts, trying to retain paying customers in their fold. Bullying (with all the behaviours and attitudes that fall under that umbrella) happens too often, and within a wide scope of children and their parents. Typically, not dealing with problems that stem from the words we use (and allow to be used) is a by-product of unawareness. I think it starts mostly because "we just don't always get it." Coaches and parents and teachers do not always witness the behaviours that negatively impact on classmates, teammates, and friends of their own children. And most certainly, understanding that even if something is intended to be innocent or neutral, even if it is intended to be funny or charming in some regard, it is often the case that the person receiving those words or gestures is in a very different place and mindset than the person offering it. German philosopher Immanuel Kant points out that information is only received in the mode of the receiver, never in the mode of the transmitter. It isn't what we say, necessarily, it's what the other person hears!! In other words, water takes the shape of the glass. It doesn't matter what I pour into, the water will never create its own shape. It only and always is subject to its receptacle.

Our words and attitudes can carry just as much positive messaging as well. Brody was a player who wanted nothing more than to be part of his hometown elite baseball team. He tried out and was cut, and was subsequently devastated. His father, desperate that his boy not give up the game that he loved, brought Brody to our training centre. His first couple of days was filled with doing a lot of familiar things in new and different ways than he had experienced before. Knowing that he was in a fragile emotional place with his feelings about baseball, I encouraged our coaching staff to purposefully and proactively encourage Brody. The two things that he heard most from our coaches were these: "You sure do know how to have fun out here," and "it's awesome to see how much you like to learn." We were all authentic with him, because the last thing he need was hollow words. There's a lot to tell you about this particular kid, and how much he thrived as a player in the following months, but we won't go into all of it here. What I can tell you is this. This young man, who was on the precipice of giving up the game altogether, continued to play, redoubling his efforts to get better. He worked and worked and began to play at a higher level than he ever had before. He found within himself a renewed joy. Part of the wonder of the story, and in no small part because of the encouragement he received from our coaching ensemble and his family, Brody ended up securing a spot with his hometown "dream" team in a later season, and has parlayed that into an opportunity to play college baseball. Clearly the power of words had a strong and positive imprint on his life.

I have always admired that my son has had a good attitude about his teammates and others around him. We've been quite proactive and direct with him through his early years about how he treats people, and he's probably overheard lots of conversations I have had with athletes and coaches about these sorts of things. So, it does not surprise me when I hear that he's a good teammate and friend.

The positive power of words can be witnessed in kids when we give them opportunities and guidance towards these principles. When he still played Little League, Matt was part of an 11U "all-star" team (which in effect was the league's 12U Majors "B-team" of some 12s and a handful of 11s). It was mostly a good group of kids and included a pair of girls as part of the thirteen players on the roster. What we didn't know till the group was well into their summer schedule was that a couple of the involved families thought that girls should not play on the same team as their boys. One dad in particular was really outspoken that having the girls on the team was "costing two boys a chance to continue playing." His son was also steeped in like-hearted patterns of behaviour and verbal expression. After one practice, at around the mid-point to the season, I overheard the dad ask a couple of the boys how they liked being on the team with a couple of girls. His voice dripped with a derisive tone. I think he was surprised by Matt's answer. "They're just two of the kids on our team, and they can play as good as the rest of us." And when Russell and Alex (a pair of very fine boys) chimed in with replies like, "Yeah, they're fun," and "They help us play good baseball," the dad's maybe-not-so-subtle attempt to undermine the girls' status was halted.

Another time, when he was playing with a 15U team, some of his teammates were grieving on some first-year guys who were assigned to the tier-two squad. Matt knew that wasn't good for either of the teams, so he asked us at home what he could do to make this situation better. It was another of those times that he already knew the correct path, and merely needed a nudge to trust his instincts. First, he and two of his friends attempted to intervene, going directly and quietly to the two kids who were doing the bullying. When this didn't bring about change, he took the issue to some of the veterans on the 18U team, young men that he had grown to respect. And they took steps to help the offender-players to see their way to better choices with their teammates. Behaviours and attitudes were appropriately adjusted and didn't need to move up the ladder to involve any coaches or parents.

So let me reiterate. "Death and life are in the power of the tongue." Proverbs goes on to say, "And those who love it will eat its fruit." The things we "say"—verbal, written, or visual—have remarkable sway upon the lives of those around us. And they are a primary part of our own diet!! Former NFL linebacker Emmanuel Acho says, "Once you realize the power of your words, you won't just say anything. Once you realize the power of your thoughts, you won't just think anything. Once you realize the power of your presence, you won't just be anywhere." Acho point us towards the concept of intentionality in our choices. Awareness leads to accountability; accountability allows us to make adjustments; and as we adjust, we can actualize our fuller potential.

How can we sum up what a purposeful and proactive approach can entail? Goethe said, "Treating people as if they were what they ought to be, will help them to become what they are capable of becoming." As it pertains to interactions with others, if we are to help kids become the best version of their best self, we need to be deliberate in showing them to look for the best in others, and to be intentional in what they think and what they say. Thumper's father in *Bambi* advises, "If you can't say something nice, don't say anything at all." This is a solid foundation upon which to build.

There are five pillars/principles for us to implement for ourselves, with our children, and in their team experiences. I suggest that these are simple, and can become easy to practice, if we choose to live them out. Let's remember always that our "tongues" are directly connected to our hearts.

FIVE PRINCIPLES OF GOOD COMMUNICATION IN GOOD COMMUNITY

1. **BE AWARE**—*your words are more powerful than you think.* "Words are the most powerful thing in the universe...Words are containers. They contain faith, or fear, and they produce after their kind."—Charles Capps, writer and pastor. Know what fruit you are growing!! If there is a problem with the fruit, it is often in the roots.

2. **BE CAREFUL**—*your words have the power to take life.* "People say sticks and stones may break your bones, but names can never hurt you, but that's not true. Words can hurt. They hurt me. Things were said to me that I still haven't forgotten."—Demi Lovato, singer/songwriter. Too often, what we communicate can be empty and uniformed. Be deliberate to avoid foolish chatter, idle gossip, and careless speech. Prune away bad fruit. Nourish the trees. And protect the crop from pestilence.

3. **BE ALERT**—*your words powerfully reveal your heart.* "If you have good thoughts, they will shine out of your face like sunbeams and you will always look lovely."—Roald Dahl, children's writer. What we say reveals more about our own character than it shows anything else. What is being revealed? Our own self-worth; our perceptions about others; level of need for the affirmations of others; are we trying to

promote others or protect our own feelings? Produce and pick pure fruit.

4. **BE INTENTIONAL**—*your words must be chosen carefully.* "Be kind. Loan someone your strength instead of reminding them of their weaknesses."—Andy Stanley, leadership consultant. Make better choices; think about the why and what of the stuff you want to communicate; consider how you are being heard, and who is the receiver of those messages. Selectively sort your fruit.

5. **BE ENCOURAGING (and ENCOURAGED)**—*your words have the power to give life.* "There are two ways of spreading light: to be the candle or the mirror that reflects it." —Edith Wharton, novelist & playwright. Share your best fruit with those around you.

As parents, coaches, and teachers it is our responsibility to model and instruct patterns of attitudes and behaviours that more effectively build, maintain, and enhance good relationships. Several times throughout this guidebook, I have visited the concept of self-determination (the opportunity for the athlete to seek profound learning through autonomy). Think about this progression, as we work towards better communication trends with and from our children:

Self-Awareness → Self-Accountability → Self-Adjustments → Self-Actualization → Self-Determination

For student-athletes to get on this pathway, the concepts must be learned; thus, they must be taught and must be modeled by the adults in their life. We are the teachers, the coaches, and the models! Does this translate into an actionable plan? It certainly does. The action plan is all about accountability.

✓ **Hold Yourself Accountable**—*You have the power to choose what you say about and to others.* It begins with us! Adults are their children's' primary role models in the realm of human interaction. When you make mistakes in this area, admit them to your kids, and make changes. "Be sure to taste your words before you spit them out."—Anonymous. How important is it to think about what comes out of our own mouths? I think we know the answer to that!!

✓ **Hold Your Child Accountable**—*You have the authority and obligation to guide your child into understanding their messaging.* Monitor what they post in social media and check in with them about what they are saying and hearing about teammates and classmates. When they are off-track, guide them back. If they do get involved in doing or saying something to others, then don't default to denial. Seek out the truth. Set a standard that they, and others around them, should live up to. Guide them to begin to hold themselves accountable (and to replicate this model with their friends and teammates). And remember how increasingly essential it has become to guard them and to gird them. Accountability must include equipping.

✓ **Hold Your Child's Teams and Programs Accountable**—*You have the responsibility to expect them to be both proactive and to be responsive.* Often, negative communication patterns and behaviours can be pre-empted by intentional coaching. Ask programs to set guidelines, expectations, and boundaries. When something goes wrong, it is imperative that the team responds immediately and effectively. If they don't already do so, model a redemptive and restorative approach to situations and circumstances. Help them to consider a pyramid of intervention, as practiced by many terrific schools and teams. In this practice, problematic attitudes and behaviours are sorted according to frequency (and severity)—typically these move in sequence from isolated event to patterns of behaviour. Encourage your children's teams to do the right thing, even when it's hard.

American author Nathaniel Hawthorne effectively sums up a lot of these ideas for us. "Words: so innocent and powerless as they are, as standing in a dictionary, how potent for good and evil they become in the hands of one who knows how to combine them." Sticks and stones are just like the words we say and the voices we hear. They can be brandished as weapons, if we allow them to be.

Or we can choose to utilize them proactively and productively, to assemble them to build a home that offers shelter and comfort. They really are the power of life and death!

The power of these words is in our hands, in our mouths, and in our choices. What **WILL** we choose for ourselves and for our children?

17. Don't Dare to Compare and Complain

"Grumbling is the death of love."

—Marlene Dietrich

A number of times as we have been walking through this parent's guidebook, I have either alluded to or directly talked about a core concept of sport development. That is, "love of the game." There's so much we can do for our children to help them grow in this love, to pursue their passion, and have better and better experiences through their relationship with proper supports. However, in the same way that schooling can drive the love of learning out of many children through the patterns and systems that shape behaviours and quell creativity, organized sports can quench passion for play like a wet blanket over a fire. We are quick to blame coaches when players decide to quit their sports, and sometimes we should be. However, I suggest that when children leave athletic pursuits for reasons related to team culture, or just basic levels of enjoyment, sometimes it is just about their inability to live up to the expectations, comparisons, and complaints of the adults around them. I'm sure more than a few of us have witnessed and/or tried to escape distasteful behaviour patterns in the stands and on the sidelines, in the parking lots, and at hotel lobbies and restaurants. We have witnessed assorted parent-groups huddled about to exchange their thoughts and feelings about their own players and the children of other families. They expound on coaches' choices, the relative status of the team on which their kid is playing, and the program in which they are enrolled. What we see sometimes developing in the patterns of these interactions is a treacherous terrain. Dr. Nicole Beurkins writes, "What kids need more than anything is adults in their homes, schools, and communities who are aware of and actively working on their own emotional and behavioural regulation." Are we driving the love for the game from our wards by our attempts to compare? Does grumbling and complaining diminish their passions?

Dale Carnegie, in his most famous work, pointed out that, "any fool can criticize, condemn and complain—and most fools do. But it takes character and self-control to be understanding and forgiving." Comparing and complaining—grumbling—is a huge problem in the underbelly of our teams, and for the healthy development of individuals (both kids and adults) who are intersecting with those sports programs. Too many children and parents are battered by those running commentaries.

Let me illustrate. There was an encounter with some parents who were comparing four shortstops, all of whom played in the same program. It was early Sunday afternoon, just before the first game of a doubleheader at a marvellous ballpark. I was walking past a small group of verbally animated parents, initially unaware of what it was they were talking about. If I had known, I would have been significantly more reluctant to join in with their conversation and would have attempted to be more agile in escaping their query. Two of the parents were the mom and dad of one of four boys that were being discussed. The other three also had kids of the team and were just as involved in this dialogue as the other two. It turned out that my son was also included in the subject matter they were pontificating over.

"Steve, come here, you know about this stuff; let us know what you think." And they went on to tell me that what they were so animated about was comparing the four shortstops who were the primary middle infielders for their respective squads. I should let you know that all four of these boys were part of the same organization, but assigned to different teams within that program, based on the coaches' decisions as to their ability to contribute at each of the teams' different levels. The question was put to me. "We know each of the kids—Alejo, Matt, Josh, and Brian—are on different teams, but don't you think that they're all basically equal as players?"

I am not always very smart, but on that Sunday afternoon I was smart enough to know that that's a pretty dumb question for me to try to answer. We should probably put this into some additional perspective. The three teams that the parents were observing were designated by the program to play at different levels. One team was comprised almost exclusively of 18U players, most of whom were candidates for post secondary baseball at schools in the US, and most were already signed or being recruited. The second group was also 18 U, but the squad was mostly seventeen- and a few eighteen-- year-olds who were hopeful to play after high school. The third group was all sixteen-year-old players, but still played in the same 18U league, and were designated as a group of future top-prospects by their academy, and many of them were projected to be with the top-tiered group the following summer. The four boys being compared by these parents were assigned to different groups. Alejo (whom you have read about earlier) was sixteen, but assigned to the 18U group that was at the highest level. Josh and Brian, both eighteen, split time at shortstop and second base with what the coaches deemed as their tier 2 group, and my Matt anchored the infield with the 16U team.

It did not take me very long to reply to this group's question. I said that it would not be appropriate for me to comment on the relative standing of these four players. These parents decided to press me on it, insisting that I formulate some official response. And so, after little bit of hemming and hawing on my part, I decided to give them the most honest answer I could give without being offensive to anybody else. I said, "Well, I'm not going to compare all four, but I can tell you this. My kid, Matt, is a pretty good shortstop, I think, but I am his dad—and a lot of college folks, provincial team selectors, and national team scouts think so too. I can tell you this though, Alejo Lopez is a significantly better player right now than my kid.," I then went into a little bit of explanation as to why I thought so. I also made a point to say that I would not ordinarily compare any players to one another like this situation was prompting, but in that they had insisted that I have an answer for them, I felt somewhat okay to try to "objectively" compare my son with another player who I thought was better. And I chose not to say anything about the other two. However, I did add this. "You know what I really do appreciate though? There's a really small group of kids who play here that pro scouts and college recruiters are talking about and coming to see play. Most of the boys here are not in that category. But there are a lot of players here who are getting recruited who otherwise wouldn't be, because coaches are seeing them anyway, mostly because they are coming to see Alejo."

Sometimes parents compare and complain because they believe that every player is equal. Other times, it appears that the basis of those grumbles and mumbles is those parents attempting to prop up their own egos, in convincing themselves that their kid in on the same footing as an athlete as the acknowledged "best players" on the team. But as UCLA coach John Wooden aptly said, "We're not equal in size. We're not equal in appearance. We do not all have the same blessings and gifts. We were not all born in the same environment. But we're all absolutely equal in having the opportunity to **make the most of what we have.**" And in that, there is a key—players are not equal, but they can all be treated equitably. That is to say, when we (parents) stop comparing and complaining, when we avoid thinking that everything and everyone is "the same," then we can see more kids reach towards deeper growth, and more meaningful experiences. There is a role for ratings and rankings in sport, of course. This should be left to the scouts and knowledgeable coaches, and not be in the hands (or coming out of the mouths) of parents!

Let's be reminded from a couple of earlier accounts. Remember the story of two pitchers from Chapter 4, and the dad who was comparing his son, "Junior," to another pitcher on the team? Even though the numbers were similar, the real story that those numbers each told were very different. While that father was trying to assuage his own ego about his son, it's interesting to note that neither of the two players was much inclined to measure himself against the other. They were good teammates. There was little uncertainty between them or amongst the squad about the value each had to the team, and that their roles were remarkably different. It was only the dad who felt compelled to compare.

Similarly, consider the two brothers that we looked at in Chapter 3, and the dangerous and debilitating effect that coach expectations and comparisons had on Robbie. He felt insufficient when he was measured up to Richie. Compounding this was the role their mother had in reinforcing the trying circumstances, heaping more and more expectations upon Robbie's already loaded-down shoulders.

Here's another example. Josh and Adam are brothers that I coached in high school basketball. Adam was in grade twelve (a HS Senior, in US lingo) when his younger sibling made our team in tenth grade (sophomore). They could not have been any more different as young men or as players, though both were wonderful people, good players, and immensely responsive to coaching. Yet again, this is a story of the younger sibling struggling to survive under the withering and unrelenting heat of comparison, and having had a legacy of teachers and coaches who had habitually treated the younger as someone who should have been replica of his older sibling. Neither our head coach nor I found it hard both to see the distinctions between the two brothers and to recognize and confront the pattern of prior experiences that this family had struggled through—and good on the parents who had been willing to bring this forward to our staff. We had several talks with Josh about his uniqueness and identity, and his role as being distinct from his older brother. It took some deliberate effort on the part of our staff, and working in partnership with his family to help Josh free himself from the years of burden from those comparison was a challenge. Even after his brother graduated and went on to play collegiately, Josh still did not ever reach his fullest capacity as an athlete. He ended up playing after high school, at a division level a bit lower than his brother, but I still wonder what he might have done if otherwise freed from the early weight of those unfortunate comparative expectations from others.

In some circumstances the comparisons that we are confronted with are mired in a deeper narrative, and have someone else's agenda attached. I think of the story about a kid named Mike from one summer's Ripken selection progression, in our early years of doing the Ripken Canada teams that were playing at the CRWS. We were in final processes of selecting our team that would compete for a Canadian championship, and in our efforts to work cooperatively with local youth teams in the selection framework, I would regularly consult with coaches from the teams and leagues from which we were picking. One of those coaches, Rick, had a son that played for him, and that boy was a candidate for our team. That player was on our bubble, to be honest, and I believe that his dad knew it. Rick had coached three of the other candidate players with his league All-Star team, and one lad in particular was also from his house league group (in addition to their rep squad). This boy, Mike, was tracking into our top nine possible selections, so, our staff was prepared to offer him a spot. It was around this time that Rick decided to "help us out with our player selections" and asked me for a meeting in which he wanted to offer more insight into each of "his" players. It turned out that he especially wanted me to know that Mike had "more baggage as player" than perhaps I was aware of. So, he told me, "Peter, and Joel, and Mike, and Javier are all about equal as players" (about which he was not entirely correct, BTW). He went on, "But you need to know that Mike is always so sad after every game. He is just always sad, and regardless of what has happened he just won't cheer up and celebrate with the other kids when the games over. He might not be what you're looking for in terms of what positive team members look like." For me, having had the experience as a coach and educator that I've had, it was not that difficult to see that Rick was trying to set up a negative comparison of this boy, so that his own kid might have a better opportunity to make our team. Fortunately, I knew enough about Mike and his situation to know the immense loss that he had experienced earlier that year when his mother had passed away after a gruelling illness. So, I was able to say to Rick, something to the effect of, "Of course he is sad. How could he not be? Do you have any idea what this boy has been through?" And I left it at that. Later in the summer, after Rick's kid had made our team, I took a few minutes with Rick while we were at the world championship. I let him know that he had put his own son's opportunity on the chopping block, because of the comparing and grumbling about another player-candidate.

Author, professor, and editor Moises Silva writes that, "Nowhere does the self-centred heart of a man more quickly take control then through the machinery of criticism and the promptings of self interest." It certainly is not hard to find ample examples of people who compare and complain because they are exhibiting some form of self-interest. And as much as we can try to convince ourselves that "I'm just trying to help my child," in reality we are unwittingly bringing poisonous malcontent and damage to the individual and to the team. Just because our societal context seems to have grown to believe that this sorrowful pattern of commentaries is the norm, it most certainly does not have to be!

What, then, should we do to confront, challenge, and defeat this pattern?

What you think you see as a parent, whether real or perceived, are like stones. Motivational writer William Arthur Ward challenges us with this idea. "We can throw stones, complain about them, stumble on them, climb over them, or build with them."

Complaining and comparing hearts tear down; humble hearts build up. Not just in some things but in all things. Problem A is grumbling/complaining—especially when we let it fester, percolate or steep. It becomes like an infection. Grumbling or complaining is an internal unrest that becomes external negativity, it's a self focused reaction when were not getting our own way. Problem B is disputing/comparing—letting it spew out or spillover. This is when the infection becomes a contagion. When those grumblings become more vigorous or virulent, they become infectious.

Jessica Jones, in her piece *Love What You Have* warns, "Negativity and complaining are like a virus. It only takes a little bit of exposure before you are completely overtaken. Then the more you feed it, the better the climate for the virus, and the worse your attitude becomes." In this era, when we have faced (and are still facing) a pandemic, do we need to expand any further on the dangers of exposing one another to illnesses?

Here are some core principles upon which we can understand what grumbling and disputing brings as risks, and what a humble heart can do to help us.

1. ***Complaining and comparing hearts tarnish the experience for everyone.***
   a. Your words reveal your character, and your character matches up with what you profess. Not everyone's kid is the best playing in the program. And even if they are, you don't need to point it out.
   b. Grumbling is an external manifestation that brings conflict and division. Put aside your own "stuff" for the betterment of your child and their teammates. Rather than sling mud, perhaps help with the clean-up.
   c. We are trying to view the experience through a pane of glass—this gets dirtied and blurred by the smudges of grumbling, comparing, and complaining. Sometimes we need to clean our panes, even if it makes us see things from which we were hiding.
   d. However, humble hearts radiate light on others, and lets them shine and sparkle. When light shines on others, it shines on our child as well.

2. ***Complaining and comparing hearts frustrate passion in everyone and everything.***
   a. The surest method and quickest way to kill a team is to let grumbling fester and poison the experience. Remember what Albert Einstein said. "Stay away from negative people. They have a problem for every solution." The world has enough of this in it already. Help to make your child's team a place of health and safety.
   b. When things get outside of our own prescribed moulds and expectations, we can become self-indulgent, and we sew discord from it. Open your

mind and your heart, see that things may not be the way you think they are.

c. Grumbling and disputing as behaviour and attitude comes from an orientation towards being self-serving and self-satisfied. Ask yourself why it's so important for you to hold your child above the others with whom they train and compete.

d. Everyone is touched by grumbling, even if we think we're doing it in secret. However, true unity, because it takes the long view, brings personal and program peace. (Refer to Chapters 14 & 15 for reminders about this).

e. "Parents: the influence you have on your child is infinite. One conversation or snide comment can ruin the substance of your child's team. A team sport needs each player to support the team effort. Don't tear that down. Support the entire team and let the coaches handle the coaching." This insight from John Beck, educator, coach and consultant, is valid for us all.

f. Humble hearts energize that passion—these bring life and nourishment to the program. They are not just medicinal; humility is an inoculant against the illness caused by complaining and comparing.

3. *Complaining and comparing hearts diminish the opportunities for all*.

   a. Grumbling and joy cannot coexist—don't rob your child of their joy. It's not just other parents and coaches who hear and are affected by discord—kids cringe when they hear it, too!

   b. Remember, when others hear you grumble and dispute, it has impact on the impressions that decision-makers have about your kid. That would be tough to have happen to your kid, if a school walked away because of how you talked about others.

    c. We have to get out of our own way, so we don't get in the way of our kids—and remember that "joy" doesn't mean you're happy; rather it means that you find satisfaction and peace in the circumstances, trusting that you can learn and grown through them and from them.

    d. It's to realize that grumbling and complaining and comparing only costs all those involved more opportunities to grow and to exceed beyond where they're already at.

    e. However, humble hearts amplify those opportunities, especially as we work together for the common goals we share with others on our team.

A favourite poet of mine, Robert Browning, scribed about discontent and discord. "And the muttering grew to a grumbling; and the grumbling grew to a mighty rumbling; and out of the houses the rats came tumbling."

Perhaps take a moment to consider his thoughts.

And ask of yourself...

What good does comparing and complaining do? Does it do any good at all?

What does it ACTUALLY accomplish? What are you really validating or modelling for your children when you grumble and dispute? Are you trying to have the cutest puppy in a room full of warthogs? Are you infecting the organization? Or would you rather invigorate experiences for everyone?

Negativity and complaining **ARE** like a virus, at the very least. Perhaps these attitudes and efforts are even worse than that. Bridget A. Thomas, from *Every Day is a Gift*, writes: "The world already has enough complainers. Let's spread light by practicing gratitude."

It sure does seem like we could use more of that in our world!

18. Better than "My Bad"

"To make a difference is not a matter of accident, a matter of casual occurrence of the tides. People choose to make a difference."

—Maya Angelou

"Character is tested, revealed, and further developed by the decisions we make in the most challenging times."

—Tony Dungy

How many times have you watched a game, in person or on a screen, in which one of the players has made some kind of misplay, and then immediately says or gestures a form of responsibility indicator? "My bad," they may utter. It used to be a good thing. In those moments when a player sincerely owns the mistake and acknowledges to his teammates that he's aware of it, it can be golden. While it still can be a good thing for an athlete to do, too often it seems to have become some form of throwaway gesture, an act to make it appear like the player is a good teammate. It seems to be a pretense. Truth be told, sometimes I see these acts as some form of "faux-remorse" and wonder if they are really holding themselves accountable.

At times, it is even worse. What has become more and more commonplace is the ways in which young athletes and their families treat teammates, opponents, and officials. They spew words, gestures, and body language that scream out negative messaging. These derisive attitudes certainly discourage others. Whether merely dismissive or abjectly degrading, these types of interactions have become increasingly problematic in youth sport "culture." How about those sarcastically toned "I'm sorry" afterthoughts that we regularly encounter? Athletes need to be "better" than this. We all need to be better than this. And it is up to us as parents to teach them, and to model for them, how to better interact with empathy, accountability, and responsibility.

Character matters! Personal and individual accountability and responsibility are building blocks to good character. These are also part of the foundation of any good program, classroom, or family. We cannot merely hope that these essential attributes "just show up." They must be expected, taught, modeled, nurtured, and refined.

Because "this is The Way."

It certainly is not hard to find examples of people who are not a part of the way. I was watching a youth baseball game a while ago. One boy was pitching and got a batter to hit a ground ball to the third baseman. The defender "booted" it, which drew a glare from the hurler. Most notably, the pitcher's mother loudly and immediately with a disdainful tone, yelled out, "Oh come on, Billy, help out your pitcher!!!" Ironically, this mother was silent two innings later when her son, who had moved to play third base at that point, made a similar error on a relatively easy grounder.

Here's another incident that I witnessed recently at hockey rink. A player on one of the teams, the "captain" as appointed by the head coach, over the course of that game was consistently chirping at a linemate. It appeared to happen whenever the other kid didn't pass it at the right time or missed a shot attempt that the captain had sent his way. There's a margin between helping a teammate get better, and being a bit of a jerk. This young athlete had not yet learned that difference. It didn't take me long to see what the source of the "captain's" behaviour pattern was. In the stands, as the game proceeded, I was able to figure out who the parents were of the two players I am talking about. The Captain-Dad was sighing overtly and gesticulating profusely, and making not very subtle comments about how his son "deserved to play on a better line with players who know what they are doing." "These players can't play." "This is Tier 3; they should know what they're doing by now!!" His comments were loud enough for me to hear them from about forty feet away, and were threaded throughout the game. Almost all were exclusively directed at the linemates of his child. At about 45 minutes into this hour-plus-long episode, the other parent had heard enough, and briskly asked the first father to "quiet himself" (not exactly those words). Their verbal interaction got more heated, and the two "adults" took their discussion outside the rink.

Earlier in the book I mentioned a basketball player named Tanner, and what sorts of things his father did from the stands. Tanner was not innocent himself. He had a terrible habit of gesturing at teammates when a pass went askew, among other things he would do. His facial expressions and hand actions were the stuff of legend in his community. He was even worse with his body language whenever he felt a call from the officials did not go his way. He was perceived as a substantially self-indulgent young adult. Years later, his former school mates still recall him as a person that they would never want to work with.

Enough incidents, when examined over time, indicate a pattern. The world has certainly changed...or it sure seems to have. Things that we would never have been permitted to do or say a generation ago seem to have become common attitudes and behaviours. That they are so readily perpetrated by parents and modelled by professional athletes across media platforms only serves to compound the issue. I cannot imagine ever have gotten away with what is so commonplace in youth sports today. Once, when I was playing baseball, one of my teammates made an error behind me while I was pitching. I did not respond very well, making my anger at him quite obvious. The coach came out, and I was expecting him to say that I was right to be upset, that my shortstop needed to make that play. But that was not what happened. Coach told me that I was being a selfish punk, and that I needed to grow up. And he reminded me that if I wasn't going to strike out every batter (and that was not going to happen!!) then I better treat my teammates as if I would like them to make plays behind me. My mom happened to be at that game, and afterwards asked about what she had seen. When I explained, she added some additional wisdom. "That had better be the last time I see you try to embarrass your friends."

Not everything is a quagmire of negativity. There are still coaches and programs and parents who do good jobs in promoting respect and appropriate conduct. Though isn't it interesting? These folks seem to have become the exceptions, rather than the "rule of thumb." I am certain that I am not the only person who has witnessed a family leave a program or generate a conflict with a leader when their child is challenged to adjust an attitude or behaviour. Can we do anything to help calm the stormy seas?

Well defined and intentionally executed perspectives of responsibility and accountability are desirable qualities in students and athletes that can carry forward from the field of play into other aspects of life. My friend works for a major player in the energy sector, in a role of leadership within a significant department. Rather than permit his group to take an oppositional stand (us vs them), he encourages the team to take an individualized approach to improvement. He models and leads his department to undertake "a continuous working at making ourselves better than we used to be." When he works with all of the members of his team through these exercises, he is attempting to help them to reframe their perspectives. Rather than complain about what is or is not being done in other departments, he asks his team to do a few things that they appear to have not done very intentionally before. He asks them to suspend their criticism of others; after all, he suggests, "when we make them an 'adversary,' we are just making our own work that much more challenging." They are then asked to critique their own practices, and to suggest ways that they can be more effective, both in manifesting their own set of tasks, and in the manner in which data and information is shared with others. The team is also asked to become familiar with diverse aspects of the department beyond their own job description, in order to develop broader knowledge and deeper empathy. My friend knows that his team needs to be coachable; thus, he spends ample positive effort in helping them learn to be coachable, so that they are dependable, consistent, and knowledgeable. This is a terrific approach: the team seems to be taking on the challenge of accountability in their approach to personal productivity. Not surprisingly, the team has begun to function more effectively and more efficiently. He reports, as well, that the ripple effect, as his team intersects with other aspects of the corporate structure, has begun to manifest positive consequences to the company.

Patriots coach Bill Belichick year after year is able to construct competitive teams in the NFL landscape. Their consistency is remarkable, in spite of the ups-and-downs of rosters and players in professional football. "Success isn't all about talent. It's about being dependable, consistent, coachable, and knowing what you need to do to improve," he says. If we are not accountable within our own self-pursuits and responsible in our own choices, how can we ever attain some collegial and collective accountability as a team?

Sometimes the matters of dependability are about concerns that are much deeper than talent or athleticism. At times the outcomes that we incur are the by-product of the choices that we make. Reality is tough. Our choices always lead to consequences (whether positive or not), and truth be told, the consequences that we create are not limited in their scope to just ourselves. Our team, for example, was playing Greece in the opening game of the 1998 world championships, in a hostile arena in downtown Athens. Our squad was battling ferociously, and we trailed that very good Greek team for much of the game. With only a few minutes remaining, we finally got back to almost even when one of our guys committed a stupid and unnecessary foul while we had possession. It was away from the ball on our offensive side of the floor. His selfish act could not have come at a worse moment. Retaliating for something that had been left uncalled by the officials a few seconds earlier, this player had thrown a stiff elbow at his counterpart, ostensibly to "get even." As he was in the process of doing this, one of our other guys was releasing a three-point shot—a shot that went in, which would have given us a two-point lead with only a few minutes to go. It would have been our first lead of the game. More significantly, that hoop would have added to the positive momentum that we had been building. Unfortunately, the basket was waved off.

Adding insult to injury, Greece was awarded two free throws, which they made. On the subsequent inbound play, the same athlete who had committed the dumb foul (clearly in a state of frustration) attempted to throw a pass to half-court which was intercepted and led to an almost immediate three-point goal by our opponents. Our coaching staff was attempting to make a substitution while this was happening but some of the FIBA rules in that era were restrictive. After that made basket, we were able to get the ball up the court, at which time the very same guy then missed a shot that perhaps he should have passed up. In the space of less than 45 seconds, largely in part because of one selfish decision (my interpretation, of course) and then the fallout from it, the game had gone from possibly winable to practically out of reach. The score had turned from could-have-been "up by two" to "down by eight points." The momentum had swung un-mercilessly to the other side, and much of whatever "life" we might have had had been sucked out of our bench in those few heartbeats. Years later I had the opportunity to get together with that former teammate, and during the course of a lovely evening, we talked about those moments. He maintained that he was "just competing," and that he "had to show that guy he couldn't get away with what he'd done." I translated his position as either unwillingness or inability to readjust his perception, and to grow in his own awareness.

The road to self-determination *(profound learning through autonomy)* **involves adjusting our paradigm.** It is essential that we take a look at our own worldview and determine if and where we need to adjust our point of view. There is an account I have heard about elephants and ropes that bind them to stake. The story goes that from the time they are born, elephants in captivity are chained to firmly planted posts in the ground. The pachyderm may pull at the restraints, and struggle against its limits while young but to no avail, as the post in the ground is too deeply entrenched and the chain is unrelenting. Over time, the elephant "learns": if well treated, the beast will stay within its boundaries without struggle. Intriguingly, when older and trained this way, an elephant will not pull against the restraint. Often, the post and chain are replaced with a light rope and small stick that would be easily plucked from the ground.

Nonetheless, the animal stays put, and works within the frameworks of its permitted experience. This is not to suggested that we should be focussed on behaviour mediation and modification. Not at all. However, the reality of our world is that most aspects of social structures are geared towards influencing attitude and behaviour patterns. If we are going to allow forms of conditioning to shape our children, why not be more intentional about to what ends they are being conditioned? Consider the journey of those young baseball players that I had noted earlier, those who were doing extra practices, hitting in cages. Early on their sessions were coach-directed, and as time passed the daily plans became more and more of their own creation. They began to design and implement their own activities and monitor their own efforts. Into early adolescence and through their high school years these athletes displayed a level of work ethic, coachability, and trustworthiness with the teams that they had advanced to, that was noted by coaches around the country. Their capacity to be concurrently both autonomous *and* within the expectations of their coaches was instrumental in generating opportunities to play collegiately. These boys had learned to be accountable to themselves and to each other. From that base, they were then able to expect accountability from their cohorts. They were conditioned towards self-direction, and it carried forward for them into their future prospects.

These were aspects of **empowerment and equipping**. Parents with whom I have worked through the decades have wanted their children to be the "best that they can be" in the sport. At times it has been a trial for some families to grasp and to grapple with how to most effectively encourage their children towards the sort of autonomy we are talking about. It is often just as much a struggle for coaches. Early in those dialogues with families, we have to make a series of early outlook recognitions. First is to acknowledge that one of their patterns has been (often inadvertently) to redirect or remove responsibility from their child when looking at what has happened in games or at school. This is a point of great discomfort for many parents. Families have to be willing to recognize this behaviour pattern, one that allows for the opportunity to elude, evade, or escape responsibility, consequence, and accountability. Sport, like life itself, does not really come with many guarantees. None of us are entitled to whatever we desire. Too often programs and families enable behaviours and attitudes that may at surface level appear to be harmless. But if not checked, any small bit of dirt can turn into a dangerous infection. We need to be cautious that in own approaches we don't conform to these same patterns. We have to fight against enabling our children to not be challenged, and the pratfalls of thinking they are entitled to an outcome that they have not yet fully earned.

This is a tough part of the journey. Yet, it is ridiculously important. It is not difficult to see that there are many speed traps, potholes, and possible accidents on that road, many of which are unexpected or unseen. "Patrick" is an athlete I have known since he was nine years old. Based upon his athleticism and ability to play the game, he was often one of the top prospects in his age group. He almost always passed the eye-wash test. Unfortunately for Patrick, the closer he got to high school graduation, fewer of those schools that had initially been recruiting him continued to express interest. More and more reports about Patrick making bad choices were getting back to college coaches. As an only child of very eager-to-please parents, Patrick had developed habits of pushing the boundaries of the authority figures in his life, whether it be teachers or coaches or high-level staff of elite programs. His parents had rarely corrected his behaviours or held him accountable. With this pattern, and because some teams he had played for had overlooked some of his wrongdoings in order to keep him active on their rosters, it appeared that Patrick had begun to believe that he was untouchable. So, when he was "disinvited" from his spot with the National team program for his 18U year, he and his parents presumed it was someone else's fault. And as potential schools dropped by the wayside and he was left with very few opportunities for post high school scholarships, the family could not be made to understand why so many programs had changed their minds.

"Harry" was a terrific athlete who could have been a very good player. Occasionally, though, he had run-ins with certain types of authority figures. There was one time in which Harry was "goofing around" in the outfield while his 13U team was making a mid-inning pitching change. One of the coaches from the staff took exception to his efforts at dancing a jig, preferring that the young athlete would better serve the team if he would just "respect the game." That coach asked me to "straighten up that kid between innings." When I attempted to talk with Harry, trying to indicate the importance of the other coach's concerns, he brushed it off. "Well, that's HIS f***ing problem." I was not prepared to let that slide and explained to the player some of the dynamic that he was inflaming and that he needed to take a step back and grow up a little bit. After the game, he had talked to his parents, and they confronted me. "How dare you say these things to our child." They expected me to "be on our kid's side"—not realizing that by calling him into accountability, I actually was! They would not consider that their son had done anything possibly questionable, let alone wrong. From that platform, why would they even imagine that he should take responsibility? Where, then, could accountability ever fit in?

So, what is a solution? What can we learn from these stories? Combatting this conformity to the patterns that we need to reject becomes increasingly imperative. The answer is to seek transformation. Becoming, and then being, the "best version of your best-self" is not only about developing skills and athletic prowess. It takes more than executing plays and gaining competitive experience. It takes a conviction to ongoing renewal. It takes character.

Empathy (making the effort to see from someone else's perspective) is the doorway to awareness, making it possible for responsibility and accountability to be the benchmarks of our children's character. As these benchmarks are developed, we see their capacity to be self-directing grow. And then they recognize that everything has consequences. When we make good choices, positive outcomes are more likely to follow. Just as true is that bad decisions often lead to penalties we would rather not have to face. Reality is tough to avoid, even if we try to. Rather than show our athletes the path that avoids consequences, or absolves from taking responsibility, let's guide them towards a road that embraces the opportunities to overcome challenges. After all, kids become responsible by working through responsibilities.

Hall of Fame basketball coach George Raveling talks about the relationship that accountability and responsibility have in development. "Growth, learning, unlearning, relearning, and seeking the truth has no finish line. We must use adversity and circumstances that are out of our control as teaching moments while focusing our attention on the controllable with excellence, enthusiasm, and positive energy." You see, Self-Directed Athletes are engaged in their **"A-GAME."** This interconnectivity can be interpreted in a number of manners. The first is as a *cycle*: each element builds towards the next, progressing forward, around, and eventually back to a similar point at which the cycle began. Presumably, that process will have enhanced the understandings and practices of the individual. The second might be an *upward spiral*. Similar in that it cycles, this process adds a dimension. The cycle moves upward and to some degree outward—as if expanding its areas of imprint. In this model, the movement leads back to "awareness," and in this scenario that awareness is at a new point in the journey. It is heightened and more articulate. And the third image could be a *ring*. This image infers that the elements are all integrated and united in holding the form. The images smacks of an enduring and persevering commitment to purpose, in which all the aspects are working together with a sense of eternal strength. Perhaps it is all three.

AWARENESS → ACTION → ACCOUNTABILITY → ACHIEVEMENT → AFFIRMATION/ACCEPTANCE → ACKNOWLEDGMENT → AFFINITY → ATTUNEMENT/ADJUSTMENT →

Let's briefly look at what these segments mean.

➢ **AWARENESS**—being conscious of things; being informed; being teachable.
➢ **ACTION**—the process of doing; manifesting change
➢ **ACCOUNTABILITY**—being responsible for choices

➤ **ACHIEVEMENT**—accomplishing or carrying out tasks; struggling with the changing zone that we encounter (as per previous chapters)
➤ **AFFIRMATION/ACCEPTANCE**—an intrinsic declaration /willingness to adhere to new circumstances and conditions; growing commitment into conviction.
➤ **ACKNOWLEDGMENT**—recognizing, admitting, and confirming truths; external indication of internal learnings
➤ **AFFINITY**—believing in the process and the progress you are making, even when the results don't match up right away. Seeing the similarity of characteristics, suggesting there is relationship between all aspects of life (sport, school, friends, family)
➤ **ATTUNEMENT/ADJUSTMENT**—adjusting and acclimating to a new understanding, leading to the next level of awareness.

As the individual becomes more **self-aware** and thus more **self-determining**, they grow in the capacity to be **self-directing** in each of these elements. The athlete is still open to and responsive with the insights and input of others but is no longer solely reliant upon them. And at this point of the maturation process, the person does not elude or evade input from other. They are moving away from the trappings of enablement and entitlement **towards the freedoms found in equipping and empowerment**. Baseball coach Jeff Leach puts it into this perspective. "Developing a clear sense of who is responsible for what is more important than always 'doing well.' This is the key to raising a self-driven child."

I regularly ask high-level high-performance coaches about what separates athletes that they have coached. Consistently, they point to a challenge that is becoming prevalent in sports, in learning communities, and within families. Most people, they tell me, rarely reach their fullest opportunities, often from reasons related to self-defeating attitudes. In other words, many athletes give in or give up too early, or are satisfied with "doing well" or being "good enough." More troubling is how many coaches and teachers point out that these patterns are part of the everyday world. They suggest that our society is populated by individuals who are mired in personal insecurities and feelings of insufficiency. The patterns of that world have led to habits within kids and their parents to see mistakes or problems as someone else's fault, or to always excuse them away. The separator for those who **actually do** reach levels of personal excellence? Those who persevere towards success take responsibility for their own choices and for the challenges and consequences they encountered. They become resilient.

Here is a hard truth about the world for them. It's not always someone else's fault!!! Pursue empathy, take ownership, be accountable, and embrace responsibility. John Wooden, the dean of all coaching wrote, "Be more concerned with your character than your reputation, because your character is what you really are, while your reputation is merely what others think you are." Character—the stuff that your child is "made of"—really does matter, and it's up to us as parents, teachers, and coaches to aid our young people in deepening and entrenching good character.

Not unlike a large segment of people, I really enjoyed *the Star Wars* spinoff, *The Mandalorian*. The protagonist, like most well-developed characters, was comprised of a wide range of qualities, attitudes and behaviours—both admirable and admonishable. Perhaps he was "only a hero in a piece of fiction." There is still, however, a lesson in his saga for us. What strikes me is this: the Mandalorian existed according to a code, and breathed in the conviction that he was called to live up to it, to adhere to it, regardless of circumstance or situation. His choices were dictated by the content of his character, and destined by the convictions of his code.

Why not us as well?

After all, "This is the Way."

19. The Perfection Paradox

"Present over perfect living is choosing 'real over image,' 'connecting over comparing,' 'meaning over mania,' 'depth over artifice.'"
—Shauna Niequist

Recently, I was talking with one a top youth development coach about some of the changes that we've seen transpire through the last few decades. He related a few stories about a number of kids he knows throughout the US, many of whom had chances to be good players, but gave up because they did not believe that they could live up to the expectations of others. Numerous players believe about themselves that they had to be "succeeding" all the time or they were failures. His conclusion was that the problem for so many of the prospects that he had seen was that they were increasingly being eaten up by misplaced interpretations of "perfect" and damaging interactions with perfectionism.

I know some of that struggle. "The harder you try, the better they get." These were words that were said to me by the player-coach from one of my ball teams a long time ago. Hal was the oldest player on our team. I was among the youngest. He recognized early on that I had a deep passion for the game and a fiery intensity for competing. Sometimes, though, the extremes to which I would take my efforts could interfere with my ability to smoothly execute plays. One game in particular, while playing third base, I managed to snag a hard ground ball to my glove side, fully stretched out with a diving play. I scrambled to my feet, and despite having ample time to throw out the batter-baserunner, in my attempt to showcase what I thought of as a strong arm, I ended up airmailing the ball into the stands behind first-base. It was not the first time that season in which I had botched a play because of misplaced or misdirected effort. Wise old Hal pulled me aside and said to me, "You know

Steve, you're a good ballplayer. But here's the thing. The harder you try, the better the other guys get!"

It was not the first time I had heard those sorts of things from coaches and older teammates when I was a player. While I never fully appreciated what it was that they were pointing me towards about my youthful exuberance, I have grown to appreciate the commentary to great extents now, both as a parent and as a coach. What I realize now, was that at the source of my at-times-misplaced efforts was a sense of perfectionism. This disposition derived from my own legacy of uncertainty and wanting to belong. I felt that I needed to be perfect, and sometimes even "better than perfect," in order to belong as part of those teams. It robbed me of the joy of playing and eventually tainted my love for the game. I could never believe that I ever lived up to the expectations of others. After all, I rarely achieved to the level of my own expectations. I was chasing an illusion of "perfect" from my damaged spiritual and emotional uncertainty, a pursuit of perfectionism that I could never reach.

For me, just as it is for so many young athletes, the premise of "perfect" was an elusive concept. The pendulum in my world would swing from one side to the other, and the range from euphoria to despair was extreme. Sometimes I was really good, but I could not be perfect in everything at all times. Herein lays a conundrum—in the world of sports, we crave for excellence, and we are compelled to practice till we get it right, until we are perfect. Yet, perfection as a goal is practically unattainable. Michael Jordan, arguably the best player of all time in basketball, by the end of his career had missed more shots than anyone else in NBA history. The best hitters in professional baseball get out more than twice the number of times they get hits. Even Wayne Gretzky did not score a goal every time he had the puck in the offensive zone. How do we reconcile the pursuit of perfect?

Doesn't it seem to be a paradox? In a very real way, this perfection pendulum is very much exactly that. A paradox **is** a statement that is seemingly contradictory, or is opposed to common sense, and yet is still perhaps true. Allow me to present this, then, as a paradox. In sport, improvement or growth

Steve Lloyd

demands that the participant pursue perfection. However, when athletes get trapped by the detrimental aspects of "perfectionism" it can de damaging and, at times, destructive.

Does practice actually make perfect? One of my high school coaches was a disciple of the teaching of John Wooden. Mr. B., though, still made the principles his own. He did not adhere to the idea that mere practice makes perfect; his clarification was that "perfect practice makes for perfection." I have adapted his mantra with something for my own journey. In my world, this means that the emphasis needs to be on progress through purposeful process. There is little point, after all, in doing thousands of repetitions of "not quite right." The person will just get really good at doing something wrong. Recently, I was remembering two players that I had coached as "little guys" in a conversation with someone who had also coached them both with Team Alberta when they were older. Player A was the bigger, stronger, and more "successful" athlete when the two were in Little League, but Player B over time caught and surpassed his friend as a baseball prospect. Their former elite coach asked me what the difference was in the paths of the two players. My answer was deliberate. "Well, Player B typically did two or three hours of practice a day with **his** dad, and Player A did two or three hours of extra practice with **HIS** dad." Huh?? What was the difference? One of the dads was a coach, someone who was willing to do right things right, and knew how to do this. The other was great at being a dad, but their extra time was taking lots of additional reps without really getting better. One was using the present to become future-prepared, and the other was replicating past patterns that would help the boy be good enough now.

How could doing extra practice not help? This may be contrary to generalized opinions, but doing more of the same was not necessarily better for that one athlete. In the same way, I have seen more cases than I have cared to witness of gifted young intellectuals being given more work to by their underprepared teachers. Too often these students have needed challenge and adversity, rather than to have been stuck in getting "more perfect in things they had already mastered." It has led to too many children ending up as gifted-underachievers. It happens in schools, and it happens in sports.

It is also possible to see the parallax that perfection sometimes is. Parallax is the apparent displacement or the difference in position of an object, as seen from two different points that are not on a straight line with that object. It has to do with perception. In other words, what we see—or, more pointedly, what we **think** we see—can be remarkably different from what someone else sees, especially when they are seeing it from a different vantage point.

This can be true in at least a couple of scenarios. The most obvious is what happens when two people see an occurrence from distinct angles. It is also a matter of perspective within the individual. Have you ever "seen" what you are looking at in the dark and been sure what it was? What happens to your perception when the lights get turned on?

We encounter a parallax opportunity when we help our children to address the goals that will they chase. Will it be "the process" or will it be "the product"? Along with kids, we must ask: In the pursuit of that activity, are we seeking to be perfect in process, or do we pursue perfect production? Answering this question is imperative. The former is within reach and can lead to autonomy; the latter is a Quixotic quest and is a path to frustration.

Perfectionism is seen in athletes who primarily attach their value to what they are producing. These are learned behaviours, and we have become increasingly conditioned to believe in them. In some regards we see it as youth sports pretends to be versions of professional leagues. Major league players in all sports are paid to perform; their level of pay is determined by what value is attached to their statistical output. Where this has become somewhat perverse is that the emotional and psychological "token economies" that are chained to student-athletes' personae are at times overbearing. A great problem with perfectionism is that it foments an internal belief system that only attends to results. It too often presumes that failings are more final than they are.

As we teach and model for the student-athletes in our life, there are several other guiding questions to which we can point them.

Steve Lloyd

- ➤ Is their perfection pendulum like a rhythmic time piece? Or is it a wrecking ball at the end of a chain?
- ➤ What does the pursuit of perfection indicate? What does it protect or promote?
- ➤ How do the perceptions and projections of others (especially key influencers) imprint or impact?
- ➤ Do they build & bless or do they bind & blind?
- ➤ Do they propel or do they paralyze?

Which way will that pendulum swing? Do we have the power to alter its dynamic in the life of our children? Herein lies an apparent paradox. Are our student athletes striving towards goals that are impossible to attain? Or can we aid them in suitably setting attainable goals and measures? Let's look at a few case studies of young athletes who tried to work through their own early perfectionistic tendencies.

Tyson is a baseball and volleyball prospect. He's a terrific multisport athlete who at his school also plays basketball and does track. While always among the top performers in both his school and club volleyball teams, and a perennial rep-team player with the local baseball league, he consistently puts unrealistic pressure on himself to "do better." When he was younger, and his teammates would make errors when he pitched (which was not uncommon in his league), Tyson would personalize those outcomes. He would then insist within himself that he needed to pitch better. I could see in him a lot of the issues I had faced as a teenage ballplayer. Whenever his volleyball squad would lose, he tended to shoulder much more of the "blame" for that outcome than one person could reasonably assume.

Truth be told, some of this came from a commonality in communication patterns from an assortment of the coaches he'd encountered. He had regularly heard from various team organizers that he had so much potential. And that as a leader, he needed to be a better example to his friends of "everything." The combination of these messages had begun to squeeze in on Tyson, and the subsequent tension he was beginning to feel was starting to restrict his capacity to play with the joy and freedom every athlete deserves to experience. He was convinced that unless everything was a favourable outcome, he was letting down his teams. This bubbled over in both of his primary sports. Despite having amazing parents, who had tremendous perspective, Tyson owned and operated a worldview that was a bit off-centred.

I have known Tyson (and a lot of "Tysons") for a long time. We had been chatting about these tendencies for a few years, when an opportunity arose to bring a lot of lies into focus. Tyson was asked to try-out for a regional volleyball 15U team. His region has the largest population base in the province, so being invited as one of thirty to make a twelve-person team was remarkable enough.

I asked Tyson what he wanted to accomplish—naturally, his answer was that he wanted to make that squad. My next question was about how he would do that. He replied, at first, that he would try to be the best player there, to which I offered him my typically skeptical and quiet look. He then proceeded. "Well, I guess I will have to show the coaches that I am one of the top players there." This time he was a little more uncertain. Still from me, nothing much more than a few pensive nods. He finally revealed what was really on his heart. "I don't know, Steve, but I really want to be on this team, and I don't know if I can perform well enough to do it."

What followed was the beginning of a series of conversations. We chatted about setting aside the idea that making the team was really what to strive for. We talked about a better outlook. I challenged Ty to think about what he would look like, as the best version of his best self. When he was able to describe what that would resemble, he then began to explore with me as to what it would take for him to be that guy leading up to those try-outs. He agreed to work at this, and to "bring that person with me to the evaluations."

In effect, he confronted his misperceptions about perfection, and redirected his efforts to focus on what he could control—his process. And he did great. He made the team and was among the better players at the Alberta Winter Games. His reorientation to perfect and perfectionism are also seeing positive growth in other areas of his life as he approaches graduation.

I first got to know Aido when I was coaching his older brothers. As the third of three athletes, he had developed a tremendous baseball presence by the time he was ten. He had exceptional skills and work ethic. He was committed to practicing to precision. In his early days, he faced little challenge in his baseball world, and was easily the best player in his age group in the area. This became a problem for him, one that was hard to avoid. At the time there were no real alternatives for a gifted player to move up to divisions for which he was not yet age qualified. He quite literally dominated, both because he was a talented and adept player, and because most players in his league were not. When he travelled with our programs (both our travel team and our Ripken teams) he was among our better players. He encountered for the first time that he couldn't get everyone out all the time, or reach base in almost every at bat.

When he was finally age-eligible to move to our region's top elite program, Aido found that his game results were not always there. His problem? He was often trying too hard to not get out, a very different mindset than what it takes to have quality at-bats. The pitching was better, and he needed to adjust his approach. He needed to learn that to swing and miss was not going to be the problem he perceived. He knew intellectually that he could never have a perfect batting average but needed to learn this emotionally and spiritually. Over time, he grew dissatisfied with just being good enough to be part of the program in which he played. He sought to raise the level of his game, and in conversations with several folks that he trusted he was getting a similar set of encouragements. From me it was things like this: "Your mechanics are fine, and your strike zone management is excellent. If you want to throw harder, then throw harder. Don't concern yourself with where the ball ends up, just be athletic and throw with intent."

When it came to hitting, he got similar advice from Al, his most trusted instructor, and from Matt as well (who Aido grew up watching practice and play at home). It was all some version of, "You have a beautiful swing, and you have great early pitch recognition. Trust them: stay loaded on your platform a tiny bit longer and explode your hands through the zone at full speed." That is baseball lingo for stop doing things safely and assert yourself in that situation. He began to understand that it was no better to hit a ball weakly for an out than it is to swing and miss. And once he adjusted his body's balance and rhythm to his new approach to "rip it," his season took on a whole new level of authentic success. He both changed his outlook on what mattered (process over production) and also gained new perspectives on the respective journeys of his older brothers in their sports, and what his parents had accomplished in their workplaces. His process orientation has led him to collegiate baseball at a very good program.

Jonah, as a raw arm, had outstanding upside as a young player. He was also that kind of kid that showed aspects of intellectual giftedness in his ed-psych profile. The way that his life circumstances played out, Jonah had a tendency to overthink most things—this is a problem with coaching very smart kids. Jonah, as that type of kid, wanted to pitch perfectly every time he was on the mound. When he missed his spot, or bounced a ball, he would begin to tighten up, as if trying harder was the answer. He would spiral downward—miss; ruminate; stress; try harder; miss again; have his whole body tighten, and so on. This was a pattern that he needed to overcome. He struggled with results. He was willing to try to learn from what was happening but didn't know how. But he had not yet learned to adjust his perspectives. He tended to assign an unhealthy ratio of his self-worth on the results he would generate in games. It took a lot of insight and effort on his part and with his parents help to practice parallax. He began to internally shift his viewpoint of the events, and reassess them from an alternative perspective. He set aside the immediate outcome (whether it was pleasing or troubling to him) and began to ask himself what he was learning in each of those moments. He then worked to apply those learnings to a commitment to improve, thus turning them into self-directing lessons. As more time passed and as he understood and trusted the process, he was able to transfer his between-games introspections into in-games adjustments. Over the course of a few months, he had begun a transition from being tossed about by externals and momentum, to building for himself a foundation that can develop into authentic self-determination.

Clay is a fantastic young man. He's still a terrific friend of my son, and they were teammates for a number of years. Clay had a masterful repertoire of off-speed pitches as a youth player, and in batting practices and scrimmages could befuddle his teammates. Yet, his capacity to perform in games was an enigma—or rather it was his lack of capacity. Somewhere on his pathway, he had developed a gameday version of "the yips." He struggled to throw strikes, regardless of the quality of his lead-up bullpen sessions. On at least two occasions, I witnessed him pitch sixteen consecutive balls to batters for four successive walks in games, before being given the "hook" by the coaches. Clearly, something was getting in the way of Clay's ability to transfer practice excellence into game-time performance. Through it all, he remained an incredible teammate to his friends. We never really figured out what the source of his in-game battles with the baseball was, but one thing does really stand out. His struggle never appeared to get the best of him. That he went on from high school and was an outstanding student at university and into post-graduate studies is no surprise. He made some pretty excellent choices through his baseball experiences to grow in other areas of his life. It is a valuable lesson to see that his pursuit of the process in one area of his life made a positive imprint of pursuits of perfection in others. What some may see as failures (the baseball results) are actually part of remarkable success (who he is becoming)!

Jessiya and Kayla are two high school basketball athletes that I had the privilege of coaching. Jessiya was a senior at our school, and Kayla was a sophomore (grade ten in Canada). Within our 2A division our team was quite good, and I give a lot of the credit for that to Jessiya. As a multi-sport athlete who excelled at a number of sports (she ended up playing collegiate volleyball and was recruited by a few schools for basketball as well), Jess had been well raised by excellent parents. Her mother, in particular, was an educational psychologist and she and her husband had raised their daughter to be a self-aware, balanced, and confident person. She also was very athletic and her 6'1" length only helped her in her sports pursuits. She made it a habit in her life to pursue the perfect process, well ahead of settling for only perfect-ish production. She would not be satisfied in her classes, for example, with just getting a great test score from mastering the content. She hungered to know the "why" behind the material, and to master "learning about the learning."

Perhaps what most impressed me that season was how Jessiya reached into the life of her younger teammate. Kayla, though a tall and strong athlete at 6'2" (yeah, I know, imagine coaching a high school girls' team with these two in the middle of it!!), struggled with how to fully believe in herself. Her junior high coaches had made her feel that she had to statistically dominate every game she played. Kayla had developed a reluctance to try to be at her best because of those burdens she had carried from grades eight and nine, believing she was failing too often with previous teams. Her parents had to talk her into trying out for our school team!

Through their church, Jessiya had known Kayla for years prior to their only season playing together. Jessiya had the temperament was a natural fit for what I would ask her to take on. Part of our daily practice routine was for position specific skills work, and Jess and Kayla were consistently matched up. The key to this work was that Jessiya would relentlessly focus on the process and purpose of what they were doing. Combined with our staff's deliberate focus with the whole team on long-term progress over game results, what began as a minor shift in her perspective became a cascade of change in Kayla's orientation. Kayla realized that her best version of her best self needed to pursue a better intrinsic process, and not place value on herself based on her numbers, or even how much she had contributed to whether we had won a game. Jessiya also continually modelled joyfulness in competing, and was particularly persistent in showing Kayla how much fun they were having. It was incredible to be part of this wonderful transformation. What a marvellous effort by Kayla and her parents! By changing the viewing point, moving from one spot to another, Kayla was able to see herself in an entirely new way. She parlayed this new point of view into very successful junior and senior seasons and moved on to play at a high level with a university women's basketball powerhouse. This was, in no small part, a by-product of the mentoring relationship she had had with Jessiya, and that she had confronted and defeated aspects of perfectionism that would have likely hindered her otherwise.

What seems evident in all of these situations is that each person's capacity to succeed was somehow based on permission to "fail." Each had some weight on them from extrinsic factors connected to their results or with the opinions of others. Each had an intrinsic permission that they needed to give to themself. They became aware. They each needed permission, freedom, comfort, and capacity. These four concepts work together in a pattern, establishing the framework.

Awareness → Permission to Risk → Freedom to Fail → Comfort to Struggle → Capacity to Excel

This progression is foundational for our students and athletes to work towards defeating misplaced perfectionism, and to develop autonomy. It establishes a perspective that can open pathways for self-determination.

We also have to deal with the issue of "time in space" in which our young people are predominantly residing. One of the things that I have always said to those that I have coached is, "What is about to happen is a lot more important than what just happened." Whether a victory or a defeat, they need to move on to the next moment. That moment needs to be in the "now." Perfectionists, though, alternately live in one of two timeframes—the past and/or the future. Regretting what has already happened or being anxious about what may occur can be crippling. Neither of these are very helpful in functioning to full capacity in the present.

Those who pursue "perfect in the process" have their feet anchored in the present. Coach George Raveling tells us, "The past is gone, and the future is yet to come, so wherever we are right now on our journey is the starting point to begin and build. As we continue with grace and gratitude, let's cultivate the courage to step into the fire of self-discovery, self-discipline, and self-leadership each day." What he is telling us about staying in the process is important. Perhaps even more poignant is that he compels us to understand that this process keeps its feet in the moment. Even as the process concurrently evaluates the past, and plans for the future, it lives, strives, and thrives in the present. Raveling continues, "Today is a precious gift of possibility. What we do with it and where we focus our attention is more in our control than we think. Let's use the time wisely, earnestly, and without fear or regret."

Let's take a few moments to compare and contrast the dangers of perfectionism to the possibilities of embracing the pursuit.

Contrasting Perfection Paradigms	
Perfectionism	Pursuing Perfect
• Worships production.	• Process is the driver.
• Values results over anything else.	• Values progress ahead of outcomes.
• "Be better than an opponent."	• "Be better than I was before."
• Is held hostage to the perceptions and projections of other.	• Maturely manages perceptions and projections.
• Can be paralyzed by obstacles.	• Is propelled by challenges.
• Often grieves the past.	• Learns from the past.
• Fears the future.	• Is preparing to be "future-ready."
• Willing to do things "right."	• Wants to do "right" things.
• Tends to bind up participants, restricting and conflicting internal liberty.	• Builds proactively towards permissions and freedoms.
• Is often blind to realities needed for growth.	• Blesses with truths that need to be struggled with.
• Failures feel final.	• Failings fuel future.

If it is unhealthy for our children to be entrapped in perfectionism (that is, primarily attaching their value to what they are producing), what, then, can we encourage them to pursue on their perfection pendulum? Allow me to suggest three areas:

"Perfect" in Perspective: Coach Dave Gallagher makes an insightful comparison. He asks prospects and parents to examine what he refers to as the hitter's mindset during a plate appearance. "Performance stress for an MLB player may be fear of failing front of 50,000 fans, and millions watching on TV. For a little league player maybe mom, dad, and grandparents are watching. For a high school player, they will have friends from school there. It's all relative. Learn to perform under stress!"

There are a few things at play in perfecting our perspectives: we have to be aware that what our kids are experiencing may not be the same as what we see. We have to help show them how to have alternative points of view. Often it means to see things more clearly, and other times it is just confronting things that are wrong.

It also means that we look way down the road. Beginning the journey with the end in mind is almost always a better choice. When we look at what is happening through the lens of what we are planning for, then we have opportunity to inform our journey. When we know that we need to struggle to grow, then we embrace "getting comfortable with being uncomfortable."

"Perfect" in Passion: When he was young, I made this sign for my son's wall. "Your own vision compels your own decisions." This is a huge component in self-determination. He knew early on that he was the key to determining what he could accomplish.

The passion towards becoming the best version of your best self applies to every aspect of life. This passion also embraces the realities of living out the consequences of your choices. This passion turns dreams into goals, and goals into plans. It moves a person from involvement towards commitment, and commitment to conviction.

One of the t-shirt slogans I have one day said I will make for kids is this: "If there is no struggle, there will be no strength." It will be their passion that will get them through the tough times.

"Perfect" towards Process: Usain Bolt said in an interview, "Worrying gets you nowhere. If you turn up worrying about how you're going to perform, you've already lost. Train hard, turn up, run your best and the rest will take care of itself." In a roundabout way, Bolt is telling us to be dedicated to the process.

Progress is all that really matters. Mark Twain said that, "Continuous improvement is better than delayed perfection." Be better today than you were yesterday. It involves doing right things right, and looking towards being future-ready. Process involves having a goal, setting a plan, and sticking to it. Process involves assessment, authenticity, and adjustment. It stays on course, with direction from its "north star." I found this item online at TheDailyCoach. I think it sums it up nicely. "You were born to be real, not perfect. Life is not about perfection. Life is about progression. During the daily grind, dare yourself to return to the present moment and silence that doubt. Never stop trusting the process on your self discovery journey."

Embracing perfection does not mean we have to be swallowed by perfectionism. We need to confront the patterns and powers out there that are sucking kids into believing that their worth is based upon their results, whether it is in sport, in school, or on social media (with their numbers of likes, friends, or followers). Wouldn't it be wonderful if we can help them to not be trapped in that mindset?

Is "perfect" attainable? We know that there is a complexity to answering this. As a goal in sports-based production, the answer is no. Making every shot, batting 1.000, never getting tackled, or winning every outcome is out of reach. But we can teach our children to strive towards perfect process. It is in that striving that we can reach towards what Vince Lombardi said decades ago. "Perfection is not attainable, but if we chase perfection, we can catch excellence." This is something we would like all of our kids to reach towards and eventually achieve.

20. So Do You Wanna Get an Ice Cream?

"Have you ever noticed how parents can go from the most wonderful people in the world to totally embarrassing in three seconds?"
—Rick Riordan

In the early years of coaching Matt and his teams, he and I would do as much extra practice as he wanted. For the four summers that I coached him in summer rep ball with LL (each year, ages 9-12), most weeks we would spend about three hours every weekday morning at the hitting cages and Little League field that was half a block from our house. We would invite his teammates and friends to join us; each summer most of the team was there with us during most of the mornings. Why did so many kids come for extra "work"? there were several reasons. The first thing was that all of the kids who joined in wanted to get better at their sport. They were doing terrific learning and the reps the players got were purposeful in getting them "future-ready." We had developed an environment in which the players could co-teach their teammates and learn from one another. They had begun to lay stones in the foundations of their own self-determination. The optional extra practice time, while vigorously paced and focused, was a lot of fun. The kids really liked being together. No one ever got grief for taking a break, and if a teammate did goof around "a bit too much," the other kids would ordinarily correct it.

Looking back, though, the most significant factor in those players coming for the optional sessions was what they could count on afterwards. Many days, most of our crew walked over to our house in Glenbrook, to have lunch (we went through truck loads of sandwich stuff, fruit and veggies, chicken strips and Kraft dinner every summer) and then immerse themselves in downtime. Friends would play some video games, maybe watch a movie for a bit. Many days, the kids had brought along their summer book, and would spend an hour quietly reading (part of the expectations for the teams I coached). Inevitably, as long as the weather didn't get in the way, the group would make their way out to the park beside our house and play...something! It's amazing what kids can do when we stop programming everything for them.

A majority of the parents from our team bought in whole heartedly. Who doesn't like their child being actively engaged in positive fun stuff?! Some even started to work together to bring in lunch stuff once in a while. Mom or dad could drop off their player with us on their way to work and pick them up on their way home. It didn't hurt, either, that parents could see the fruit of their child's work ethic in the quality of their play on the field.

There's something else about those summer optionals that carries some significance as well. *Unless it was really important or really funny, we made a point that what happened in practice, stayed in practice.* With very few exceptions, the coach didn't talk with players about what they had done or not done that day, unless the player brought it up. When the practice was over, we left it at the field and in the cages. This is a lesson that we can apply to our own families.

Not every situation is like this though. Let me share with you about the ordeal for a kid we'll call "Andy." For two summers I coached him with a core group of nine-and-ten-year-olds, in summer select baseball. About halfway through the second summer I began to recognize a pattern developing with this particular kid. Whenever he thought he had played well, and especially when he thought he had performed poorly, Andy would ask Matt to invite him over to our house for a sleepover. Andy's dad was more than a little bit overbearing. Andy told us that after every game his father wanted to rehash every play, especially the errors or outs. "Here's what you should have done." "Why didn't you do this?" From the kid's POV, it was just as bad when he pitched well, or had a few hits in a game. "See, this is what you should be doing at every bat!!" And the child didn't like that his dad was consistently comparing him to the other players on the team. Andy just wanted to have fun practicing and playing, but his dad's insistence for a constant feedback loop was sucking the joy out of the experience.

Russell and Dan, on the other hand, seemed to have had great postgame talks. When our kids were both eleven and twelve years old, I got to coach in spring season with an amazing guy named Dan. While not a particularly strong technical coach, he was amazing with the kids, and good with the parents. Dan would do really cool things to help redirect refocus our young players in moments when they might have been feeling extreme measures of stress. One thing, for example, was when he would make mound visits, most usually when the pitcher had been struggling with something. The old saying is that you can't teach during an exam. Something Dan could do very well was to help a child relax. For example, when he would arrive at the mound to see a player, typically he would do something like ask them if they had seen the latest Spiderman movie. "I thought it was pretty good, but maybe there is to just too much kissing, what did you think?" He had a capacity to change the child's focus almost instantaneously, diverting attention from the anxiety he or she was feeling, and redirecting them towards something a lot less threatening. He also was quite deliberate in having the athlete turn their eyes away from wherever his parents were sitting as he talked with the player. As the mound meeting wrapped up, Dan would say some version of, "Oh yeah, so let's just relax and do what you can do. We both know you can get the ball to the catcher. Let's have some fun." His postgame talks were just as epic. They were always focused on who had fun and wondering "what we learned today."

I asked Dan's kid what it was like to drive home with his dad after practices and games. Russell explained that they rarely talked about any particular play, or very much about the games at all, and almost never did they bring up anything about personal statistics or team results. Ordinarily, Russell indicated, they just talked about the things that they were going to do later that evening or the next day. Let me be clear, though, that Dan's players and teams through all the years (whether we coached on different teams and with the same squad) were always given the opportunity to practice and to improve in every aspect of the game. They were shown how to be competitive, the kind of competition the strives for being better that they were the day before, rather than just being better than the teams they were playing against that day. All of this was done with fun and joy at the centrepiece of the experience. Regardless of the final result of the game, or the outcome of any individual aspect within it, Dan was determined that every child would want to come back next day. To that end, he tried to make sure that every drive home from the field was an enjoyable experience for his own kid, and any teammate with him.

Interaction and conversations with our children are imperative. But sometimes, and probably more often that we'd care to admit, our kids don't want to debrief with their parents after practices and games. Can we blame them? Most adults are no different. A few years ago, I did a workshop with a couple of other coaches. The sessions were all recorded on video, and we had taken the time to get written feedback from the participants at the end. It had gone pretty well, and I was worn out in that "this was a good day kind of way." When we went out for some wings after the seminars, one of the young guys with whom I had presented wanted to talk about the day. He was feeling an urgency—about his contributions; about viewing the surveys while they were still fresh; about "what could have gone better" anxiety that most of us have probably felt at one time or another. I let the guys know that we were going to talk about it all the next day, after we had had our own time and space to process. And I advised them, "When you know you have to debrief, make sure you wear clean underwear." My point was this: being able to engage productively in feedback loops takes readiness and willingness, and is based upon proper timing.

This is true of adults in the workplace. How much even more so is it evident for children in sports, then?

Good communication between parents and children is essential. I am in no way trying to discourage anyone from engaging their kids after games and practices. But there are better things—and more important matters—about which you can chat. This will usually help to open doors later for talk about the other stuff.

Steve Lloyd

The folks at Champion Parents (a really terrific social media platform) list what they say is all that ever needs to be said by a parent about their child's sporting events: "I love watching you play"; "I'm so proud of you"; "I believe in you"; and "I love you." I really like this point of view. What is the best thing to talk about with a young student-athlete on the way home from one of their games or practice? Adapting what they suggest, I almost always I recommend some version of this: "*Wanna get an ice-cream?*"

There are countless variations and combinations of conversational openings that are like this. "Are you hungry?" "Should we get a Slurpee?" My friend Dan would often take the opportunity on the drive home with Russell to talk about their plans for the upcoming winter's ski season (the boy was an elite downhill skier, as well). The bottom line is the dialogue is almost always better when it's about something other than what they just did or didn't do. This is especially poignant when we recognize children are increasing conditioned to feel that their efforts are relentlessly judged, and that their value is based upon their performances. This is unfortunate and it is wrong. The ride home should be a safe and comfortable time and space, in almost all circumstances. And they should be steeped in unconditional love.

There are some exceptions to the timing of these guiding principles—that is, there may be times when what I am suggesting a bit later in this chapter has to be suspended. These two scenarios should be uncommon. The less frequently they have to occur, the more effective as a parent-communicator we can become.

1. When there is an obvious **Need for Intervention** (at a point of immediacy or urgency).
    a. Has there been something that has happened that demands an immediate response?
    b. Does the athlete need to be "checked on or corrected" regarding a behaviour or attitude that could be problematic in their future, if not nipped in

234

the bud? We don't want dirt to stay in a wound. Cuts are dangerous, but infection is deadly.

2. When the situation presents an immediate **Opportunity for a Valued Teachable Moment** about an essential learning (typically not something about executing a sports play).

   a. Was there something observed about his/her character or values (whether something to admire or admonish) that we needed to address? Typically, if not in the urgent category, mention it in that moment, and then tell them that we would defer conversation about it till later.

There are **six guiding principles** to learn to practice in communicating with your student athlete. These are sound precepts for coaches, and perhaps even more essential as pillars for parents.

➤ **The Cornerstone Always Remains the Cornerstone.** It starts with some version of "I really love to watch you play." It could as easily be, "Watching you compete inspires me," or "It is really awesome to see you work hard at something you love to do." Even in those times our son was not playing, we knew we could still affirm in him many other important aspects we could see (or would want to see) that could shine through. In his freshman year at Iowa Western, we went to watch the team play at the JUCO World Series, in spite of the fact that Matt was an injury red-shirt that whole season. We got to see how he interacted with his teammates, and the level of leadership development he was being schooled in by that program. I was able to affirm him, telling him how wonderful it was to watch him be a teammate. What do you think the messages Matt received from us? That **he** is more important than whether he is playing or not; and that his character will always carry more weight than his skills and abilities. A cornerstone is designed to be solid and immoveable. Figure out the most important values to your family and affirm them in your child through the processes in sport.

- ➢ **Seek to Understand before You Try to Be Understood**. What is their state of mind, or condition of their heart? Are they emotionally/spiritually/socially enflamed after? Is whatever you have to say really more important than what they need to hear (or not hear)? Too often adults don't listen, or just as bad, they half listen with the intent to reply. Seek to hear and learn, rather than speak and teach in those precious moments that follow games and practices. Cherish the quiet times of the ride home when those times are quiet. Celebrate the times when the chatter in the car may seem pointless and know in your heart that these moments are actually investments in later conversations.

- ➢ **Ask Yourself This Essential Question**: What are you adding to their experience during and after the game? Realize that they just want the drive home to be a drive home. There is an old quote I like, "Before kids can play like a pro, they must enjoy playing the game like a kid." Talking about "anything else" on the way home helps the child to normalize the events that just happened (whether outstanding, neutral, or horrendous) and keep them in better perspective. We looked at this concept to a little more depth in Chapter 2. And in those times that something may not have gone the way that your student-athlete may have wanted, ask yourself this question. "If I try to talk with them about this, will it make the situation better, or will it make it worse?"

- ➢ **The Nature of Unconditionality** is the backbone of a strong body of communication—specifically when balanced with holding them accountable for their choices and actions. Everyone needs grace in their life—especially children. Grace with our kids means that they know there is nothing they can do that would make you love them more, nor is there any thing they could do that would make you love them less. Often when talking about their performances, it can sound to young athletes like we are adding what we can call conditional language tags to their efforts. They hear *"when you"*, *"because you"* or *"if you"* as pre-conditions for "and then I am proud of you" and "so I love you". These three words (if, when, because), once tagged onto the messages of results, are dangerous to a person's belief about their value. It is hard to live up to these kids of conditions.

This is not to say that there is a lack of accountability. Children suffer damage if we dismiss or disregard their "hiccups", shortcomings, or failings. This is not grace. When they have wronged someone, or done something they should not have done, they only get better by being held accountable in a loving, grace-filled manner. This is true of every aspect of their relationships and is just as true in their outcomes in sport. However, when in sport, if the failings or triumphs are only about what they appear to be producing, then more often than not conversations about those can wait a little bit.

➤ **"Let Things Be" for a Little While**. Sometimes (probably more than we think) we need to practice silence. Not just not speaking but actually quieting our minds and heart to openly listen. Give them a chance to test the waters. Create space for them to say what they want to, so they can say what they need to.

Early in my career in working with young people, I had to learn the intentional practice of letting things be. In those times that we weren't actually putting out a fire, most of the tough situations I have had to work through were easier to deal with when we let emotions calm down a bit first.

➤ **You Can't Teach During an Exam**—and not many people want to do the test again right after they've finished it! Timely feedback can be very useful, but rarely is it timely for the student-athlete when they are still in the midst of their event. Be intentional about what and when feedback and our parent-based insights are offered about how they have played (if at all).

Using the platform of these principles in our own family became more and more organic as time passed. Both the emotional dynamic and content areas were fluid, changing as Matt got older. When he was really young, the conversations mostly included discerning if he had fun, and what he liked to do. In all honestly, in the early days it was hard to separate being his coach from being his dad, and there were times that I struggled. But mostly, with the help of my wife, and a few coaching friends, I was able to apply what I expected of the other parents to my own situation. When he was playing for me, the parental-based conversations typically included:

- Did you have fun today? What was the most fun thing?
- How intentional was your preparation? Did you feel like you were ready to try your best?
- Did you get quality rest?
- What did you eat today? Did you think you did a good job taking care of your body?
- Did you feel like the stuff you are working on in practice is coming out in your games?
- (Sometimes) Do you know what I learned about you while watching you play?

Keep in mind though, these chats were rarely immediately after games. Mostly, our post-session dialogue was about where and what he wanted to eat on the way home!! And then he would "shut himself off" for a while and go to sleep in the car. These freedoms were essential components of his process. That era also involved a series of choices to discern and separate "when I was his dad" from "when I was his coach." In the one role we talked about the process of being a person, and in the other it was about the process of being a player. And, of course, there were significant conversations about when those two threads would have to intertwine.

It got a lot easier for me when he moved on to other programs. Later on, when he began to travel with various elite level teams, I would ask about how practices and games had gone. When it was time to talk together, I still focussed on process over production. This carried over into his college days, and now into pro ball. It was very freeing to make the transition from his coach to being an occasional consultant about his game.

These are some question areas that I have engaged in with Matt (and other players) through the years:

- Did you experience joy today? Tell me about something that was really fun.
- What did you learn about yourself and about the game?
- Did you make the plays that you had opportunity to make?
- Did you hit your "spots"?
- How did your swing feel? Any really good swings?
- Did you barrel up any baseballs?
- Did you see the ball well? Were you able to time up?
- Did you enjoy competing?
- What are you doing to help yourself regenerate and recover?
- How is stuff going for you away from work?

Sometimes, I still attempt to ask him about particular things that have happened in a game, or when I get to watch parts of his practices. Usually, this comes up when I am curious about a situational approach or wonder if what I thought I saw was what had actually happened—this is my innate desire to learn and apply. I still like to inform my own coaching practices!! When I have these sorts of questions or comments, though, it is almost never in the space and time immediately after a game. And I almost always start with, "I have a question about something I would like to learn about. Is it a good time to ask now?"

I think that there is a solid premise in this—if it is valid to respect the emotional/intellectual/spiritual landscape of a mature professional athlete in regard to feedback loops, then why wouldn't we be as intentional with our children?

Still to this day, every inquiry I try to have with my son about his sports life is centred in the principles that I have noted above. And the underlying foundation to it all is reminding him that I love to watch him play, to compete, to strive, and to work at becoming the best version of his best self. He hears regularly what I think of him and his future in sport. But more often, I let him know how proud that I am of the person he is, and is becoming. I encourage you to do the same with your children.

Danny Norris, head football coach at Gilbert Christian School offers this insight. "My parents told me before my games: 1) Have fun; 2) play hard; 3) I love you. Parents: the most impactful thing that you can do for your student athlete is to love them and not to coach them. Watch the change in their attitude when you simply tell them, 'I love to watch you play.'"

Most parents are not coaches in the sport that their children are pursuing. But parents **are** the primary mentors and models for how a child will navigate through life, and journey through their complex interactions with the world. Trying to coach them in their sport may not be possible.

But guiding them through the practices and games that is "life"—now that's something we all need to be intentional about.

And maybe this is something for which we might want to develop better practice plans!

21. A Roadmap Story

A "roadmap" is a key body of work that details out your journey to the vision or master goal.

There are two critical elements to your roadmap:
1. Establish your vision
2. Establish your current state

Setting these two elements (that truly reflect who you want to be or the result you want) with an accurate assessment and accounting of your starting point sets the tone for the rest of the roadmap work.

Six Key Elements of Roadmap Execution

1.POLICY	2. MISSION	3. STRATEGIC GOALS	4.TACTICS/ACTIONS	5. STRATEGIC OUTCOMES	6. VISION
Guiding principles. Your "WHY".	What you represent.	Which choices you make towards your Vision	How to achieve your Strategic Goals	Observable and measurable results of your Strategic Goal	The future you seek.

The Vision Statement–Starting with the "End in Mind"
Although the "Vision" resides at the end of the roadmap, one needs a directional cue to develop the roadmap. Beginning with the "End in Mind" provides that target for all our precedent goals and actions to work towards. In the realm of performance sports, an example of a vision could be: **Play Collegiate Sports.** How might a family work towards that vision?

Using this simple and succinct vision plan, you can start your journey in understanding **why** you exist and seek this purpose, **what** values and ideals you represent, and **which** strategic goals you need to perform to achieve your vision.

1. **The Policy**

The roadmap Policy statement is a deliberate document of decisions that guides your work to achieve rational outcomes leading to your vision. These specific decisions on behaviour are implemented as a protocol for daily work. As you build your list of Policy statements, this will guide how you will behave as you work towards your vision. Some examples might include:

"When I work toward my vision, I will…"
- Empower myself and the team to perform with operational excellence.
- Establish and measure key perfromance areas.
- Build on strengths of each team member or coach.
- Develop a culture of values, pride, ownership, and professionalism.
- Expect feedback opportunities for continous improvement.
- Search for ways to best utilize all resources.
- Encourage and audit data driven decisions.
- Encourage partnership/participation of all parties and integrated external resources.
- Be ambassadors of trust and fair play.
- Search for and utilize the best teachers, tools, and technology in this sport.

2. **The Mission**

The Mission Statement is the culminating body of guidance that will be shared across your vision. The Vision, Policy and Mission are the intertwining elements that converge the unique work within your roadmap to a single point, which is your Vision realized.

A mission statement describes what you represent and are willing to fight for. A mission statement can be very simple. They can be built into slogans like some of these: Perfect Practice makes Perfect; Commitments Matter; Fair Play; Integrity; Win or Learn; Support the Success of Others; Hustle Takes No Skill.

One my programs consistently use is "Be the best version of your best self."

3. Strategic Goals

Strategic Goals are "What" we do to support our vision. They are large bodies of work that are designed to focus our efforts in a prioritized and purposeful way. It's key to develop your goals in a prioritized way based on authentic measures of your starting place. This ensures that we are building a solid foundation for growth.

Before your strategic goals can be worked, one must understand the true current state. It's never surprising that there is a gap between a person's belief in their view of their status, and what the reality is. Developing Strategic Goals to Self-Actualization can create large gaps between the goal being worked and the vision attained.

Based on the reality of your current state, what high-level strategic goals could be put into play that close the gaps on the road to your vision? A limited example could include: baseline ability evaluations; independent skills specific coach assessments; or where you "fit" with competitive team and programs.

One caveat to the strategic goals to consider are "People, Process, Technology and Data" as subgroups for your work. For example, when aligning on a strategic goal like "earn a spot with Team Alberta 18U," consider tactics and actions that include People, Process, Technology and Data. This could drive some actions like:

- Targeted tryouts and camps, attending "showcase events."
- Psychology of sport—learning to embrace failure.
- Metrics, software, and applications to better understand technique, and sports specific analytics and metrics.
- What to measure and what to ignore.

Below is an example of a specific targeted goal for a performance athlete. Note that this is a framework and can be adapted as a template for other specific targeted goals. Each category is filled with generalized and guiding suggestions and can be articulated for each as appropriate. You can do this for each goal, in the scope and sequence of the overall development plan towards the end-game Vision.

	Tactics & Actions	People	Process	Technology	Data
Strategic Goal — *Earn a position with Team Alberta U18 program.*	Develop athletic abilities: list specific matters.	Who do you rely on to work on this?	What do you need to do? Where? When? What is being measured? How is it being tracked/monitored?	What is being used to measure?	What does the data indicate? Has there been growth?
	Refine skills: identify and target skills; compartmentalize aspects of each skill set	Coaches and teammates; will you use lessons and additional coaching?	What do you need to do? Where? When? What is being measured? How is it being tracked/monitored?	Are you using video? Do you have the right equipment? Access to training site?	Before & after? What are the metrics revealing?
	Increase Game Play and Game Speed; gain Experience; compete	Does the game schedule align? Are you playing with and against players?	What measures will track progress in the process?	What feedback is available to you? Narrative? Visual? Empirical?	If using statistics, are they reliable?
	Enhance mental and emotional aspects; gain confidence.	With whom are you working? What are you reading to help?	Sessions with mentors; professional insights; reliable authors	Journaling; ongoing dialogue	Tracking emotional and psychology engagement is practices and games.

As a helpful part of using this framework, think about clearly categorizing the two distinct areas of "Tasks to still be done", and "practices/measure that are ongoing." For example: Blue = Work to be completed as part of the task or area; Red = Measures for sustainment, which are all within the Process Stream.

4. **Tactics and Actions for Strategic Goals**
   (Particular to Each Goal)

Tactics & Actions are the detailed bodies of work that determine "How" you will achieve your goal. A strategic goal can be a simple statement, but the Tactics & Actions can be very extensive in complexity and quantities under each goal. Consider the subgroups of people, process, technology and data for each tactic or action.

These tactics and actions across the people, process, technology, and data may be completed in a set time period, but some may be too comprehensive to be achieved in one year and span two or more years. From this point, each Tactic & Action needs to be measurable. Measures can be a metric for the initiative or for process sustainment.

5. Strategic Outcomes

Strategic Outcomes are the successful result of the integrated roadmap to the vision. It's only successful if the outcomes are in direct support of the Vision. Unsuccessful outcomes need to be re-integrated and/or adjusted into the roadmap.

Strategic Outcomes are a combination of initiative completion and or improvement / sustainment in process measures.

6. Verify Vision

The validated collective Strategic Outcomes are measure points for the successful completion of the **Tactic and Actions** support of the vision. As you can see, simple goals and moderate tactics and actions can get busy. It takes a great deal of effort to build this roadmap within one function, let alone several integrated ones. The key here is that the capital and emotional investments in the first stages as it relates to time are often high. Once the multi-year roadmap is complete there is only a periodic review and edit to account for work completion and changes.

22. Some Key Question Areas When Talking with College Coaches

A few things to keep in mind before talking with a coach/recruiting coordinator and/or visiting a campus.

- Typically, it seems best to **NEVER talk about athletic scholarships** or the school's willingness to help with the cost of going to their institution, **UNTIL THEY bring it up**
  - This noted, once there is clear indication from the recruiting coordinator that you are a priority recruit, scholarship and other financial aid needs to be part of the discussion. This "moves the needle" and helps to align both parties in the recruitment process (no sense in spending time considering somewhere that won't match up to the player's financial requirement.
- **Understand that scholarships are only guaranteed for one year** (typically one year renewable) and that you must produce on the field in order to be assured of a four-year experience in that program (two-year for JUCO). A collegiate coach's job is based on winning games. In baseball, there are scholarship limits at each level that do not come close to matching the number of athletes on the roster. Know that it is extremely unusual for someone to get a full ride in baseball.
- **ALWAYS try to do some research** prior to talking with the coach—you will still ask a bunch of the questions noted below, but it would be good to know some of the answers already and to see what they say—good to know the school team nickname, for example! The *tone of the program will be set by the Head Coach*. **Try to speak to present and former players/parents** regarding how the day-to-day functions of the program are worked out, and how they got along during their time at that school.

- **Know yourself and what type of coaching philosophy & methods works** best for your motivation, production, and development. You will want these to match up.
- Unless it's impossible to do (like during a global pandemic), **making a school visit** to any program that you are considering (that has interest in you) is very important. And remember that there is a lot more to finding your fit that just the baseball facilities and cool gear!! So,
  - ➤ Plan comprehensive school visits prior to making a commitment.
  - ➤ Be sure to visit when classes are in session.
  - ➤ See the residences and dining halls.
  - ➤ Make visits to more than one school if you have multiple recruiters. Official visits are ideal (indicates that the school has significant interest), unofficial are advisable otherwise. If an official visit is not possible, and if your family can manage the expense, it is much better than no visit.
  - ➤ Compare multiple schools prior to making a final commitment. Be reluctant to commit until you have a chance to visit the school—examine the rules and guidelines about this when you start to get into invitations, or begin to plan on your own.
- You will be involved first with an assistant coach/**recruiting** coordinator. **Expect to Meet with the Head Coach** in regard to the role, playing time, and developmental philosophy. The Head Coach will have the final say in all of these areas. You need to hear from him before you make your commitment.
- **Coaches HATE IT when** parents talk more than, ask more questions than, or answer for the student-athlete/prospect /recruit.
- While **the decision where to go is mostly up to the athlete** (*and the coach at the school!!),* it is **essential to keep mom and dad in the middle of the dialogue**—often it is helpful for the first few conversations to have the parents "listen in" until the recruit gets more comfortable.

- Take notes—it will be impossible to remember everything from all the schools
  - Create a doc or Excel sheet, stretch out some spaces between each question to take notes—use the question template that is included in this section.
  - Also, highlight the most important questions in each area for you.
  - Label each "interview," with the date and school, and name of the coach you talked with. Include the phone numbers and email.
- Always know **what governing body** the school is part of (NCAA I, II, or III; NAIA; JUCO).
- **DO NOT BE SEDUCED INTO PRE-JUDGING LEVELS**—there are great opportunities with top-notch, terrific fit programs at every jurisdictional level.
- **If (when) coaches ask you to make a commitment**, ask them when the latest time is that you can let them know. Be respectful and ask if he can give you a few days to talk about stuff with your parents. Do not mislead any coach about having offers or interests that don't exist. They will find out!!
- Understand that **Verbal Commitments are not binding** and you can say as such. Continue to be openminded about possible alternative options prior to signing a National Letter of Intent.
- **When they ask you when you plan to wrap up recruitment**, be honest—so you will need to know if you want to finish this process by the fall signing date or are willing to extend to the spring. But rarely will it be a bad idea to say, "I really want to find the best fit for me, and hope I can do that with a school by the fall, but I don't want to rush into a commitment unless our family feels like it is a great fit."
- It is extremely important to always keep in mind that coaches, especially in college baseball, talk all the time with one another. **Do not mislead coaches** about anything, or misrepresent any reality associated with your recruitment.

It is imperative to always remember that you, your family, and your advisors/coaches should be 100% dedicated to finding the best possible fit for you as a person, student and baseball player.

Based on what I have heard from dozens of coaches in multiple sports, I have listed question areas in an order that will most impress upon good coaches. These are things that you want him/her to know are important to you. In other words, the athlete's questions about themself as a possible player in their program gives coaches a great sense that they are not a self-centred person, and are a legitimate prospective student-athlete that will be an asset.

Academics and Personal Development

➢ Coach, I think I am interested in (this area of study). What can you tell me about that program at your school?

➢ What type of school scheduling does your school operate? Is it semesters, trimesters, or quarters? How does this work for the baseball players?

➢ Is there someone (a current player/grad/professor) I can talk with about my particular academic interests?

➢ If I decided later on that I wanted to switch to a different program of studies, is that possible?

➢ Can you tell me the success rate of your school's graduates that qualify for Graduate Studies? Same question about the team? What do most of your players do after they finish here?

➢ Do most of your players graduate? Do most graduate within the four years?
  o What happens to players who finish eligibility before they finish their degree?

➢ Do you have someone on staff or in student services that is a baseball team academic advisor?

➢ What do you do about Study Hall for the team? What academic expectations does the program have for the players?

➢ What can you tell me about the academic supports for the baseball team? Tutors, accommodations etc.

THE SCHOOL and the Community that the School is in.
➢ What are a few things that the school is "known" for?

➢ Tell me about school spirit.

➢ What is the cost of attending your school for a Canadian/out of state student?
  o Tuition/books/fees
  o Residence / accommodation
  o Meal plan
  o Travel

➢ How do I know if I qualify for academic scholarships at your school?

➢ Does the school have any aid packages to help students from out of state/out of country make attending more affordable?

➢ What is the nearest airport to your town? How do you get there?

➢ What can you tell me about the town?

➢ How close to the school are places to eat? What about grocery stores and other stuff?

➢ Do you get support for the program from the community? What can you tell me about the fan base?

➢ To what extent (if any at all) would I need to have a vehicle here with me?

Values, Character, and Program-Culture
➢ Coach, would you mind telling me the things that are most important to you?

➢ What are the most important things that form the core values of your program?

➢ What do you expect from your student-athletes? What happens when a player strays away from your expectations? (If he asks you why you are asking this, it is because you have seen/heard about some programs that have not disciplined players and have seen things go wrong—but don't "tell stories.")

➢ Can you tell me how your program lives up to what it says it believes?

➢ What do you think I will learn most from you if I am a part of your program?

➢ What are some of the "non-baseball" activities the team does in the community?

Player Development
➢ How do you help players get better?

➢ Are there any off-field development opportunities (like leadership training, etc.)?

- Could you tell me about your strength and conditioning programs?

- Have you had very many two-way players?

- Whom do players communicate with about stuff?

- What characteristics and qualities do you want in a player?

- What are the expectations and opportunities for summer baseball connected to this program?

The Baseball Team
- Please tell me about the conference your team plays in.

- What does your non-conference schedule look like in a typical season?

- Where do players in the team live? Is there a player residence? Do all freshmen live in residence?

- Are there team meals?

- What does the fall program look like? If an NCAA school, ask how they work this into the NCAA rules?

- What does team travel look like?

- Can you outline for me what a typical weekend series or game day looks like?

- Typically, what's your approach to player roles and playing time?

- How long have you been coaching here? What should I know about your coaching style?

Questions about Me as a Possible Student-Athlete
- Coach, why are you recruiting me?

- Does the school help with the paperwork needed to be able to go to school there?

- What does a first-year player need to do to earn a spot in the lineup?

- I want to work at being the best player I can be. What would be your plan for me to have an opportunity to be that?

- *(If applicable)* Right now, I am a two-way player—will I have an opportunity to try to keep doing that? What does it look like to be a two-way guy for you?

- What kind of player do you think I can be?

QUESTIONS/ANSWERS FOR WHEN THEY DO START TALKING ABOUT SCHOLARSHIPS
But do not be the first to bring this up, until it is clear that they want you to go there!

- "Thank you for that offer. I will have to talk with my parents about how that fits into our overall ability to pay for school.

➢ What does the scholarship cover? What are the terms of the scholarship? One year, renewable? Four-year commitment (almost never really offered)?

➢ "If I also qualify for an academic scholarship, is "stacking" allowed? (Stacking means it is permitted by the school, conference, and jurisdiction to accept both athletic and academic scholarships at the same time.)

JUST FOR YOUR FAMILY

This is not for discussion with the coaching staff initially. If you are serious about this school as a possible landing spot, then look at the team stats from the last few seasons to see patterns of playing time for freshmen and sophomores, and who could be coming back to school.

Concluding Comments

"The world is changed by your example, not by your opinion."
—Paulo Coelho

Making a New Year's resolution can sometimes be a good thing. Often a fun or trite thing to do, many people make promises to themselves and then drop them in the following weeks. In its truest form, though, a resolution can lead to remarkable transformations in a person, an organization, or even a society. Resolutions are introspection-based-decisions to make changes either in behaviour or attitude, typically compelled by a recognition of aspects of one's life that are not going the way that we want them to. Changes are sometimes hard to want, and often even more difficult to execute. At times, we need help to even see that change is helpful, or at times, necessary. We began the small journey of this book with hope that can lead to change. And it is with that hope in mind that we wrap up with these final thoughts.

This guide was designed to offer an opportunity for us to examine practices and procedures that we have with our children and to assess whether we might be resolved to do better; to clarify and articulate our work with them as they seek after excellence in their pursuits. One day, their sports life will be over. Will they get to choose when that day is, or will they be "told"? How far along the journey will they have gone? Will they have played in college? Earned a scholarship? Played professionally? Or did your family set more foundational goals? Will your child become the person, spouse, parent that you have hoped they could? Will sport have been the "end"? Or will you have done your best to help them see it as a means to the greater end?

It really is a tough world out there, and the stories and concepts that we have explored can assist us in clarifying what the goals and practices might truly be for them to have reached their fullest opportunities. As parents, most of us would agree that there is little that is more important to us than our children. I hope we have been able to cut away some of the things that are hinderances and roadblocks to the most noble journey—that of becoming the best persons we can be, and helping them do so as well. I hope this collection can help you to see a destination, and to find a pathway that works for your situation. I hope it helps you to locate and set your eyes upon a North Star.

The book has focussed on the importance of guiding principles. Staying on the mission before us is paramount. This book, I hope, can help us in finding and adhering to a "True-North." Think about early explorers, in the times before maps. It was imperative to stay oriented correctly, with a good compass aiding in staying the course. We need the same conviction of purpose, with clarity of mind and heart—setting our eyes on the prize.

This conviction is built on a Vertical Vision rather than Horizontal Short-Sightedness.

It keeps the heart on the Destination, as our eyes remain on the North Star, using the Compass to find and retain orientation for directional changes and course adjustments. Unlike the problems we encounter when only seeing the horizontal, it (vertical vision) is not sidetracked by pit stops, shiny-new-attractions, and dead-ends. It stays on the route, and works through, over, and beyond road-stops, roadwork, and roadblocks.

It is characterized by purpose-driven process; the principle that values progress ahead of production. It understands that long-term investments are preferable over quick payouts. A vertical vision puts into perspective the reality that immediate gratification is an addictive trap. It understands that seeking prosperity, profit, or gain ahead of (or rather than, in some cases) growing character is a very dangerous path to walk. It does not sacrifice the future-ready for happy-ish today. After all, "what good does it do for a man to gain the whole world if he loses his soul?" Vertical vision knows "who" these things should be about, and "who" they should be for.

And vertical vison knows that the "why" is the central question that sends us on this the expedition.

It remembers that the mission **IS** the journey; the mission is not the destination.

Several times through this collection, we have looked at some lessons from films that I have found meaningful. As we wrap up, let's think about some wonderful checkpoints that someone encountered on their trip. We find these in another favourite of mine, *Field of Dreams*.

➢ **The Mission Discerns Diligently**
"Listening in the cornfield."

The story begins with a man hearing something that no one else can hear. He makes the deliberate choice to begin to listen to what it says. In the film, Ray was challenged by a disembodied voice in his cornfield to do something ridiculous. That mission spoke to his whole being, and he was driven by the conviction to plow under a significant portion of his crop. In its place, he built a ball field. His conviction was compelling. Be certain of the truths about the journey and those who are part of it with you; caution yourself about false or secondary messaging; watch out for the "dogs" and detractors. If there is a voice in the cornfield that is your True North...well... you know what to do!!

➢ **The Mission Plans Purposefully**
"If you build it, he will come."

Inward choices led to outward actions. This was an act of faith on the part of Ray Kinsella—in the same way, securing our hearts must be faithfully anchored to hopes for things not yet seen. When we are patient and insightful, we can see that intrinsic values & motivations can deliver extrinsic value and manifestations. And even if some of those around us cannot yet see what we are truly building, don't let it matter.

➢ **The Mission Traverses Truthfully**
"Stay the Course."

So whispers the voice. It is an ongoing journey. And just like in the film, we will experience obstacles, changes and adjustments. Having put "first things first" already, keep your heart on the destination and eyes on your guiding star. Move your feet along the path, and get them back to it, should you stumble or stray. Stay laser-focused on the purpose. And keeping moving towards the goal.

> ### The Mission Views Vertically

"Is this heaven?"

What an insightful question that Ray's father asks in the story's marvellous payout. The *he* of "build it and he will come," has arrived—John Kinsella is there to play. And the *his* of "ease his pain" realizes that the dream all along was his own; to redeem his relationship with the father he had lost. When Ray points out that they are actually in Iowa, John's answer is breathtaking. "Seems like heaven," he says.

And I suppose it is. They have arrived at a moment of fulfillment and restoration, not just a location. And in staying true to the course, Ray's trust in that vertical vision is honoured. Ray's journey, which had begun with one end in mind, turns out to have had a significantly different outcome. But it is that the journey was still undertaken that is the story! Trusting that an end would come, and that whatever it ended up being would be what was for the best, is our lesson in this film. We see lived out through that character's conviction something that perhaps we can all hope to embrace. He lives a confidence towards a hope not yet seen, and in something which will not change—a faith that the pursuit of the mission is worth the journey. Ray Kinsella's conviction is compelling. Oh, that we all should be so convinced.

Setting our eyes on the right goal is up to each of us. This book makes the case that our goal can be to help our children become "their best versions of their best self." We all know that this involves more than just wanting to arrive at a destination or attaining a reward. It has to be about more than just acquiring the prize. This book hopes to shed light where there may have been shadows. I hope we can help student-athletes to "win their lives," instead of settling for merely "winning their games."

To this end, we must develop insightful, caring, knowledgeable and intentional planning. It starts at knowing where we are at (and authentically working at understanding where we "really" are). From this point, we can begin to set and execute a course. We need to be their best role models. As Dr. Bethany Hill asserts, "Co-regulation is the best form of discipline we can model for children and youth."

I hope what you have found in these pages has been helpful; the journey you are undertaking with your student-athlete can be one that is full of joy, and ought to be. But there are pratfalls and potholes along the way. All the extra "stuff" around youth sport creates a convoluted landscape. Especially as a kid pursues performance-oriented endeavors, we can see the road is full of possible distractions and dilemmas, and potential dangers or demons. It is a challenge to discern who are friends and what are foes, isn't it? What are the elements on the path that will be helpful, and what should we put aside that can hinder or harm? Are we willing to consider that sometimes the things that we need most to get out of the way, are us? Parenting is hard enough! Performance-based sport, with all its bells and whistles, with all the promises and sales pitches, is seductive. And it is easy to get caught in its traps. Thus, we must be aware, so that we can be intentional.

Progressing in sport is a wonderful goal. The dream of playing at "the next level" is something worth chasing. Jordan Burroughs, the five-time World Champion and Olympic freestyle wrestling gold medalist, reflects on the purpose of sports: "To prepare kids for the path, not to prepare the path for kids." This book has been intended to offer to you a collection of guiding principles and practices to help focus on what is most important in helping make that possible. I hope it also helps you to filter out the "noise" around your child's opportunities, obstacles, and obligations. I hope it can assist you in helping your child determine their own future, and to become the best version of their best self.

Let's resolve ourselves to help clear their paths of all the unnecessary debris that they shouldn't have impinging upon their journey. Be diligent; be purposeful; be truthful; and be vertically minded.

It's a challenging enough time in a challenging world for our kids to grow up in. It's already a difficult thing to play any performance sport after high school. So, let's do everything we can to not make it any more challenging...

...Because the game really is hard enough.

The Game Is Hard Enough

Acknowledgements

My life has been the product of Grace. It is only by His Grace and Mercy that I have walked through this world. Thanks first to God, and His work of reconciliation through Christ alone. Your Hand has guided and provided and protected throughout. I submit this work for Your Glory and "count all else, but loss" (Phil 3:8).

In this world and on this journey, Leslie Ann, my wife of over thirty years—it has always started, and will only ever end, with you. You have been the bedrock for our family and have always made it possible for everyone in our family to follow our dreams and helped us to get back to our path whenever we faltered. You have been loyal through struggles, prayerful and faith-full in adversity, and purposeful in your stewardship. There would be no life in our family (figuratively and literally) were it not for your patience and perseverance. You are the person I most want to live up to. And in spite of my failings, you, Leslie, are the epitome of Grace in my life.

To Rebecca and Matt, I am so grateful to be your dad. You have consistently reminded me through the decades of the chasm in life's journey between "wanting to be a good parent" and actually "being one." And that there are many ways to be exceptional. You both are that—exceptional—in so many wonderful and dynamic and unique and extraordinary ways, and the two of you are the heartbeat of my life. You have each taught me much about Grace, both in what you have given to me, and in those times that you needed it yourselves.

Steve Konchalski, Coach K, who has been a constant mentor, guide, and friend for over forty years, and has shown me more about being a father, coach, and teacher than any one person could deserve. You have imprinted upon my life and the journey of my family in ways that you will never fully know, and more deeply than I would ever have hoped or imagined that day when we first met in your office in 1980. God put us in each other's life, and He has shown me so much about Grace through you.

There have been dozens of close friends along the way that have challenged me to grow. Thank you to David, James, Jennifer, and Rob W, from those formative years to the present. Who would I be without you?

Thank you, Stu, for letting me be part of your road. And thank you especially to Mike (who would rather not be acknowledged) for encouraging and equipping and empowering me, and so many others, in so many ways. You are a paragon of all that is good and right in a man. Grace shines through you.

And where would I be with The Garage Guys? Wise and intriguing, compelling and challenging, interested and interesting, these men are models for what our world needs these days. Thank you to Brent, Duff, Layne, Sheppie, Jimmy Hockey, Reitz, and Shawsie. And Robbo—what can I ever say or do to acknowledge and appreciate how essential you have been? You, as much as anyone has ever done, have guided me as you've walked alongside me through some very dark and hard times. You have challenged and encouraged me to finally compile and construct these principles and practices into this collection. You have helped me to see that my "voice" in these matters is worth lifting up. And that the world needs to hear these messages.

Thank you to coaches: Greg, Chris, Gary, Ramon, Marc, Jeff, Amron, Braydy, Allen, Neil, Bernie, Richard, Mr. B, Augie, Doc, Raz, and so many others—I have learned so much from you and because of you. This journey would not have been what it has without the wonder of working with so many incredible young athletes, who are too many to list, and some of whom still continue to be significant parts of my life. I am blessed by you. Thank you to so many of the families and those moms and dads who would be part of any coach's "dream team." Your relationships with your children and your intentionality to help them become their best selves has inspired me.

And though it may seem peculiar, I also want to say a thank you to some other consistent companions in my walk through this life. To pain, adversity, trial, and struggle—I say thank you. You have not been strangers. And yet, you have not defeated me. To fear, and loss, and hurt—you have made me a better man. And to the Black Dog—you know what you are—you have been my Beast. Without you, there would be no struggle, and no strength to overcome. It has been good to pickle that beast!

And finally, to a friend and colleague who planted seeds of possibility in my soul and taught me to trust that they could grow and thrive. I will ever be thankful for you, Cal.

Steve Lloyd

About the Author

It has been a forty-plus-year journey working with children and their families that has led Steve to constructing this book. A career in helping professions that has seen him serve in youth justice, social services, refugee housing, youth ministry, and schooling has informed Steve's life journey profoundly.

Growing up mostly in rural Nova Scotia, Steve played multiple sports as a kid, through his high school years and into young adulthood. He attended St. Francis Xavier University, where as part of the basketball program, he earned a degree in Literature and History ('84), and was mentored by legendary coach Steve Konchalski, in life even more than in sport. Almost two decades of working with kids and parents in other fields led Steve back to Antigonish, where he garnered an Education Degree ('02). Since then, the Lloyd family has lived in the Calgary, Alberta area, where Steve has, at different times, worked as a teacher, run baseball programs fulltime, been a consultant, and has coached both sports be loves.

In the sports world, Steve has coached high school basketball in the Toronto area, in Nova Scotia, and in Alberta; he's coached at grassroots, junior high, and high school levels. He's consulted and assisted with the collegiate basketball program at his alma mater and served for four years with the Senior Men's National Team in a variety of capacities. His baseball experience has ranged from the early coaching years in his hometown as a student, to consulting with elite programs around North America. During his years in Alberta, Steve has coached Little League, both in house-league and summer "All-Stars" from 2005 to 2009. In 2008, he founded Coyote Baseball (a development-centred performance youth program), created Ripken Canada, and later, Alberta Cal Ripken Baseball (for 9-to-12-year-olds) to expand opportunities for player development in Calgary and beyond. Under Steve's leadership, Ripken Canada teams based out of Alberta represented this country in eight out of ten years ('08, '10, '12, '13, '14, '15, '16, '17) until his retirement from full-time baseball. Prior to that retirement, partnering with several corporate leaders in Calgary, Steve designed and implemented the establishment of Coyote Den in 2015, which remains one of Calgary's premiere year-round baseball training centres.

Just as he has throughout the last thirty years, Steve continues ongoing work with coaches, athletic departments, and business leaders around North America. His consulting agency, *Patch29TeamBuilders*, offers programs for teambuilding, culture development, and family and player advisement. Steve's current research and writing project is centred on concepts related to "coaching towards character, climate, and culture," and is intended for coaches, teachers, and culture-managers everywhere. He continues his passion for coaching kids and families, in sport and through life. At the time of publication, Steve has worked with hundreds of kids who have moved on to collegiate athletics, and a handful who have advanced to professional ranks in their sport.

Steve resides in Okotoks, Alberta with his bride of thirty-plus years, and their snuggle-pup, Snoop. Steve and Leslie have two great kids, Rebecca (a student) and Matt (who lives at home in the off-season) and have been part-time "parents" to dozens of athletes who have lived with them through the years.

Steve Lloyd

Appendix: Additional Resources

OVERLAPPING ROLES IN SPORTS DEVELOPMENT RELATIONSHIPS
A Venn Diagram by Rob Arseneau and Steve Lloyd

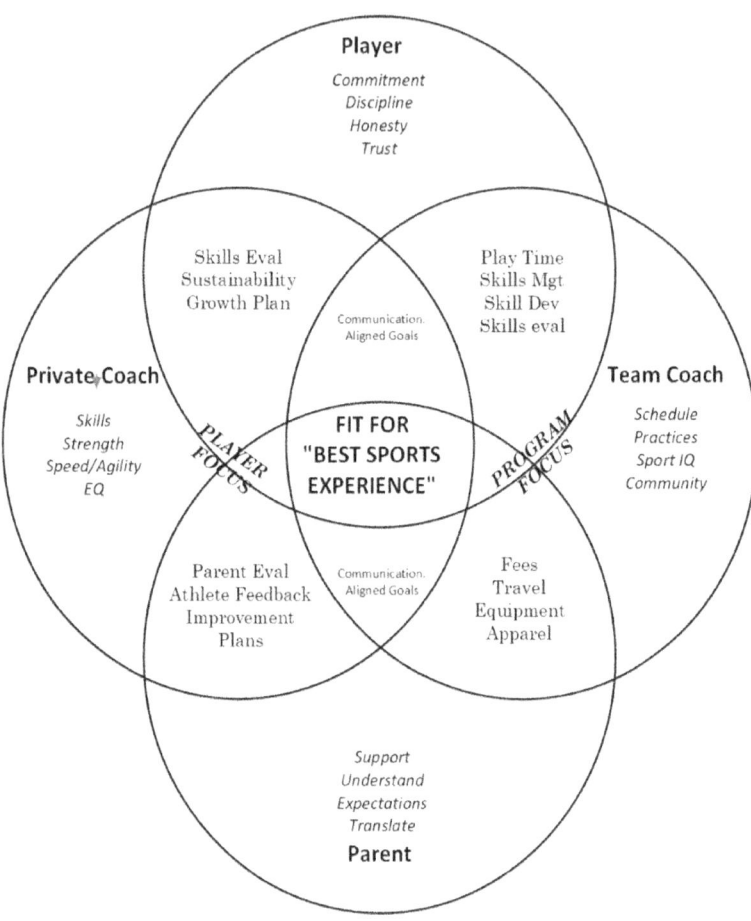

Parental Roles with Young Athletes

By Chris Reitsma

When thinking about the role that parents play in athletes' lives, I am automatically drawn to my own experience as a young athlete and how my own parents shaped my experience.

There are many horror stories out there of how a parent's outlook and attitude has ruined a young athlete's experience. Expectations and pressure are the two words that stand out as momentum killers. Parents that live vicariously through their children and want them to make-up for or redeem the father's past athletic failures are easy to detect. Parents that have unrealistic expectations take the joy out of the game for so many youngsters.

My parents were the exact opposite. Deeply rooted in the view that sport should be fun was on the top of their list. I did not feel pressure from my parents because they always wanted to support me in the things that I loved. If they don't love the game as young athletes than they will never reach their ceilings. My parents believed in reaching your potential by working hard and being discipled at the craft I chose. When I didn't have a great game or was upset by an outcome, my father would just simply ask me if I had prepared properly mentally and physically. He used the analogy of being able to look in the mirror after a game and ask yourself if you had given your all during the event. If the answer was yes, then I could sleep soundly knowing that sport is never perfect, and I didn't have to be.

They were my biggest fans attending almost every game sitting in the background and just enjoying the athletic experience. The only pressure I felt was put there by myself. My parents believe in God, and that we are all gifted differently. I would glorify God by being the best I could be in my given area of giftedness. If my giftedness was in a different area than sport, then their expectations of hard work and discipline would apply in the same way in that particular field.

Burnout of young athletes is a very real thing especially in this age of sport specialization at a young age. My father would always tell me that he wanted me to play multiple sports in high school. It was very important to him for me to develop in areas other than just Baseball. Quick twitch muscles such as sprinting, jumping, catching, and passing in Basketball and Volleyball allowed me to become more well-rounded as an athlete. He was also smart enough to realize that the window that I was able to compete in these other sports was small and to enjoy the high school moments. I see way too many kids specialize too early and come down with sport specific injuries at a young age. I also see the mental burnout of these athletes when they get to the end of their high school days and realize that they have not reached their goals and have not experienced any other activities.

Parents, be your kids' biggest supporters while teaching them the value of hard work through sport. Stay away from creating pressure through your own expectation of success. There are only a very small percentage of athletes that will reach the pinnacle of sport, and those athletes are the ones who are gifted in special ways athletically and the ones who are able to compete for the love of the game.

Drafted and signed in 1996 in the first round by the Boston Red Sox, Chris Reitsma pitched in the Major Leagues for seven years (Cincinnati Reds; Atlanta Braves; Seattle Mariners), retiring as a player in 2007. He represented Canada in baseball at the 2008 Olympic Games. Since then, while running some successful businesses, "Reitz" has served for years as a coach with Canada's Junior National Team and been a scout and cross-checker with two MLB organizations. In addition to these, Chris has coached with a number of youth baseball programs and helped with coaching and other leadership within the school community in which he grew up. His parents, Mike (a pastor) and Ruth (a schoolteacher), served faithfully in their respective roles for decades. Chris's kindness, insight, and integrity can be traced back to his remarkable family.

No stranger to philanthropy, Reitz has been, among other things, a spokesman for the Parkinson's Society of Southern Alberta and is the founder of Reitsma's Relievers*, whose mission is to benefit at-risk children, youth, and their families.*

What Parents Need to Know

By Allen Cox

There are core three questions that I feel parents need to deal with, as they consider having their children being part of the world of competitive sports or any performance-based pursuits.

What do parents need to know about performance sports today?

The world of sport has moved rapidly from community-based to pay-for & travel-type teams. It can be great for athletes.

It's taken on a bit of a "big business" aspect.

Parents need to be aware and discerning. Not everyone delivers; not every program is committed to character growth and community. Look for longevity, and sustained success in what really matters. Do they practice more than they play?

Look for opportunities that willing to work as part of a complete team for the sake of the student-athlete: communication and coordination amongst the family, the school, the travel team staff, private lessons, and the high school coaches can make a world of difference for a player.

Insist upon and model good communication with all the stakeholders.

What should the role of parents be in the journey of their student-athlete?

It begins with three basic premises that should NEVER go away:

- GET INVOLVED with them in all aspects of their life, FOR THEM!
- LOVE ON 'EM!! Unrelenting and unconditional love is the foundation.
- Do all you can **keep the game (and the journey) FUN!!**

As the child has opportunity to advance in their sport three other things:

- **RESEARCH** every team and program you are considering: know the distinction between promises, and deliverable goods; know in whose hands who you are about to leave your kid.
- **INVEST** more than just money and be aware that it should not just be an expense. Invest in instruction and development; invest in competitive opportunities; invest is their schooling; invest in them becoming quality people. Always remember that your fees are not guaranteeing an outcome—it is only offering an opportunity for your child to grow through!
- **TRUST**—as hard as it is, at some points in life we have to hand our children over to others. It's hard to do. If you've done your work, it now just takes trust. Trust your discernment about those to whom you have entrusted. Trust your parenting to have prepared your child. Trust the process, and the checkpoints along the journey. And perhaps most of all trust your kid!!

These pillars are not just good for sports. They're excellent standards upon which to raise your children regardless of what they do.

And remember, even though lots of folks think so, kids really haven't changed that much. They still want to come to their sport to have fun; they still want to play and enjoy themselves; they still want to be trusted to grow up.

What has changed are some things around our kids. Stats are perceived to be more important that being a teammate. "Getting mine" is valued by the world more than being a good teammate. More than ever, kids are not expected to be accountable when they screw up. And a huge change is what many athletes hear on the way home from practices and games—umpires, and coaches, and the field conditions, and their teammates: everything else is blamed for what has not gone the way the parents like.

What are college coaches or scouts looking for in a prospective recruit?

Coaches know that the person they get correlates to the player they want.

Every kid they recruit has talent. Programs are looking for the best player they can get who they won't have to babysit or coddle—or worse, bring a shadow to their world.

Coaches place high value on things like accountability; work ethic; character; discipline; teamwork; the classroom; social media habits.

Trying to get to the next level involves a lot more than just skill and athletic ability.

A final thought—coaches and scouts see a lot more than you think. So be aware of your own attitudes and conduct. Because we rarely outrun our pedigree!

Allen Cox is a Yoda!! He's coached at the high school level for decades (Owensboro Catholic and Okotoks Dawgs Academy) and served in collegiate baseball at both Kentucky Wesleyan and Georgia Gwinnett. In addition to leading several select teams and events like Canada Cup and the Toronto Blue Jays premiere high school event, Tournament 12, Allen has been a guest instructor for numerous elite programs around North America. Perhaps most telling is that Allen has coached hundreds of players who have moved on to college sports, and dozens who have advanced to professional baseball. Additionally, the coaching world across the continent is well populated in academies, high schools, and colleges with Allen's former players and colleagues. Currently with the Carolina Rays, and the GM and Head Coach of Scoutz USA out of Myrtle Beach, Allen continues to be a mentor to former players everywhere.

Steve Lloyd

Three Tips
(To Help Your Kids Achieve More Confidence)
Marc Rardin - Head Baseball Coach, Iowa Western CC

HELP THEM TO REDEFINE THEIR DEFINITION OF SUCCESS.

It's not about the batting average. It's not always getting a hit.
It's having the "right" player showing up to the field.
It's hitting the ball hard and helping the team win.
When they do that, the results will come.

HELP THEM KEEP PERSPECTIVE.

There is no reason the players can't play this game in college. There are so many college baseball programs looking for ballplayers. For most of kids, this means they could be playing for at least another six to eight years!!

So, if you had a bad game today (and some days you will), it's not the end of the world.

**HELP THEM TO REALIZE THAT THEY DON'T HAVE
TO BE A PERFECTIONIST TO PLAY THIS GAME**

Making an error...striking out with the bases loaded...get picked off...

These things happen. It's part of the game.
You don't have to play like you're in a three-hour "timeout" for bad behavior.
It's a game!!
It's okay to have fun and it's okay to laugh at yourself.

Courtesy of Iowa Western Reiver Baseball - "A Culture of Excellence"

Two Questions I Get a Lot

Marc Rardin - Head Baseball Coach, Iowa Western CC

Two questions I get a lot from people about our consistent success:

If you could narrow it down to one thing to describe how you are doing it, what would it be? — **CULTURE**

What does it take to be a successful baseball player at Iowa Western?

My answer: Personal Character—DON'T BE A JERK!!

That means...
1. Say "Please"
2. Say "Thank You"
3. Say "Excuse me"
4. Apologize when you screw up
5. Then MAKE IT RIGHT
6. Don't screw people over
7. When you say you are going to do   something...DO IT!!
8. When you say you are going to be somewhere...BE THERE!!
9. Be on time
10. If you're going to be late...Contact them!!
11. f you can't do something...Just say you can't do it!
12. NEVER quit on your friends...They're your friends!!
13. Be FIERCELY LOYAL...Family, teammates, friends
14. Tell the truth...Even when it's going to hurt
15. Don't take shortcuts...If it was the right way, it would just be called "the way"
16. Sometimes you will mess up #1 to #14. That's okay— refer back to #4

** SUCCESS IS A CHOICE—NOT A RIGHT**

Courtesy of Iowa Western Reiver Baseball - "A Culture of Excellence"

Lessons I've Learned About Life

Marc Rardin - Head Baseball Coach, Iowa Western CC

IF YOU CAN HELP ENOUGH OTHER PEOPLE GET WHAT THEY NEED IN LIFE, YOU WILL GET EVERYTHING IN LIFE THAT YOU NEED.
Give away what you want most.

WHAT YOU CAN DO THIS WEEK: Make a conscious effort to go above and beyond, to be "present," and to help someone each day to get closer to where they want to be. Not only will this help them, it will help you.

ENERGY IS THE FUEL OF LIFE.
When you help someone else get what they want, you will be ENERGIZED. When you are ENERGIZED, you feel better, look better, act faster, get more done, and MAKE A BIGGER DIFFERENCE. Energy is the FUEL OF LIFE. Your energy is contagious, and you MUST ask yourself; *Is my energy worth catching or is it worth avoiding?*

WHAT YOU CAN DO THIS WEEK: Consciously and intentionally be an energy giver. There are too many energy vampires that SUCK the energy out of others by complaining, being bitter, being negative or telling you that what you think is wrong or to forget what you know and adopt their way of thinking. Look, I DON'T want you to adopt my way of thinking. I DO want you to be ENERGIZED by our interaction in hopes that you will get closer to the life of excellence and fulfillment that you desire and you deserve. As a leader, you must be an energy giver. This week, bring positive energy and optimism with you and refuse to complain or listen to those who are complaining to you. *Tell them to STOP.*

**STOP TRYING TO BE RIGHT AND
START FINDING OUT WHAT IS RIGHT.**
I also learned that in life there are those who WANT to be right, and those who are in search of what IS right. What is right, when it comes to best current practices, will constantly evolve. You must evolve, adapt, adjust, change with the times. You cannot live on yesterday's strategies, philosophy and way of thinking. The world is changing at a RAPID pace, faster than ever. Some of the best teachers out there may be half your age or twice your age. I have learned that you must know the age-old wisdom AND be open to new era thinking; stop trying to be right and start finding out what *is* right.

YOU ARE ONLY AS GOOD AS YOUR TEAM.
You will become the average of the five people you hang out with the most. If you are a student, and you hang out with people who have a GPA of 4.0 and 3.0, then you will probably end up around 3.5 GPA. The law of averages always holds true, and you will only be as good as your team. Every day I am reminded of this. And I was reminded to STOP trying to do EVERYTHING myself, and to rely more on my team.

WHAT YOU CAN DO THIS WEEK: Evaluate the five people that you associate with most. Know that you will unconsciously take on some of their characteristics. If you are the most energetic, smartest and hardest-working person in your group of five… IT'S TIME TO GO LOOKING FOR ANOTHER GROUP!!

LIFE MOVES FAST.
Stop!
Look around.
Do something everyday to connect with a friend.

Courtesy of Iowa Western Reiver Baseball - "A Culture of Excellence"

Steve Lloyd

On Learning That Some Things
Are More Important than Others

By Corey Eckstein

Looking back over my seventeen-plus years of coaching, I find it fascinating to see how I have personally evolved and matured as a coach. Each experience that I have gone through, both on and off the field, has shaped me into who I am today.

Coming off an injury at a very young age that I never recovered from, I was quite bitter when I first started coaching and felt that the game had been taken away from me. I felt it owed me something. It was a pity party early on and I was too young and naïve to realize the imprint that a coach can have on a child's LIFE! I was blind, full of ego, and quite frankly all I cared about was the "W." Playing and coaching in a small town, I figured that people should just respect me because I was THE Corey Eckstein. I learned in a hurry that this was simply not the case.

I've been fortunate enough to be around some good people over my career in baseball. I am a firm believer that everyone needs a "sponsor" in life, someone who may open a door when you least expect it, and that turns into something far beyond anything that you could ever have imagined. I also believe in lifelong learning, in self-reflection, and in studying successful people. I have always been infatuated with seeing what personality traits work best as leaders in a workplace. And I have been blessed to come across a number of mentor-types that have helped to shape me. My foundation for success has been building a career around trust and relationships. I joke with people all the time that I sure as hell don't have my World Series Ring because of my playing career!

At the age of 24, I had my first "A-HA" moment, an event that changed my course, transformed me, forever. It was a Saturday night after a double-header and I was so tired that night that I remember purposely turning my ringer off because I wanted to go to sleep and didn't want to be bothered. Around 2am, I woke up to my phone buzzing over and over and over again. It was one of my players who was frantically talking with me, in tears, because his friend had just tried to commit suicide and he didn't know who to call. I was the first phone call he made, the first lifebuoy he reached out for. He could have called anyone that night but he decided to call me...his coach.

For whatever reason, this moment completely changed my outlook on how I want to be remembered. It reformed what I believed is important in pursuing this coaching passion of mine. I realized that it was more important to help them win their lives (as one of my coaching friends has said) than it was to win games or seasons. The irony in all of this is that my program started to win more games as soon as I started investing more time outside the game of baseball into the lives of those kids that I was coaching.

I would like to say this to all those moms and dads: As a parent, find coaches who go above and beyond the job description. Find coaches who spend more time investing in players' lives outside of baseball. Find coaches who are vulnerable enough to show their own lives outside of baseball. Find coaches who can respond to adverse situations in a positive manner. Find coaches who show their players what it means to be a good father and husband. Win the people battle!

Yes, parents, you do spend a lot of money to have your sons and daughters develop on a field and in the game, but the real question you need to ask yourselves is:

"Is your child going to be a human being longer than they are a baseball player?"

You know the answer, and that the one thing is significantly more important that the other.

Corey Eckstein is the Director of Player Development & Personnel with the Ontario Blue Jays Baseball Club*, one of Canada's top youth baseball programs. Prior to join OBJ, Corey built the Abbotsford (BC) Cardinals from the ground up; not only at the upper level of baseball but also at the grassroots level with his* Sandlot Baseball Program, training players from 6-18 years of age from the Abbotsford area, truly growing the game in his hometown. During his time with the Cardinals, they took home five British Columbia Premier Baseball League (BCPBL) championships while placing over 80 players into post-secondary opportunities and seeing 11 players selected in the MLB First-Year Players Draft.

His dedication to coaching, character development, and modelling professionalism has taken him all over the world, including spending three years with the Canadian Junior National Team with whom he was a part of two Silver Medal wins at U18 World Championships, both in Cartagena, Columbia (2011) and Seoul, South Korea (2012). In addition, Corey has served as an Assistant Coach at numerous additional showcase events across Canada and throughout United States. This includes (so far) five years at Tournament 12 (hosted by the Toronto Blue Jays Baseball Academy) and two years at the New Balance International Series, held in Houston and Boston. He has also served as an Area Scout with the Kansas City Royals, with whom he has earned a World Series ring.

The Game Is Hard Enough

An Argument for Multi-Sport Pursuits

By Duff Gibson

Why do we want our kids to play sports? What do we want them to get out of it? The answers to these questions are almost universal. We want them to be active and healthy and we want them to learn those life-lessons about dedication and teamwork, like so many of us did when we were young. Not surprisingly, we also want them to be successful, and that's where things can get tricky given all the different options and pathways a young athlete might choose.

There are a number of moving parts here, so let's start with what we know for sure. Certainly not every kid is the same, but there is a great deal of research showing that the number one reason why kids play sports is for fun. The number one reason why kids quit sports is because it gets too serious and therefore ceases to be fun, and this has been shown to be the case with up to junior-aged athletes. To be clear, because the concept is often mischaracterized, this isn't about everyone getting a trophy, and this is absolutely not about making it less competitive. My experience is that competition and the challenge of sport *is* the fun part. Why is fun relevant? Because it's tied to motivation, and it relates to burnout. As a former Olympian and Olympic coach, the greatest athletes I've known each had qualities that contributed to their success relating to mindset and work ethic. They were also the kids who never had the fun taken out of it.

One very simple way of keeping sport fun is to make it seasonal. By switching from sport to sport over the course of a year, in simple terms, you leave them wanting more. Early specialization, or playing only one sport for the entire year, is something that has become quite prevalent in the last few decades and in a sense, that's to be expected. Many kids would happily play their favorite sport all year long if we let them. Many parents are afraid their kids will get left behind if they don't. We want the best for them, but early specialization has a number of significant consequences relating to burnout as well as an increased rate *and* severity of injury. Something I wouldn't have anticipated, is that early specialization is also associated with an increased risk of leading a sedentary lifestyle after they quit!

Despite the risks, some have argued that sports like hockey and soccer are so technically demanding that in order to compete at an elite level, there's no other option. This assertion does appear to be true with regard to gymnastics and figure skating, but these are also sports in which there have been world champions at age sixteen and younger, and therefore everything happens earlier, whether that's good or bad. You could also argue that gymnasts *are* multi-sport athletes. With respect to hockey however, the data suggests National Hockey League players typically didn't up the intensity or frequency of training until they were about fourteen, right around when they tended to specialize in the sport.

There are undoubtedly successful athletes from a variety of sports who were early specializers, however, they are the exceptions rather than the rule. In a survey of American summer and winter sport athletes who competed in at least one Olympics between 2000 and 2012, athletes averaged three sports per year until age fourteen and 2.2 sports per year until eighteen. Even after eighteen, American Olympic team members still averaged more than one sport per year. Of course, if you exclude gymnasts and figure skaters, those numbers are even higher.

Perhaps the most definitive study ever of high-performance sport was published in the European Journal of Sports Science in 2014. Not only was the sample size massive at 1558 athletes, but the caliber was also excellent, involving German national team athletes from each Olympic sport. The study found the factors contributing to adolescent success either had no relevance or were *negatively* correlated with success as a senior athlete. In other words, what makes someone a great ten or twelve-year-old athlete, either doesn't matter or actually makes them *less* likely to be successful beyond that point. Specifically, the study concluded that starting earlier, specializing earlier, as well as high-intensity sport-specific training were all shown to be associated with adolescent success. This might be the single biggest reason why it persists. Playing one sport for the entire year, whether we push them to do it or they're begging us to play, really *works*. Unfortunately, the benefits are fleeting.

In contrast, world-class senior athletes typically started later, specialized later, and played many other sports prior to specializing. Essentially, it's the opposite set of conditions. The study also found no relationship between hours of practice in their primary sport as an adolescent and how successful they were as a senior athlete. These results were found to be consistent over time and independent of sport. In addition to burnout and the increased risk of injury with early specialization, according to this study, it's actually counterproductive to senior level success. So, with all the negative, why are we still having the conversation? It's not the most optimistic way of looking at it, but as David Epstein points out in *Range*, there are very few people promoting early specialization who don't also benefit from the belief that it's a good thing...or perhaps a child's last chance. At the very least, when it comes to your kids, it would be worth the time to seek out advice from someone not associated with a youth sport program.

The one aspect that seems to fly under the radar is athleticism. If you've played a variety of sports, you're a better athlete. You've built a foundation that lends itself to *all* sports. I've personally heard the manager of a AAA baseball team, which is one step below the major leagues, say they're not looking for ball players—they're looking for athletes. They believed they could teach the baseball part, but there's only so much you can do if there's a deficit of speed, strength, balance, or coordination. This is also why you have a storied hockey coach like Brent Sutter saying he can tell the difference between multi-sport athletes and those who have only played hockey. Multi-sport athletes in addition to being less injury prone, have in essence, better prepared themselves for novel environments. I once saw a clip of Steven Stamkos, captain of the Tampa Bay Lightning, lurking at the side of the net as a shot was taken. The rebound went straight up in the air, Stamkos choked up on his stick and scored through a very narrow gap with a motion similar to a bunt in baseball. The point is that the move is not something you would ever practice in a hockey environment. Young athletes succeed largely because of early skill acquisition. As athletes get older and the technical proficiency starts to even out, it becomes very difficult to hide a lack of athleticism.

So, this is a critical message for parents and coaches: specializing in one sport before *at least* fourteen years of age is not an effective strategy to help kids one day achieve their true potential. In fact, it might be stacking the odds against it. If you're worried your child will get left behind if they *don't* specialize at a young age, unfortunately as the system exists, you could be right. However, we need to be aware of the consequences of such a decision. As we better understand the research and its implications, it's my hope that parents will begin to make changes in the best interest of their children from within organizations. My friend and former teammate, Nathan Cicoria, is in the process of doing this with his daughter's soccer club. Instead of the organization constantly fighting with families who want their kids to play other sports in addition to soccer, he has proposed they transition into Calgary's first soccer *and* hockey club. He's getting some support and I really hope it happens because it's a brilliant idea and I think a number of organizations will follow suit if just one takes the first step and shows that it can work.

Sometimes we forget the original purpose of sport and why we have our kids involved. It's of value to re-examine such things from time to time. Without question, there are competing forces involved. But if the goal is for our kids to love what they do and therefore lead healthier active lives, and learn those life-lessons about dedication and teamwork, then multi-sport is the foundation. If the goal is for our kids to be the best they can be, then it's no different.

Adapted with permission from *The Tao of Sport* by Duff Gibson.

Duff Gibson has spent the better part of three decades in a hotbed of Olympic sport. As an athlete, Duff was a provincial champion speedskater, a national champion and national team member in bobsleigh, and then a world and Olympic gold medalist (Torino 2006) in the sport of the skeleton. As a coach he led six different athletes to podium finishes at the world level. Competing against, working with, and learning from numerous world-leading athletes and coaches has provided Duff with a breadth and depth of experience few others have had. Having moved on from coaching after the 2014 Sochi Olympics, Duff launched Dark Horse Athletic in early 2016. Dark Horse is about developing physical literacy, a growth mindset, and, above all, inspiring kids to participate for the love of sport.

Who Do College Coaches Want to Sign?

By Jeff Mercer

I feel our job (as a coach) is to provide two major resources to players: one is to provide instruction and constructive critique; the other is to reinforce the trust and confidence we believe the athlete should have in themselves if they've done the requisite work asked. That covers the vast majority of the issues we encounter on a daily basis. Student-athletes face mental health issues, family concerns, relationships and the like, all sorts of things that we need to foster growth through: these are normally handled through a strong personal relationship built through the trust placed in you to coach them regularly.

Through that lens when recruiting, we're looking for a player that we feel is open and eager to learn, and then, after that, who has the aptitude and capacity to translate that work into confidence. I often hear how the game is mostly mental, how if you work hard enough you can be the best. However, the reality is no amount of mental training or physical work will allow some athletes to outperform their physical ability. We're all bound by physics and, to a greater degree, genetics. Most athletes won't play professionally through no fault of their own. They just aren't able to physically compete at that level.

If for a moment we took professional athletics away as an option, what then would any coach value in a student-athlete? We would want someone we enjoyed being around daily, the positive attitude, pleasant personalities that we prefer in the rest of our daily lives. Life's hard enough without being surrounded by a group of people who chose to only view the negative in every positive situation. We would want to be with someone who has an open mind and enjoyed being coached and instructed, without having their feelings hurt and bruised by an unbiased evaluation of their current ability. Have an educated opinion, but be willing to adjust if the evidence is overwhelming against you. I personally enjoy a passionate conversation on a controversial topic. When most topics in athletics become controversial it is often because you've done things a certain way your entire life. I want athletes to have personal opinions and come to a conversation prepared, but if we go through that process and find that one of us is obviously correct, the other need to be flexible enough to adjust: the coach included!

As a coach, keep in mind, my playing career is over, and I know it. I'm not living vicariously through you. I'm coaching because I enjoy being part of the game and I enjoy seeing the joy that success bring others. If you agreed during the recruiting process that you "want to play professional sports" or "be the best version of myself," I know how to do that. But it's going to be hard and very uncomfortable at times. Regardless of how uncomfortable it gets, if I don't push you through those moments then I'm not holding to my end of the agreement and that makes me a liar. And I'm not a liar. Make sure you're capable and willing of doing what it takes to achieve YOUR goals, and don't be shocked when I hold you accountable to what you said you wanted to do.

Jeff Mercer
Head Baseball Coach: Indiana University

In his first season as head coach, Jeff Mercer led the Hoosiers to the 2019 Big Ten Regular Season title, earning Big Ten Coach of the Year honors. The conference title was the seventh in program history for IU and the first since 2014. Coach Mercer has put together a 72-47 record in his first three seasons at the Hoosier helm. His squad also earned a spot in the NCAA post season in 2019. Mercer, a native of Bargersville, Indiana, is widely regarded as one of the top young baseball coaches in the country. Known for his strength as a recruiter and talent developer as well as his innovative use of advanced analytics, Mercer was named the 2018 Horizon League Coach of the Year with the Wright State Raiders. Mercer brought a winning background to Indiana. In his time as a head coach (2017-18) and an assistant coach (2014-16) at Wright State, he has been a part of three Horizon League regular season and conference tournament titles, three NCAA appearances, and a combined record of 199-92 (.684). The Raiders won four NCAA tournament games over those three appearances, having reached the regional finals twice.

Qualities of a Youth Coach

By Steve Konchalski
St. Francis Xavier U & Canada Basketball

As parents, look for coaches who have a habit/legacy of doing these things.

They...

- ✓ Make it FUN for the kids!

- ✓ "Coach people, not players." Develop a relationship with ALL the players—show student-athletes that they care about them off the playing field as well as on. Treat their developing players the same as the more skilled players.

- ✓ Put the emphasis on putting forth the player's best effort. "Success is peace of mind which is a direct result of self-satisfaction in knowing you did your best to become the best that you are capable of becoming."—Hall of Fame Coach John Wooden.

- ✓ At all levels, emphasize SKILL DEVELOPMENT. Avoid specialization at the early ages as kids develop physically and mentally at different speeds.

- ✓ Are POSITIVE! "Whisper critique, yell praise."

- ✓ Teach SPORTSMANSHIP as well as RESPECT FOR OFFICIALS and model it themself.

- ✓ Teach your children as players how to be a GOOD TEAMMATE.

✓ COMMUNICATE WITH THE PARENTS their values, expectations and coaching philosophy early in the season, answering any questions they may have.

✓ With older youth, challenge their more skilled players to succeed, giving them guidance preparing for the next level.

✓ Create an environment where the players will be excited about wanting to continue to play next year!

Steve Konchalski is Canadian collegiate basketball's winningest coach (919 career victories, with .615 career win percentage), and led his St. Francis Xavier University program to three national championships and nine AUS conference championships. In his 46 years at "X," the X-Men went to 18 U SPORTS championship appearances and made 42 AUS playoff appearances (with two post seasons cancelled).

*Coach K also served as the head coach of Team Canada for four years (1995-98) and was an assistant coach for 16 years prior, **coaching in three Olympic Games**. He was a member of coaching staff of the Canadian U19 team that won the 2017 World Championship in Cairo, Egypt. Steve has been a member of Canada Basketball's Counsel of Excellence since 2009.*

*Coach K has been **inducted into four Sports Hall of Fame**, and in his "retirement" is consulting with and mentoring coaches from all over the world. The "Dean of Canadian basketball," he can offer a wealth of experience and insight to players and parents about the landscape of youth sport.*

An Anecdote

By Steve Lloyd

Something happened in the summer of 1998 that planted a seed which over time and through some caring choices eventually grew to bear fruit. I hope that there is a lesson in this anecdote for us all.

In Chapter 15, I shared a story about something that Dr. Cal Botterill did with our team, the night before we departed Canada for a very long road trip that culminated at the World Championships. His question to each of us, and to all of us, was: "What do you bring to this team?" Let me tell you about my answer to that question. Cal had left me till the end (intentionally, he later told me), and I had listened intently to this collection of amazing men each outline what their roles were, and what they had hoped to offer. It was remarkably humbling, and I knew by the time it was my turn to speak, that I had no choice but to honest, vulnerable, and real.

"I am the only person in this room that doesn't 'deserve' to be here." I went on to elaborate that each of them truly represented the best of the best of what they did, and that they had all earned their spot. Each of them deserved to be part of this team. And that I was not like them, at least not in that regard. *"I am here because someone else allowed me to be—someone else gave me this opportunity to be here."* I was there because of Grace—and it was not something I could ever "deserve." So, I promised them that they were "my guys," and that I would serve them to the fullest of my ability and from the depth of my heart. In serving them and our team, I would try to have "earned it" by the time we were finished. It was, for me, very much like the scene at the end of *Saving Private Ryan*.

I was overwhelmed by the response from my teammates—they stood and applauded. As Cal wrapped up the meeting, my heart swelled as each of "my guys" embraced me. The spontaneity and sincerity that poured from them into my spirit was life-breathing. It's a moment that I shall never forget.

After we were done, Cal had a private moment with me. He said to me that he left me till the end on purpose. That he knew that I had something to share that this group of men needed to hear. That in a room full of leaders, someone needed to show them the value in serving. And then Cal challenged me.

"This team needs YOU, Steve. You are here because we need you here."

My journey changed that day. Cal entrusted me with some treasure and helped me to set my feet on the path that has led me "here." Back then, I thought the treasure was our team, and its mission. I was not entirely correct. The treasure was me. My calling. And by Grace, and Grace alone, I seek to live out that which I have been called to be.

Made in United States
Orlando, FL
12 April 2022